Praise for *Africanizing the School Curriculum: Promoting an Inclusive, Decolonial Education in African Contexts*

"A profound, insightful and scholarly discourse on transforming and decolonizing colonial school contexts and curriculum that have continued to neglect the lived experiences, voices, histories and cultures of African educators and learners. Afful-Broni, Anamuah-Mensah, Raheem, and Dei have carefully compiled a volume that addresses and acknowledges that African voices and cultures matter in educational contexts. Their collection will be of interest to stakeholders interested in transforming and Africanizing school curriculum and school contexts."

—Edward Shizha, Ph.D, Professor in Youth and Children's Studies,
Wilfrid Laurier University, Brantford

"Africanizing the Curriculum is an outstanding work that impressively persuades us to shift the way we perceive, interact with, and locate African education and its curricular designs and outcomes. By insisting, in both its descriptive and analytical formats, on centering contemporary schooling, learning and related epistemologies, on the continent's rich Indigenous contexts, this Reader distinguishes itself by concretely affirming the urgency of transformative curricular, policy and counter-racism possibilities. It is with this topical and temporal immediacy that Africanizing the curriculum represents the best current critical intervention in the area, and will surely benefit scholars, students and policymakers."

—Ali A. Abdi, Ph.D, Professor in the Department of Education,
University of British Columbia, Vancouver BC

"In the African worldview, education in all forms is a right but not a privilege. It is a natural way of life, a must happen and a must have - the way of life and socialization of our people. This work on Africanizing education is the solution to achieving sustainable education and development in its real sense. The human resource development and the unemployment issues that we face as a result of providing what I call an 'artificial' education does not fit into the natural life of the African. I can't wait to see a full implementation of the solutions provided in this work. That way, there will be minimal if not zero, unemployment, and most critically, the potential of Africa and Africans will be unleashed as we become fully equipped in our own style to utilize the human and material resources that abound us."

—Prof. Olivia A. T. Frimpong Kwapong, Ph.D,
Department of Adult Education and HR. Studies
Dean, School of Continuing and Distance Education
College of Education, University of Ghana

AFRICANIZING THE SCHOOL CURRICULUM

Africanizing the School Curriculum

Promoting an Inclusive, Decolonial Education in African Contexts

EDITED BY

Anthony Afful-Broni
Jophus Anamuah-Mensah
Kolawole Raheem
George J. Sefa Dei

Myers Education Press

GORHAM, MAINE

Myers Education Press

Published by Myers Education Press, LLC
P.O. Box 424
Gorham, ME 04038

Myers Education Press is an academic publisher specializing in books, e-books, and digital content in the field of education. All of our books are subjected to a rigorous peer review process and produced in compliance with the standards of the Council on Library and Information Resources.

LIBRARY OF CONGRESS CATALOGING-IN-PUBLICATION DATA AVAILABLE FROM LIBRARY OF CONGRESS.

13-digit ISBN 978-1-9755-0459-5 (paperback)
13-digit ISBN 978-1-9755-0458-8 (hardcover)
13-digit ISBN 978-1-9755-0460-1 (library networkable e-edition)
13-digit ISBN 978-1-9755-0461-8 (consumer e-edition)

Printed in the United States of America.

All first editions printed on acid-free paper that meets the American National Standards Institute Z39-48 standard.

Books published by Myers Education Press may be purchased at special quantity discount rates for groups, workshops, training organizations, and classroom usage. Please call our customer service department at 1-800-232-0223 for details.

Cover design by Sophie Appel.

Visit us on the web at **www.myersedpress.com** to browse our complete list of titles.

Dedication and Acknowledgments

We dedicate this collection to the faculty, staff, and students of our research centers: the Centre for School and Community Science and Technology Studies, University of Education, Winneba (UEW); the Centre for Integrative Anti-Racism Studies at the Ontario Institute for Studies in Education (OISE) of the University of Toronto, Canada; and the Institute for Educational Research and Innovation Studies, UEW. The centers and the institute have been in academic collaborations over the years as part of knowledge mobilization and dissemination on African Indigeneity and the search for new educational futurities for Africa.

We are thankful to the Institute of International Education for the Carnegie African Diaspora Fellowship Program (CADFP). CADFP made it possible for professor George Dei to spend the summers of 2015, 2016, and 2019 at the UEW, Ghana, to collaborate with faculty, staff, and student initiatives on Indigeneity and African schooling and education. We also acknowledge graduate assistance on this work from Ernest Akrofi Obeng and Rukiya Mohamed of the Department of Social Justice Education, OISE, University of Toronto. Finally, we owe a deep gratitude to Chris Myers of Myers Education Press, Gorham, Maine, for publishing this book.

Contents

INTRODUCTION

Africanizing the School Curriculum: Promoting an Inclusive, Decolonial Education in African Contexts: An Introduction

Anthony Afful-Broni, Jophus Anamuah-Mensah, Kolawole Raheem, and George J. Sefa Dei

Rejuvenated Soul

WE ARE PART of the consensus that education is key to human development. The development of any nation or community has a powerful bearing on the education of its citizens. Education is key to the foundational work of nation building and the maintenance of nations in a mutually constitutive relationship. This involves education that happens both in formal school sites, as well as nonschool/nonformal educational settings. This understanding is often valorized for Africa, where, for too long, national educational systems have been critiqued for their failures to provide the human power necessary for development to take off. If we accept this premise of education as crucial for human development, some questions become relevant: What type of education are we talking about? How should this education be delivered, to whom, by whom, when, and why? Who should be the (multiple) stakeholders in education delivery? And how do we ensure that all citizens have access to relevant education? For this book, we are propelled by a key question: How do we ensure that education is not simply available and accessible but that it is also fundamentally equitable to all?

Throughout the discussion, we use *Black* and *Africa(n)* synonymously. We appeal to a broader audience but are also partisan in our particular focus on Black and African learners. We see synergies and convergences in *Black* and *African*. We are unconvinced by the intellectual politics that deny *Black* as a term relevant to discuss the African experience. As we point out later, *Africa* transcends the continent and simply a physical space. Being "Black" and Blackness daily confront the African diaspora. *Black* gestures toward a radical politics of group affirmation rather than simply skin color or phenotypes. But we do not imply skin color is irrelevant—far from that. We also capitalize *Black* to speak to our shared histories, agencies, and resistances as a political and communal people who have survived the Middle Passage, enslavement and genocide, segregation, and the continuing daily assault on our bodies, spiritualities, and futurities.

Our decision to write this book is based on the discomfort we have regarding the current state of affairs in African and Black education. There are many challenges, but we cannot be overwhelmed. We look for possibilities of Black and African educational futurities. One of the editors, George Dei, has been a Carnegie African Diaspora Fellow, visiting the University of Education in Winneba, Ghana, in the summers of 2015, 2016, and 2019. Our collaborative ventures and discussions have put us on the path of gathering knowledges and perspectives in book collections on the question of Black and African education, linking issues between the continent and the African/Black diaspora. We bring a conscious gaze to our intervention on African and Black education starting from the continent itself and extending a read of Africa as more than a physical space. Africa is beyond its boundaries. In fact, we theorize Africa as a social construct with global implications beyond the mere physicality of geographical space. This is where ideas of African education as education for global learners can appropriately be lodged and interrogated. Our intervention is intended to reach this broad audience and to register that no matter where we are located and how we are situated, the education of the Black and African child affects *all of us* as Black and African educators worldwide.

As African scholars, we need to understand and respond to the depth of our own intellectual imprisonment and the failure to collectively think through viable solutions to the myriad challenges of African education from a critical, African-centered vantage point. Our refusal to do so reflects a cultural, moral, and intellectual failing. This failure has also forced us to become "intellectual imposters" in the (Western) academy and its colonial satellites on the continent and in the global diaspora (Nyamnjoh, 2012). Many of us have parroted worn-out Eurocentric theories to explain the African predicament. At times, we become resentful or suspicious of any claims of African Indigeneity. We fall into the trap of the universalization of Western scientific knowledge. Yet, this science, for the most part, concerns the particularities of Western Europe. We can think of the many times African scholars who attempt to espouse African-centered ideas, and cultural or Indigenous knowledges, have been called on to defend the merits of their scholarship. Alternatively, they are met with demands to "translate" such knowledges into their Western equivalents, as if they can be translated as such or cannot stand on their own. When one looks at it critically, those doing the questioning are themselves trapped in Eurocentric blinders. The harshest critics or cynics of African Indigeneity are African scholars ourselves!

It is about time we exercise our intellectual agencies by offering African-centered and Black-centric standpoints to subvert the aggressive, capitalistic, and Eurocentric ideologies that insist on consuming all the intellectual space unto themselves. Our bodies, cultures, histories, and experiences offer important ways of knowing. In fact, we make no apologies for asserting this fact. We must think through solutions to our own problems and challenges using our own cultural paradigms or modes of thought. This does not mean that we do not engage other bodies of knowledge. But we have a responsibility to assert African ways of knowing as legitimate and valid in their own right and unencumbered by Eurocentric evaluations and standards of what constitutes knowledge and how such knowledge must be produced, interrogated, validated, and disseminated internally and globally.

Long ago, a Ghanaian intellectual exhorted African scholars to begin to "pioneer new analytical systems for understanding our own communities steeped in our home-grown cultural perspectives" (Yankah, 2004, p. 26). We could not agree more and pay heed. Although others have been on this road for quite some time, they are only a handful of scholars. We must all take up this call. We must all rise to this intellectual occasion and imperative. We can begin by reframing our curricular pedagogical, instructional, and communicative practices in schools and classrooms. We can reclaim our rich intellectual traditions by using our Indigenous languages in our collective pursuit of relevant, responsible, and partisan education and scholarship. While "Africanizing" the curriculum rests on buy-in from university administrations and other scholars on the value of Indigenous knowledges (e.g., such that Indigeneity is not only an add-on or alternative knowledge but is centered), we can also acknowledge our individual responsibility in the intellectual spaces in which we are situated to fight this battle. Arguably, "Africanizing" and "Indigenizing" the academy can be a distinct political project from the more difficult work of decolonization. This can be taken up as such by university administrations and those in power *precisely because* it is taken up as a more superficial add-on rather than requiring actions to dismantle and rebuild. We argue for "Indigenizing" (and, by extension, Africanizing) as a sort of reinvention of the African and Black academy in ways that lead to truly decolonial ends (see also Hewitt, 2016, and Taiaiake et al., 2004, in different contexts).

In discussing the Africanization, Indigenization, and decolonization of education, three issues need to be emphasized: (a) the relationship between colonization, capitalism, and education; (b) the relationship between education and nation building/sovereignty/autonomy; and (c) the role of the embodied learner in their own education.

Making these connections helps us ground a critical understanding of where and how to proceed with Black and African schooling and education. In fact, the connection between colonialism, capitalism, and the role of education cannot be overemphasized. We are still struggling through the vestiges of colonial education exacerbated by capitalist imperatives leading to stark global inequities. Education can allow people to "live well" (Gudynas, 2011) and to live out their dreams and aspirations. For example, we need education that emboldens the African learner to think deeply about what it means to pursue so-called African development (e.g., whose conception of "development," how, what, and why?), the relationship to the Western capital to this education (e.g., is there a goal of local autonomy and self-governance for Black/African education?), and the need for Africanizing/Indigenizing education (e.g., what role does African-centered education play in liberation/in relation to the "African development" and the question of local autonomy?). These are not just words, phrases, or ideas with contested meanings and understandings but also critical issues on which local peoples' survival depends. For example, *through* the relationship of the "postcolonial" African state to the ongoing colonization of African peoples, Western financial institutions have become arbiters of life and death. These external financial institutions continue to have deleterious consequences on the autonomy of African education and the sovereignty of the African nation-state.

Writing in a different, but related, context of North America, Glen Coulthard (Yellowknives Dene), an Indigenous resurgence theorist drawing on Fanon and Marx, argues for the urgent need for Indigenous Nations on Turtle Island to reject a "politics of recognition." Coulthard (2014) links his criticism of this strategy, a criticism of the Canadian state and colonization of Indigenous Nations, to capitalist writing:

> The federal government has invigorated a struggle for Indigenous self-determination that must challenge the relationship between settler colonization and free-market fundamentalism in ways that refuse to be coopted by scraps of recognition, opportunistic apologies, and the cheap gift of political and economic inclusion. For Indigenous nations to live, capitalism must die. And for capitalism to die, we must actively participate in the construction of Indigenous alternatives to it. (p. 173)

We find this intellectual reasoning and stance relevant for our own work. It is important for us to interrogate the ways power and knowledge production work so as to be able to subvert the dominant frameworks of Western modernity and globalization. In particular, we must reflect on the role and place of race, social difference, and Indigeneity as significant forces and entry points in decolonizing education in transnational communities. The issues of marginalization, exclusions, and the dynamics of social oppression reveal mutually intersecting forces within broader social and political systems beyond schooling and education to structure society. It is significant that we interrogate conventional ways of knowledge production as to how racism, capitalism, and heteropatriarchy work within social formations to inform schooling and education and, consequently, create the urgency and imperatives of educational change.

For too long, "postcolonial" African/Black education has contended with issues driven by neoliberal capitalist economic agendas making education more of a privilege than and right. Neoliberalism has been a new way of colonialism in African education. In current educational contexts, there is the primacy of markets determining educational choices and decisions of nation-states. For example, as noted in Dei (2008), the commercialization/privatization of education in Africa has led to funding being disproportionately allocated to certain fields (e.g., natural sciences, technology, engineering, and management at the expense of the arts and humanities), as well as Western control of African intellectual property pursued under the guise of global knowledge. As globalization continues to exacerbate global inequities, the role of education in helping address rising poverty levels and social inequities has received attention in scholarly debates, writings, and public discussions (see Mundy, 2008; Mundy et al., 2016). A global capital modernity is marked by the coloniality of Western education. For example, the internationalization of (higher) education to meet Western standards and accreditation, the rise in "overseas" study programs, and research and teaching/training partnerships and networks (see Teferra & Altbach, 2004) have mostly benefited the West's capital interests and further shunned Indigenous African initiatives to think through African-centered education. The hegemony of free markets, deregulation, competition, individualism, privatization, and restrictive definitions of education to serve corporate market interests has produced colonizing forms of education.

Whether in African or North American education, there has long been class-, gender-, ethnic-, religious-, and sexual-based privileges clearly revealing ways equity considerations are left on the sidelines in the neoliberal educational agenda with futile calls for "accountability," "quality," "standards," "excellence," and "competencies" in education (see Dei, 2008, 2019). This trend has simply promoted colonial education in the context of global capitalism. We term this development the drain of the global political economy on Black and African education. We need new decolonial educational approaches that constitute a life-sustaining source for Black and African nations and communities. It calls for a rethinking of the relationship between education and nation building/sovereignty/autonomy. Education must be geared toward strengthening local knowledge and cultural resources and further engender human capacity building to respond to African-centered problems and community needs.

It is for this reason that the role of the embodied learner in their own education becomes equally important. Learning must be embodied, meaning developing a sense of ownership and identification with the process of educational delivery. Education must speak to learners' lived experiences. Teaching, like learning, must also be an emotionally felt experience. It must evoke or awaken spiritual, cultural, and psychic memories. The learner must bring the self to the learning and teaching process, and this process must empower the self and the collective to know their ancestry, heritage, histories, identities, cultures, communities, and the power of their human agencies and Indigenous resistances. Education must be holistic and spiritually affirming of the African/Black learner's sense of self, culture, identity, and developing a sense of purpose and meaning in life. Education is more than material gain. This expansive understanding of education can be attained through teaching, learning, and the administration of education that begin with the self and the collective—whether as a teacher, a learner, or an administrator. Education alien to the soul, spirit, body, and mind is not transformative education. Education that fails to begin with the self is a decontextualized, de-rooted education, one not anchored in the foundations of human existence. An embodied learner "owns" their knowledge and education but not in the sense of a private acquisition. It is more of a social identification and a shared connection with the educational process. This is the problem of colonial and colonizing education that removes learners from their past, heritage, histories, cultures, identities, and Indigenous knowledge systems and spiritual values. This form of colonial and colonizing education splits the body from the mind, soul, spirit, and psychic selves. African and Black learners need a different form of education—a decolonial and anticolonial education.

It is important to assert that decolonizing African education encompasses a reassertion of Africa at the center of knowledge discovery, validation, and dissemination in its totality and not simply de-Westernizing educational policies, procedures, and approaches (Asante, 2003). Africa should be at the *center* of global Black diasporic knowledge production. Africa must be our intellectual anchor. Africa must be the source of our knowledge generation and rejuvenation. Our identification with African is physical, cultural, emotional, and spiritual. Any African/Black scholar who fails to make this connection only reveals the shortcomings of their claims to know Africa and the Black experience. Knowledge about Africa speaks to the urgency of curricular, pedagogic, and instructional changes in the current school system. These changes cannot be cosmetic: They must be foundational and radical enough to subvert the current order of schooling and education about Black/African peoples. Transforming schooling and education about, and on, African and Black peoples to schooling by and for African and Black peoples requires that we critically interrogate the current structures for educational delivery—structures and processes for teaching, learning, and the administration of education.

In this vein, the book addresses some of the key issues and challenges in decolonizing the African school curriculum. We focus on the necessity of decolonizing the curriculum, suggesting concrete ways of making the curriculum more inclusive and accessible to all learners. Chapters in this edited collection highlight key philosophical arguments on the necessity surrounding inclusive and decolonized curriculum, pointing specifically to the challenges and possibilities in achieving these goals in a meaningful manner. We take Africa beyond the continental geospace with an important realization that the issues facing Black/African learners globally converge notwithstanding local, regional, and national contexts. It is imperative that we draw on shared lessons and that our scholarship be able to speak across Western, colonial, geographical, and conceptual borders. Among the areas covered in the discussion are inclusion, curriculum, decolonization, ways and strategies of Africanizing the school curriculum, and the implications of local knowledge(s) for schooling reforms. We also raise some key questions: How do we contextualize Black/African education defined broadly to include school, off-school, and nonformal educational settings? How do we frame an inclusive, anticolonial African future, and what is required to collectively arrive at that future? What education are learners of today going to receive, and what is the purpose of such education? How will they apply this knowledge to their schooling and work lives and, in very meaningful ways, be able to change the political/economic/capitalist domains that continue to subjugate learners' aspirations? How do we "refashion" our work as African educators and learners to create more relevant understandings of what it means to be human? How do we challenge colonizing and imperializing relations of the academy? What are the possibilities and limits of counter-visions of African schooling and education? And how do we make school curricula inclusive through teaching, research, and graduate-training in questions of Indigeneity and multicentric ways of knowing? The discussion identifies some specific areas of an "inclusive/decolonized curriculum agenda" through educational programming and training.

In our discussion, "curriculum" is taken as a particular structuring of society: a path to travel, a course of action for educators and learners to take (Apple, 1993, 1999; Apple & Weiss, 1983; Giroux, 1981). In fact, curriculum is about everything in the school system and more. It is about a "deep curriculum" that speaks to everything about the culture, climate, environment, and the social organizational lives of schools, besides issues of the text and pedagogy (Dei et al., 1997). Curriculum is also about power: the power to construct, validate, and legitimize knowledge and to deem what is and is not acceptable. Curriculum is about values, ideas, and practices, as well as identities (class, race, ethnicity, gender, sexuality, disability, language, religion, etc.), and how they connect to knowledge production. The problem with curriculum is the ideology of sameness such as the thinking that "one size must fit all." We must recognize that imposed curriculums do not fit the needs of all students. We must redesign curriculum to challenge the "imposition of sameness [as] a provocation that terrorizes" (hooks, 1992, pp. 25–26). This volume will not just identify the challenges of Africanizing school curriculum—we also take a broader approach to decolonization and Indigenization. We seek to challenge the "banking method" of education (Freire, 1970), where there is an important place for the voice of the African student. Part of the subversion of colonial and Western ways of schooling is to challenge the dominance of the teacher and to create space for students to share their knowledges and experiences, especially in ways that center embodied knowledge.

Similarly, we take "inclusion" as breaking from the past and current order and beginning anew. Inclusion can be an action-oriented approach to education that ensures the centrality of all learners, engaging them from their identities and lived experiences and presenting education that is holistic in the making of a whole, embodied learner who is able to act for change. Inclusion represents difference and does not seek homogeneity by sweeping differences among student populations under the carpet. Inclusion recognizes the power of heterogeneity and requires the school system to take difference into account and reject an ideology of sameness. Elsewhere, Phasha et al. (2017) examine the idea of "inclusive education" in African contexts. Inclusivity is bringing every learner into the fold. Inclusion is addressing the racial/ethnic, class, gender, sexual, disability, and religious differences among learners and seeing these differences as strengths rather than weaknesses. Inclusion addresses issues of power, transparency, and accountability and further shifts the emphasis away from a mere "inclusion of learners with special needs or disabilities" to transforming the entire school system to speak pointedly to questions of social difference and power. In effect, inclusion is not special education or helping so-called deficit learners. Inclusion is not merely about being granted entry—it is also about the power to shape what happens in the classroom. Working with the tenets of inclusion requires that we acknowledge the limits of the "adding-to-what-already-exists" approach. Inclusion will require trying to create a new space. What African and Black education needs is an understanding of inclusion that is informed by the tenets of decolonization, Indigenization, and Africanization. In this undertaking, the school curriculum is an important entry point.

Decolonizing and Africanizing the school curriculum require that as African scholars and researchers we pursue educational politics of inclusivity geared to an "Africanization of the mind." The educational politics of subverting the dominance of Eurocentricity requires that texts written by the oppressed from an anticolonial stance be validated (as part of the process of multiple knowledges) to counter the dominant perspectives that permeate our academies. Creating decolonized spaces is imperative to have an inclusive curriculum flourish. Thus, in Africanizing and decolonizing the school curriculum, educators need to be self-reflective and to ensure our teaching is geared toward structural transformation. So, we ask: How do we critically reflect on our teaching practice so as to ensure that we are making a difference in terms of real structural transformation? How do we expand our pedagogical frameworks for teaching Indigeneity, ethnicity, gender, class, language, sexuality, and ability? How do we speak and work with our own vulnerabilities and complicities and acknowledge the risk of entering unfamiliar territory? How do we bring teaching and learning full circle for all the students in our classrooms? How do we bring an embodied connection to our work on promoting inclusive curriculum? What is the relationship between the "body" (as self/identity and the subject) and "embodiment" (constitutive of a set of relations, structure, feelings, and values)?

We have sought chapters that address issues such as evaluating the appropriateness of curriculum materials/resources (e.g., who, what, how, and when questions on the making of texts) that help Africanize the school curriculum. We are also interested in discussions that highlight the procedures for centering, infusing, integrating, and/or synthesizing relevant African-centered and equity materials that subvert colonial dominance. How do we critically analyze texts and materials for omissions, bias, and exclusions of experiences around questions of social difference: class, race, ethnicity, language, gender, and religious differences? How do we challenge the narratives, histories, and the canon of colonization to stem the loss of Indigenous knowledge? How do we speak of a need for reclamation/resurgence of Indigeneity? How do we address issues of availability, access, and adequacy of Indigenous, African-centered, and culturally appropriate instructional materials/resources for students, educators, parents, and community workers? How do we combine the cultural knowledges of the school, community, and local cultural resource knowledges and work with such local African Indigenous science knowledge in school teaching?

This collection of papers presents a provocative conversation upholding the possibilities of deliberate and purposeful "partisan scholarship" to address the needs of Black and African education globally. As African peoples, we have to deal with the enduring legacy of colonial education in Africa and among Black peoples and communities globally. We continue to be saddled with the ills of colonial education, which lie at the root of the major challenges in Black and African education today. Nowhere is this clearer than on the world's largest continent, where educational policies, programs, and curricular initiatives are driven by corporate market forces and not rooted in African Indigenous knowledge systems. The cynic will ask us to move beyond colonialism as the perpetrator and admit that the problem of African education lies in mismanagement and the failure of current African leadership (school and political leadership) to tease out genuine educational options suitable to the needs and aspirations of African peoples.

To interrogate our intellectual stances, we highlight two key issues for in-depth discussion: first, the possibilities of Africanized and Indigenized education and, second, the practicalities this entails within the context of decolonization and the power of social difference (i.e., a consideration of race/ethnic, gender, class, cultural, religious, and linguistic differences in offering genuine educational options for African and Black peoples). To ground the discussion, it is first necessary for us to conceptualize the understandings of key terms of *Africanization*, *Indigenization*, and *decolonization*.

Conceptualizations

Africanization

Put simply, "Africanization" is a process of making something "African" in terms of a relation of history, identity, context, politics, and the philosophy of practice. In the educational project, we conceptualize Africanization as an approach and process—not event—to achieving African-centeredness within the structures and processes of educational delivery (i.e., teaching, learning, and the administration of education, broadly defined). Africanization seeks to respond to some questions: How do Africa and the African and Black experience become the center of analysis? How do Africa and Blackness offer a prism to understand global events, and how do we teach the young and the masses about the significance of centering Africa and global Black diaspora in theorizing schooling and education? Thus, Africanization is about knowledge, bodies, and structures (i.e., implicating ideas and practices of learners and our academic institutions). To Africanize our schools, we have to take the teachings of African languages, cultures, identities, and politics as critical entry points of conversation/dialogue. We need Africanization to respond to colonialism and its narratives. This is obviously in and of itself about resistance/resurgence and, therefore, a response to colonial education. But this is not to define Africanization and Indigenization strictly in relation to Western colonization. Africanization has its own inherent value, but in the context of teaching for resistance, there has to also be a narrative from the African perspective on colonization and what it is about Africa and Indigeneity that threatens the West.

Africanization calls for sustained local community engagement and practice. For example, Dei (in press) has opined that in terms of local community engagement, African elders constitute an important source of knowledge generation for transforming curriculum and instruction in our schools. Elders are venerated and respected in African communities for their knowledge and wisdom. It is widely acknowledged that elders are an important source of cultural knowledge acquired as a result of their longevity, social experience, and knowledge of culture and history. Throughout African communities, traditional elders and leaders are seen as cultural custodians or repertoires of culture and language. Elders' venerated status in local communities comes not just from their knowing of African culture, history, and Indigenous languages but also from their perceived closeness to the world of ancestors. By maintaining a relationship with local communities, schools and educators can tap into elders' ideas by inviting them into schools as teachers on African history, culture, morality, and character education. As many others have noted, African elders' cultural knowledge is about the revival of intergenerational connections, identities, and consciousness that have long been silenced or even denigrated by the legacies of colonialism, capitalism, and neoliberalism (see also Abubakre & Reichmuth, 1997; Akporobaro & Emovon, 1994; Boateng, 1990; Burns-Ross, 2016; Cordoba, 2006; Dei, in press; Glasson & Evans, 2008; Kithi, 2004).

Dei's (in press) essay points to how elders' cultural knowledge, if integrated into school teachings, has a lot to offer regarding Indigenous sciences, environment technology, and the arts. He has argued that within the culture and political economy of education, there is a central place for the experiential and cultural knowledge of elders and their voices. These are important sites and sources of knowledge. Unfortunately, African schools and educators have so far failed to tap into such knowledge to assist the education of young learners. African elders' teachings promote the interconnectedness of all life and the living, pointing to strengths of mutuality, interdependence, social connections, folkloric production, arts, culture, the science of biodiversity, and the connections of the physical and metaphysical worlds (Crate, 2006; Verdon et al., 2015; Wexler, 2011). This cultural knowledge, examined as experiential and everyday knowing, has emerged from careful observations of nature, local environments, and cosmologies. These knowledges have been communicated to the young through storytelling, traditional ceremonies, meditation, ritual practices, and other sacred performances. These cultural and symbolic expressions reveal intricate lived realities of peoples supporting claims of (African) Indigeneity (see also Burns-Ross, 2016; Cordoba, 2006; Dei et al., 2018; Kudadjie, 1996; Opoku, 1975, 1997).

Dei (in press) argues that elders' cultural knowledges are imparted to young learners using Indigenous languages and cultural mediums of communicative expressions. Elders transmit culture through linguistic codes of sages, proverbs, fables, parables, allegories, music, poetry, songs, dances, and stories (Burns-Ross, 2016; Crate, 2006). Elders' cultural knowledge tends to be holistic, drawing on the interface of society, culture, and nature, as well as revealing the nexus of body, mind, soul, and spirit. African elders use such holistic knowledge to heighten individual consciousness, and to promote the emotional, spiritual, intellectual, and physical well-being and "living well" (Gudynas, 2011) of African communities, nations, and peoples and their plants and animals. Such African elders' cultural knowledge is Indigenous knowledge that heralds ideas of community, social responsibility, reciprocity, sharing, connectedness, relationality, and connections (see also Abdi, 2015; Abdi & Cleghorn, 2005; Bohan et al., 2009; Karanja, 2018; Semali & Kincheloe, 1999; Shizha, 2005, 2014; Tedla, 1995). By engaging African elders, we see the significance and potential of Indigenous knowledge in helping to design new decolonial educational futures within Africa and African diasporic educational contexts (see also Assie-Lumumba, 2016a; Biraimah, 2016; Brock-Utne 2015; Dei, 2014a, 2014b; Emeagwali & Dei, 2014; Emeagwali & Shizha, 2016; Ndlovu-Gathsheni, 2015). We phrase the use of "new" futures here to gesture how time is conceived of in the African Indigenous context. Like other Indigenous communities, Africans challenge Western notions of time. For Africans, we are on a path of progress, and time is conceived as circular, and the use of *new* also speaks to how Indigeneity can adapt and respond to changing conditions.

By respecting, acknowledging, and validating African elders as educators, their long experience and accumulated knowledge will allow educators to critically reflect on academic and social life as a form of decolonizing project. This process of Africanization becomes homegrown. Thus, Africanization cannot be the reverse of Europeanization—for one part not only because of its unique cultural rootedness and corresponding difference but also because of the hegemonic nature of Europeanization. Eurocentric knowledge often masquerades as universal knowledge while denying its own particularity. It also negates the relevance of other knowledges and assumes itself as the yardstick to measure the work of any knowledge. Eurocentrism *requires* the denigration of other knowledges to assert its dominance. It accordingly reveals its own weaknesses in that it cannot simply stand on its own and must rely on such tactics.

In the struggle to Africanize education, the question of "educational excellence" is paramount. To be clear, the politics of Africanization is not intended to deny academic excellence. It questions conventional, dominant conceptions of excellence that have been narrowly defined to suit particular historic interests of the West. Yet no one group has a monopoly on the definition of excellence. In effect, promoting Africanization is not a "watering down" of school curriculum or even academic standards. Africanization is about contextualizing knowledge to ensure that learners are able to identify with the processes of educational delivery. It is about ensuring that African learners can own and develop a sense of identification with their knowledge while sharing it globally. This "owning" does not operate under (Western) assumptions that knowledge is personal or constitutes private property. It is a recognition of *the source* of knowledge and legitimizing this source. It brings an authenticity to knowing and to the knowledge. But it is also important for us to acknowledge that even as we speak about Africanization, it is not a uniform process: Africa and Africanness are not homogenous categorizations. Being African is demarcated by the complexities of gender, class, ethnicity, disability, and sexuality dimensions. Our knowledge systems are complex and marked by social difference and geo-spatialization. It is also worth specifying that we are not trying to slip into "pan-Africanness" but that there are some broad commonalities that we bring forward through the use of African Indigenous to distinguish from the Eurocentric worldview.

Indigenization

As noted in the preceding discussion, Africanization assumes Africa as an epicenter of knowledge for the Black and African learner. Africanization entails framing issues with an African-centeredness in an inclusive, rather than exclusionary, mindset. Africanization affirms the pivotal role of African Indigenous knowledges and local cultural resources' base. It is this acknowledgment of the key role of African Indigenous knowledges that draws the link between Africanization and Indigenization. Fundamentally, Indigenization is an approach and process of "returning to source" (Cabral, 2000), akin to the Ghanaian proverbial instruction of "Sankofa" bird—going back to fetch the forgotten value—for pedagogy, curriculum, and instruction.

Land is not just a physical entity or place. Global Indigenous peoples share the belief that land is animate—it is filled with psychic, spiritual, cultural, and emotional memories (Simpson, 2011, 2014; Watts, 2013). Land is a site of knowing and social practice (Smith et al., 2019; Styres, 2019). Through the recognition of land as a site of knowing, we come to appreciate the power of Indigenous ways of knowing associated with the physical and social occupancy of a place. Land is about the social and physical environments and their associated knowledge systems. Land is about understanding the relations between society, culture, and nature. Land as a teacher attests to the challenges and possibilities of living and surviving in a place and a given space. Living on the land offers significant lessons for building relations among peoples. It is about relationships between humans, animals, plants, and other nonhuman beings as coinhabitants of the place, recognizing that humans are not the only beings with agency (Watts, 2013). Living on the land thus requires an understanding of our obligations to the land and to each other. In effect, land is everything for us as Indigenous peoples. Land offers us its own teachings through time, history, cultural, and spiritual memories. Such teachings constitute the bedrock of a people's claim to Indigeneity. Indigeneity is a testament to who we are (identity), our histories of resistance and survival, and the possibilities of how we see our futures unfold. This explains the synergies that are drawn between the land and Indigeneity. Land and Indigeneity are intertwined concepts. For colonized peoples, in particular, the dispossession of our lands by colonialists came at high costs, which continue to be felt today. This dispossession was a detachment of our souls and spirits from place and our collective sense of being. The reclamation of land is thus a significant part of the decolonization process for colonized peoples. Our relationships to land are connected to our shared histories, cultures, and ancestries (see also Gaudry & Lorenz, 2018; Smith et al., 2019; Styres, 2019).

It is important that land and earthly teachings be centered in the school curriculum for the education of the learner, particularly, as to their social responsibilities to place, space, and others (inclusive of the collective well-being and living well of all nations [human, animal, plants]). The land has always been a site of struggle and resistance for colonized peoples, and this history is an important knowledge base to conscientize the contemporary learner for their intellectual politics. The reclamation of our relationships to land and its teachings constitute a critical Indigenization project for schools and the school curriculum. This project requires a well-thought-out educational process that would recapture and reclaim what was/is there and was never "lost." For African, Black, colonized, and Indigenous peoples, such thinking around Indigenization suggests that "Europe is not the advent of human history" and that there was/is a world before/alongside/after "Europe." It is also an affirmation that Africa has not lost its Indigeneity notwithstanding the aims and vestiges of colonialism and colonization. This is why it is essential for the Indigenization process to require of us, as African scholars/learners, to challenge the colonial appellation of the "Indigenous." There is an African Indigeneity that needs to be affirmed and spoken about as a necessary exercise of our decolonization.

There are cartographies of Indigenous and Indigeneities. The place of African Indigeneity as a counter-vision to the colonial appellation and apparition of "Indigenous," and a salient entry point to the production of counterhegemonic knowing cannot be underemphasized (see Dei et al., 2020). As noted elsewhere (Dei & Karanga, in press), the question of who is "Indigenous" is fraught with many challenges, hostilities, denials, and erasures. African and Black peoples need to exercise caution when claiming to be "Indigenous" in places to which they are not Indigenous. This does not mean African people have lost any claims to our Indigeneities in such spaces—the recourse to Indigeneity is for political and decolonial purposes. However, Indigenous is about "long term occupancy of a place/Land" (Fals Borda, 1980)—to an ancestral "home." Africans are Indigenous to Africa and we must reject colonial definitions of *Indigenous* that are restrictive and erode the politics of Indigenousness and Indigeneity from colonized bodies (see Emeagwali & Dei, 2014; Emeagwali & Shizha, 2016; Gumbo, 2016, 2017; Odora-Hoppers, 2001, 2002a, 2002b; Otulaja & Ogunniyi, 2017; Shizha, 2005, 2014). African peoples do not simply lose or concede our Indigeneity because we were colonized or we have migrated elsewhere. Indigeneity does not leave the body. It resides in us and our cultural and spiritual memories (Dei, 2000).

The sources of African Indigenous knowledge are varied. African education focusing on Indigenous arts, crafts, folkloric productions, technology, aspects of material culture, Indigenous agrobiodiversity and the role in understanding and ensuring food security, sustainability, sovereignty, and community resilience through local Indigenous food and crop systems and Indigenous animal husbandry, all present learners with important information on African Indigenous knowledge. The relevance is not only for science and technology education but also for addressing questions of African development geared to the satisfaction of local needs and aspirations rather than the autonomy that is framed by an "export-led development" mindset (see also Akinwale, 2020; Mawere, 2015; Mpofu et al., 2014; Ngulube, 2017; Shava et al., 2009). The latter positions Africa as a drain on the global political economy rather than examining it as its life-sustaining source. In other words, this latter usually subsumes Africa under the global political economy rather than placing Africa at the center of an examination of the impact of global political economies.

The teaching of subjects is contingent on the approach to Africanization and Indigenization that schools may adopt. For example, educators can ground gender education in local African contexts from the angle of gendered and age dimensions of Indigenous farming practices and processes and traditional strategies for transferring local farming knowledge in households and communities. In many African and other Indigenous communities, certain genders hold specific knowledges, such as forest, local plants/herbs, and pharmacology; water; blacksmithing; and so forth. As in many Indigenous Nations on Turtle Island, women are water protectors, which reflects a gendered knowledge and responsibility. Similarly, as noted by Dei (in press), there are pedagogies of Indigenous science and technology for knowledge building that can inform debates about African science and questions of Indigeneity in decolonial African development projects. Curricular research on Indigenous African environmental knowledge practices and innovations (e.g., multicropping, local crop science, soil fertility, meteorology, ecology and biodiversity, Indigenous pedagogy of food sovereignty and security, food storage and preservation, pest control, animal husbandry, etc.; see O'Donoghue et al., 2013) can provide educators with cultural ways of learning and teaching Indigenous science and technology and their application in formal educational processes. Hopefully, as African educators, we can devise effective curricular and pedagogical strategies to teach these bodies of knowledge in our schools. We must start from what we know and move to the outer world. Such local contextualization helps African learners to own their knowledges and strive to make connections with the global knowledge base/community.

Decolonization

In relatively recent years, there have been growing calls and attempts to think through decolonial African education. Scholars have approached decolonization and African education from different angles. Adebisi's (2016) research calls for decolonized education in African schools through critical pedagogical approaches. The work draws on Freire's (1970) critical pedagogy to respond to the need for effective education through a repeal of "un-decolonized education." Using his own lived experiences as an African scholar, schooled in Africa with the primacy of the legitimization of colonialism in "postcolonial" contexts, Adebisi critiques postcolonial deconstructionist theoretical frameworks, calling for a political, historicized understanding and ways forward for schooling in Africa that serve local needs and experiences while making African learners relevant in transnational contexts. Decolonizing African education can be approached from many subject areas or topical issues in education. For example, d'Abdon (2016) teases out the idea of "spoken word" as different from conventional poetry or a subgenre for marginalized people. We know the "spoken word" is very much alive in Black and African communities. The author highlights the multimodality and sophistication of spoken word and describes its timeliness for pertinent conversations regarding decolonization in the South African education context. d'Abdon also addresses the dismissal of spoken word poetry from the formal (Western) academy and the problematic decoupling of "spoken-word poetry" from poetry in general. This study is particularly informative in calling for a shift from "canonical English poetry" to the use of "spoken-word poetry" to further decolonize educational perspectives in South Africa. What it points to is a legitimation of African oral cultures as significant knowledge sources. In this study, it is suggested that a shift from "page-centered" pedagogical styles—a literal reading of the canonical text—to multimodal pedagogical practices that engage different cultural modes of expression is much needed as part of teaching and learning from diverse textual and oral sources.

Similarly, African folkloric and cultural productions offer different entry points to pursue decolonial education. Nkosi and van Niekerk's (2017) work highlights the significance of Modern African Classical Drumming (MACD) as a means to advance "Indigenous African drumming epistemology" in multicultural education. There is much to learn from African drumming in terms of teaching history, culture, and communication, as well as physical education. Drumming is more than artistic expression. It is embedded in African spirituality and cultural aesthetics. Nkosi and van Niekerk's essay describes the spiritual and historical aspects of African drumming pointing to the technicality of MACD and its pedagogic lessons while positing MACD as a modern continuation of African drumming in the classroom. This essay is an example of the

Africanization of the curriculum in contemporary schooling contexts. Philosophical ideals for the teaching of Black and African education abound. Kazembe (2018) highlights the ways that Black and African peoples have historically understood "education" and passed it onto their children. For example, the author describes how Du Bois's educational philosophy can be applied to current examples of teaching and learning of African and Black thought. He applies Du Bois's educational philosophy to the sociopolitical ideas embedded in the Black Radical Traditional Thought in education and links to the larger Black freedom struggle. The author highlights the importance of Black cultural memory as an important tool and source for youth education. It is noted that Black folk knowledge has been underutilized in school curriculum development. This underutilization is revealed as part of the basis of the Black education crisis today, particularly in the Euro-American context. Consequently, there is a call for educators to employ the Black Radical Traditional Thought that points to the rich intellectual heritage of African peoples as a tool to combat White supremacy in the education system.

Without a doubt, decolonization can be messy, violent, and unsettling. The struggle to decolonize comes with battles, bruises, and traumas. But decolonization can be equally rewarding in terms of building educational possibilities. Decolonization is building new relationships in schooling, local communities, and beyond. Decolonization is also parting with colonial vestiges and breaking away from hierarchical relations and practices of colonizing bodies and experiences. Decolonization calls for critically examining the coloniality of knowledge in conventional educational practices and finding ways to disrupt Euro-colonial hegemony. Decolonization requires that we engage in counterhegemonic knowledge production that subverts the dominance of Western knowledge. In the decolonial project, we confront some epistemic challenges, including the challenge of going beyond "epistemic provincialism" (see Ahenakew et al., 2014), while insisting on the power of multicentricity (Dei, 1996), that is, to see other ways of knowledge that emanate from different geospaces as critical to understanding a more complete and holistic history of ideas and events that have shaped, and continue to shape, human growth, development, and new futurities. Emphasizing "multicentricity" to us is about decoloniality because it seeks to challenge the idea of a dominant knowledge system that becomes the standard to which everything else is measured. The idea of multicentricity challenges the dominant theories and bodies of knowledge we (presently) continue to work with for their exclusions and hegemonic practices (see also Assie-Lumumba, 2016a; Biraimah 2016; Brock-Utne, 2003, 2015; and Ndlovu-Gathsheni, 2015; in other contexts).

But we cannot speak of decolonization, whether it is of the school curriculum pedagogy or classroom instruction, without a critical understanding of what it *entails* for education. We find that, today, decolonization is very much in vogue. All who seek an understanding of radical and transformative politics use the language of decolonization. But decolonization is a deep-rooted practice that touches on the question of land and the spiritual, emotional, psychological, and cultural bonding or attachments of peoples to their place of occupancy. African schooling and education must embrace decolonization in all its complex manifestations. Decolonization is about the body, mind, soul, and spirit of the learner. Decolonization begins by developing a critical understanding of the self, sense of place, culture, and history, as well as an understanding of the relationships to laws, governance systems, autonomy, and sovereignty. The poetics of decolonization enthuses that in order to pursue counterhegemonic knowledge as "decolonial education," there must, first, be a *restoration* (i.e., a deep reflection on past, history, culture, and psychic memories) and, second, be a *liberation* (the pursuit of educational praxis informed by a nexus of body, mind, soul, and spirit). This means working with the old and new while recognizing that Indigeneity is neither static nor incapable of adaptation. But as Fanon (1967) opines, decolonization is also about freeing ourselves in order "to open up a future" (p. 161). We need a restoration of our generative beliefs and practices associated with the land, inclusive of waters, seas, and sky, and its earthly teachings to help us begin the process of decolonization as colonized and Indigenous peoples. Indigenous communities globally are governed by land and place and thus relationships (see Environmental Monitoring Alberta, 2016).

As alluded to earlier, and attested to by many Indigenous scholars, the land and the body are important sites and sources of knowing. Schools are themselves "sacred learning spaces" (Garcia & Shirley, 2012, p. 76) and coming to know through the Akan linguicism of "*Suahunu*"—what Dei (2012) has called the "Trialectic Space"—allows for transgressive possibilities. Decolonization calls for upholding the "epistemic saliency" (Dei, 1999) of the African/local/oppressed voice as both a refusal and negation of the imperial narratives. Decolonization insists on the pursuit of resistance and a commitment to responsibility by the oppressed, colonized, and Indigenous peoples to narrate our own experiences, stories, and truths. Decolonization requires that we trouble the "grammar of coloniality" (Mignolo, 2000) of science and the universalization of Western thought, that is, to challenge the ways that the history of Western Europe masquerades as a universal history of human existence. Subverting this "grammar" then becomes a decolonial education practice. It seeks to uncover, validate, restore, and rejuvenate subjugated knowledge systems.

African historian and philosopher Cheikh Anta Diop (1974) instructed that decolonization means abandoning all "reflexes of subordination" and becoming true to our authentic selves as a people with history, culture, soul, spirit, identity, and purpose. This is significant. Decolonization cannot proceed on the terms of the colonial dominant or oppressor. Decolonization that seeks to replace oneself in the position of the oppressor or the privileged is not decolonization. Decolonization is being able to affirm one's agency and self-determination for new anticolonial futures. The urgency for decolonization in Africa is that we, as African learners and educators, need to confront our intellectual discomfort and ask ourselves who among us will apply our voices, languages, history, and culture for critical discursive practice. We must question why we are not always our true selves in Eurocentric/White-centered spaces and instead seek acceptance, legitimacy, and validation in Western institutions of higher learning. Even in our African institutions of higher learning, our academies have become mere colonial satellites of the Western academy. Why? The race for internationalization is determined by the currencies of the dominant. We mimic Western standards of excellence and through such entanglements are continually colonized. Because colonialism has not ended for Black, African, and Indigenous peoples, the "project" or "task" of decolonization will always represent a yearning, a desire, and an urgency. Consequently, anyone who rejects or shies away from true decolonization does so at their own peril. But we can only decolonize ourselves: It is through resistance and daily struggles that we sow the seeds of our (collective) decolonization.

Decolonization, in effect, is marked onto bodies and spaces. Bodies and the ways we come to know and act in spaces such as schools and learning sites are important. Decolonization is thus a call for the "(re-)epidermalization" of knowledge as embodiment, as part of a search for epistemologies in dialogue and praxis. This re-epidermalization arouses a consciousness that is only meaningful when it is action-oriented. There is knowledge associated with the experiences of being Black and African. This is a knowledge conscious of one's place in the global polity and what it means to resist and reclaim one's identity, past, history, culture, and future. Educators and schools have a big responsibility in performing such decolonial tasks. Our school curriculum must be decolonized in ways that bring to the heart of teaching the question of the land in Africa. We still inhabit our land, but it can be bought, borrowed, or stolen from us, continuing to allow others to strip it away from us spiritually, emotionally, psychologically, materially, and economically.

Teaching such critical knowledge of African realities and existential conditions is part of decolonial education. This awareness for the contemporary learner is about developing the criticality of knowing to question the normal order of things within schools and in the wider society we live in. In the contexts of schooling and education, critical teaching and learning include questioning schooling practices that themselves reproduce colonial hierarchies of knowing. Decolonization thus is about fighting for equity and social justice and resisting the coloniality of power that continually afflicts relations of schooling. Decolonization is about holding to our Indigenous conceptions of the land in Africa. Again, Coulthard (2014) not long ago wrote about how dispossession of Indigenous peoples on Turtle Island has disrupted their relationships to land such that in an effort to reclaim sovereignty, Indigenous peoples are exhibiting Western ways of relating to land—treating it as private property and pursuing land claim agreements with the Canadian government and giving up, in a sense, their traditional ways of relating to the land. Coulthard (2014) pointedly remarked,

> I would suggest that one of the negative effects of this power-laden process of discursive translation has been a reorientation of the meaning of self-determination for many (but not all) Indigenous people in the North; a reorientation

> of Indigenous struggle from one that was once deeply informed by the land as a system of reciprocal relations and obligations (grounded normativity), which in turn informed our critique of capitalism in the period examined above, to a struggle that is now increasingly for land, understood now as [a] material resource to be exploited in the capital accumulation process. (p. 78)

This is what happens when the norms and values of Western capitalism encroach on Indigenous ways of life and knowing, such as Indigenous philosophies of the land as a site of knowledge, teachings, reciprocal sharing, and relationships. We need school and education to restore this Indigenous sense of land as shared property with spiritual, material, emotional, and physical connections and well-being and living well for all nations (humans, plants, and animals).

Decolonization also means African schooling and education through curricular and instructional practices. Educators must embrace a Freirean "consciousness," pedagogies of liberation, and Fanonian decolonization, all of which extend the discussion beyond our mental universe to what it means to engage in true practice for educational change. Decolonizing the African school curriculum is not just a theoretical discussion but, instead, also calls for concrete and meaningful action. Decolonization means embarking on sustained curricular and instructional practices that work with the African Ubuntu sense of "community," "community building," and "communities of differences" to ensure that the task at hand is read as a collective responsibility. This task demands action from educators, school administrators, policy makers, government officials, students, parents, and local communities. The task is also informed by a value and commitment that we are not fighting just for our individual educational success(es) but for the collective success of all as well. Similarly, African education must be geared toward local and national community development as well as future youth leadership and democratic participation. Educators and education must help young African learners define new responsibilities of an African citizenry and citizenship. Education must promote sustainable livelihoods and pursue development as a humane practice and our relationality and our obligations to Mother Earth that inform the collective wellbeing of all nations (humans, plants, and animals). This practice will include working collectively to ensure knowledge generation for earth's survival, local food sovereignty, adult and youth employment, health, housing, transport, and so on. It also means educators working with learners and learners/students' knowledges/voices to address the local and social relevance of academic scholarship in our institutions of higher learning. In teasing out the possibilities of decolonial Black and African education, it is imperative that we interrogate the links between intellectuality and political thought as well as the applicability of ideas informed by continental African and Black diasporic contexts and experiences.

Each chapter in this book offers its own critique and interrogation of Black and African education. The authors take up the subject of Black/African education from diverse positionalities, including geographic locations on the continent and the Black diaspora.

What is striking are the similarities in the "stories told" and how they point to the urgency for a search for Black/African decolonial education.

Nakanyike Musisi's chapter, "Decolonizing Knowledge in the Bosom of the 'Marketplace': Makerere University Scholars in the Age of the National Resistance Movement's Neoliberal Policies (1989–2007)," sets an important tone for the discussion with a discussion of how academic coloniality and local resistance to structural processes play out. Using Uganda's Makerere University as a case study, she alludes to the coloniality of knowledge, local resistance, and the impact of neoliberalism on institutions of higher learning in Africa. It is noted that the state strategies of the National Resistance Movement (NRM) to influence the commodification of knowledge production, and its growing encroachment on academic freedom, have become legendary. Critics have accused universities of relinquishing the mission of decolonization by now "entrapped scholars" in the belly of the beast. This chapter serves a dual goal: first, to search for productive subversive elements that refused to submit to the so-called consultancy culture that Mamdani (2007) argues produces knowledge for "capital" and, second, to map out how these subversive elements navigate between different sites of knowledge production (communities, activists, or social movements) to advance knowledge and curricula that speak to the histories of the subjugated and marginalized to facilitate new ways of imagining the future. It is argued that far from being complacent with the NRM's neoliberal policies, progressive inquiry has yet to lose the spirit of decolonization and emancipation, often interrupting the colonial episteme by tampering with the very processes and mediums through which knowledge was/is produced while suggesting alternatives to, and critiques of, old colonial problematics. Feminist and lesbian, gay, bisexual, and transgender scholarship and strategies, including Stella Nyanzi's controversial episode of work done in the different schools at Makerere—all testify to Makerere scholars' commitment—against all odds—to the spirit of decolonization, emancipation, and freedom.

In her chapter, "An Antiracist Education Critique of Curriculum Policy Reform in Postapartheid South Africa," Samiera Zafar argues that the African National Congress (ANC) government in post-1994 South Africa sought to get rid of a racially segregated public schooling system and implement a new outcomes-based school curriculum. This was viewed as an attempt to subvert and decolonize apartheid-era public schooling. In "Curriculum 2005" and other education policy documents, the right to basic education as "an immediate and unqualified right" with equitable access for all children was guaranteed in Section 29(1)(a) of the new South African constitution (Republic of South Africa, 1996a). Reflecting on these policy initiatives, Zafar argues that "the globally dominant human rights discourse that steered the transition to democracy and framed Curriculum 2005 was necessary but insufficient to decenter the colonial and apartheid-era racial contours 'baked in' to the public schooling system." She draws from the body of work of South African education practitioners, academics, and public intellectuals to outline both the gains made and the "race work" that still remains to be done. Zafar posits "antiracism education futures for the South African school curriculum and public schooling," emphasizing the importance of including decolonial, antiracist approaches in the work of educators, researchers, and policy makers. The chapter offers us insights into some of the tangible challenges of implementing decolonial education in Africa.

Historically, African educational systems have struggled with the pursuit of decolonial education. In, "'Africanizing' the Ghanaian Education System: Learning Through the Prism of an Africentric System of Thought," Patrick Radebe uses Kwame Nkrumah's anticolonial theoretical framework and Paolo Freire's liberation pedagogy to examine the impact of neocolonial education on Ghanaian students and the implications for Ghana's social, political, and economic development. Recognizing that Ghana's neocolonial education system has led students to "adulterate Indigenous languages," the implications and lessons for social cohesion and cultural identity need to be examined further. It is observed that there has been a failure on the part of Ghana's neocolonial educational policy and practice to cultivate and situate a critical understanding of the country's history (particularly its independence movement, 1946–1957) for local learners. The chapter poses a stark question: "What steps are required to 'Africanize' Ghana's education system with a view to combatting an institutional culture fundamentally opposed to the intellectual liberation of students?" Radebe sees colonial education as a fundamental problem with which to contend. He suggests that Ghana's educational culture remains "essentially neocolonial" at the moment, and the stakes are high for the country's future. The strength of Radebe's discussion lies in the careful laying out of contemporary challenges for Ghanaian and Black/African education and what needs to be done to address these problems, including possibilities for educational futurity.

The jointly authored piece by Richardson Addai-Mununkum and Nyuiemedi Agordzo Edoh-Torgah, "Decolonized Curriculum in Colonized Contexts: Assessing Ghanaian Public Schools' Role in the Decolonization Agenda," takes us through attempts to Africanize the Ghanaian education system since independence. The chapter explores some of the struggles of incorporating Africentric education in students' learning. The authors undertook a qualitative case study of six public schools where data from interviews, focus groups, and observations led to a critical analysis of the extent of Africentric curriculum development in the Ghanaian public education system. There is a complex array of theoretical, methodological, and policy factors that reveal "complex interrelationships between personal faiths, institutional ideology, and school ownership/management." The chapter highlights an important lesson that effective curriculum reforms must be firmly grounded in a broader framework of ideological and structural reform achieved through a decolonial, Africentric school curriculum.

An interesting and revealing approach to decolonial curricular reform is found in the use of Indigenous philosophies as epistemologies of decolonization in school settings. Isaac Nortey Darko, Paul Banahene Adjei, and Chloe Weir's chapter, "Indigenous African Philosophies as a Critical Thinking Pedagogical Tool for Schooling and Education," examines contributions that African proverbs, riddles, and folk stories can make to the "critical thinking process" among Black and African learners. The chapter highlights the important relationship between self-identity, experience, knowledge, and the "critical thinking process." It is argued that African proverbs, riddles, and folk stories offer key pedagogical sites and curricular sources as counter-epistemologies. Fortunately, these Indigenous philosophies are gradually gaining ground in the education of young learners offering students the opportunity to explore their cultures even deeper. We need more African educators to recognize the importance of such local cultural knowledge forms and to use these in classroom lesson plans and curricular units for students. It is an important way of ensuring the promotion of African Indigeneity.

In a more concrete and grounded way of working with Indigenous knowledges, "Spirituality and Self-Care Among Ghanaian Social Workers: Lessons for Africanizing Social Work Education" by Paul Banahene Adjei, Isaac Nortey Darko, Sulemana Fuseini, and Abigail Adubea Mills shows us a direction for Black and African educational futurity. To counter contemporary contestations of "religious rebellion, theological taboo, and uprising suspicions of sanctity as legitimate in the pursuit of social wellness and change," a serious understanding of spirituality in education must be advanced to transform African learning. This chapter discusses how 40 Ghanaian social workers, operating with different agencies in Ghana and Canada, rely on their spiritualities to support their professional practices. There are important findings suggesting that spirituality can be an effective coping mechanism for social workers and other educational practitioners to deal with profession-related stresses. Spiritual values, knowledges, and practices have allowed social workers, clients, and other community learners to connect to their emotional memories, and, by extension, their lived realities, as they shared similar stories and pains. If school educators and social work practitioners are to be effective in their practice, including fostering transformative processes of educational delivery, then there is a crucial place for understanding and engaging the spiritualties of learners and social work clients. In a colonial education system where, not long ago, spirituality was denied as "not valid knowledge" and dismissed as mythic superstition and therefore "unscientific," it is a challenge to begin to center spirituality in school learning.

In reflecting on Black and African education, our gaze must look at different subject areas. Environmental education and teaching of science are very important areas for interrogation. For example, how can the teaching and learning of environmental education contribute to the promotion of inclusive education? Louis Atsiatorme and Kolawole Raheem take up the question in their case study on "Contextualized Role-Play, Inquiry, and Eco-Management in Teaching Environmental Education in Junior High Schools in Ghana." The authors offer some leads on how environmental education (presented through environmental topics and themes) can be infused in the curriculum of schools in basic and tertiary institutions in Ghana. They call for more effective pedagogical strategies in environmental education in Ghana and Africa that have had positive effects on students' learning about the environment in other contexts. The study involved 579 junior high schools in the Greater Accra Metropolis in Ghana, and through descriptive and experimental research designs, the authors assessed "the effectiveness of role-playing, inquiry and eco-management approaches in teaching environmental education" among the young learners. Some interesting gender differences are noted, including that "females expressed more positive environmental attitude than males while males had slightly more environmental knowledge than females."

When we turn to the global challenges confronting Black and African education, one theme that must also be raised is anti-Blackness and anti-African racism in education. Rowena Linton's chapter, "Global Anti-Blackness and Resistance: Implications for Educating African Learners," explores the global question of Blackness, anti-Blackness, and education with relevance for multiple geopolitical spaces of learning. The uniqueness of theorizing global Blackness and anti-Blackness in education is revealed, drawing important lessons for our understanding of Black identities and resistance and the challenge of enhancing Black and African education. Linton's work shows that the challenges confronting Black education are not unique to Africa. Black and African students in the diaspora continue to experience schooling through colonial educational systems and curriculum that negates or devalues particular body experiences, cultures, and histories. There continues to be a deafening silence about anti-Blackness and a persistent denial of its damaging effects on the Black and African student experience. To develop an understanding of the broader scope of anti-Black racism in the global context, this chapter theorizes anti-Blackness and how such theorization connects with antiracist, anticolonial, and decolonial educational politics. Understanding such theorization is crucial for deconstructing how anti-Blackness and a colonial legacy are deeply embedded at the core of formal educational systems worldwide, thus implicating Black/African education.

How do we empower Black and African learners in the context of global anti-Blackness? Popular culture, particularly media, has a role to play in equipping learners with critical thinking and subversive skills to address issues of racism, sexism, classism, ableism, and linguicism, among others, in schools and wider society. What happens when mass media is a major medium for expressing blatantly oppressive views? Patrick Radebe's second chapter in this collection, "How the Mainstream Media Signified Ben Johnson: A Tale of a Black Canadian Sports Hero Turned Jamaican Villain and the Implications for Black Students," points to the various ways in which Canadian mainstream media "signify" Black Canadians and thereby impede the intellectual development of Black learners. A doping scandal involving African Canadian Olympic athlete, Ben Johnson, is used as a case study. The author draws on theories of "cultural deficiency" and "biological determinism" to show how media representations of Black people and their families and communities work to perpetuate racial stereotypes that inform teacher expectations of Black and African students. It is opined that this situation contributes to the poor academic performance and high suspension and dropout rates of Black learners in Euro-American contexts. We need critical media literacy to play a progressive role in the fight for social justice for Black and African learners in our school systems.

Arguably Blackness and anti-Blackness are pressing issues African education must confront. In Janelle Baptiste-Brady's essay, "Rethinking Curriculum Through Critical Blackness and African Indigenous Knowledges: A Black Educator's Response," she points out the damaging nature of school curriculum for Black, Indigenous, and racialized learners. It is significant for educational transformation to target questions of epistemology and Black erasure, dehumanization, and the related concerns of structural racism global anti-Blackness and White supremacy. The chapter looks at the "ways that critical Blackness and the principles of Indigenous knowledges can disrupt, reshape, and reimagine curriculum." Among the author's key questions for exploration are, "How can Black educators Africanize the curriculum? What are some of the drawbacks and implications of rethinking curriculum from critical perspectives?" Her discussion is situated in practical examples from her own lived experience as an educator and community worker to reimagine Black educational futurity.

The final chapter, Rukiya Mohamed's reflection "Connecting Missing Links: A Voice From the Diaspora," draws on the broad convergences in the issues of Black and African education across multiple geospaces. Oppressive public education systems play a substantial role in silencing the voices of communities of African descent, distorting history, positioning colonial knowledge systems as the sole way of knowing, and undercutting the relationship among the body, community cultures and experience, and social change. This chapter is situated in two key questions: What does it mean to provide a model of education that recognizes the brilliance of Black and African learners and apprises them of their cultural legacies? And what might happen when educators develop the capacity and competency to influence a redirection of the sociocultural purpose of education for Black and African learners? Writing her chapter as an epilogue, the author has two goals: first, to position within the diasporic context a critical regeneration of what it means to Africanize the public education system within the Canadian context and, second, to challenge you, the reader, to consider your role and responsibility in ensuring that necessary opportunities to learn and thrive are provided equitably to Black and African learners globally.

We are writing this book at a time when a viral pandemic is impacting the global community, one that is revealing and deepening the schisms in our society. Out of our intellectual responsibility and ethics, we find it imperative to broach COVID-19. Although much is still unknown about the epidemiology of the virus, some facts about our global society are becoming clear. The truth of the matter is that COVID-19 feeds on the racially oppressed. In Europe and North America, we see clearly that Black and African lives are in peril.

There is more than can also be said about the impact of COVID-19 to people currently in Africa. How are local health systems equipped to deal with such pandemics? How does Africa protect itself against global developments that implicate travel, class, and racial privileges?

Black people are disproportionately working on the front lines providing essential public services in health care, home care, personal support, sanitation, agriculture, and food services in global diasporic contexts. Historically, our communities worldwide have been impacted by a lack of access to quality, affordable, and culturally competent health care. The intergenerational impact of slavery, the ongoing impact of racism and capitalism, and the lack of legislated paid sick time mean that we are disproportionately forced to work during the pandemic. And while this is the case, health care systems have and continue to misdiagnose, fail to treat, and fail to test us appropriately. The high death rates among Black communities due to COVID-19 are apparent to anyone who truly cares about statistics.

COVID-19 is a stark reminder of global racism. Individuals and governments are resorting to xenophobia and applying the tendency to racialize new viruses that arrive on the scene. As Sun (personal communication, 2020)[1] notes, the racialization and embodiment of disease are steeped in anti-Blackness. Examples include Ebola (named after the Ebola River in the Democratic Republic of Congo) and the global epidemic of HIV/AIDS, during which we saw the subsequent treatment of African people. Both of these have resulted in the deaths (Ebola fewer than but HIV/AIDS more than COVID-19) of thousands of Africans, and although there is some attention to these by the World Health Organization (WHO) and nongovernmental organizations, neither lockdowns nor efforts to quash transmission have been put in motion. In the current moment, we are witnessing increased racism, xenophobia, and physical and verbal violence toward Chinese/Asians worldwide. Not surprisingly, African and Black peoples have not escaped abuse. We see that those who are facing racism and xenophobia globally have turned around to target the Africans within their borders. African and Black peoples are among those most likely to face the brunt of expanded state surveillance and police powers owing to emergency measures to reduce the spread of COVID-19. Wearing face masks, contact tracing, and state enforcement of social distancing will exacerbate the racial profiling endemic to policing. Interestingly, the global acceptance of wearing face masks reveals the hypocrisy toward Muslim women. Nonetheless, our main point is that we have no comfort or expectation that these new surveillance measures will disappear once the pandemic subsides. Instead, they will continue to be part of a new normal—a normal that already disproportionately targets Black people for imprisonment.

Given the travelogue of COVID-19, the implicit White racism of the "Shut Down the Shut Down Movement" only points to capitalist greed and self-centeredness. It is striking that the very people privileged and best positioned to respond well to social-/physical-distancing measures and whose lives are disproportionately spared given their access to health and wealth are at the forefront demanding that the state measures put in place to support those who are made the most vulnerable be removed! There is also a misplaced emphasis on "personal responsibility" rather than community, institutional, and state responsibility. We can only express amazement and horror when the poor are told to "eat well," as if they do not know that. The fault lines in state and institutional responses, beginning with school systems, national/state governments, and policing and law, among others, are clear reminders of the urgent need for a new global futurity.

Even if it is the case that by the time this book is printed the world has found a vaccine for the virus, most of us will never forget. The losses and disruptions in our lives have been profound. It is worth noting and not forgetting that global disparities due to colonization and ongoing forces of capitalism will also determine who produces the vaccine, who retains the patent (and profits), and who will have access to any vaccine once it is produced. However, the loss and cost have been and will continue to mount. But more important, contemporary developments highlight a crucial point: African education must be focused on leading Black and African learners to understand ourselves, our identities, communities, lived realities, and the global communities to which we belong.

The struggle for decolonial education for Black and African learners must connect issues locally, nationally, and globally. We need decolonized education that allows us to think through solutions to our own problems and that is steeped in our cultural and Indigenous perspectives. For example, COVID-19 has also resulted from the state of our world as it is: one that has crushed indigeneity in favor of progress/capitalism, stamping out traditional medicines in the process. Therefore, our Indigenous health sciences (e.g., herbal pharmacology, traditional medicine, etc.) can be strengthened as part of an African-centered educational system. In April 2020, there was a purported COVID-19 herbal remedy from Madagascar, COVID-Organics. Although the WHO and the African Union were right in insisting on more clinical testing for this herbal treatment to determine its effectiveness and safety in either prevention or treatment of the disease, a number of Southern African countries proceeded to order stockpiles of this treatment, nonetheless. Although we are in agreement that more clinical trials are necessary, just like the race for vaccine treatment in the West, there are numerous lessons that can be taken away from this development. Africa, Africans, and Black peoples could develop our capacities to find local Indigenous treatment and not be dependent on the achievements of Western medicine. We must reclaim our Indigenous philosophical ideas of community, social responsibility, mutual interdependence, relationality, connectedness, culture, history, and spiritualities. It is in doing so that we may thwart our dependence on the West and the continued colonization of the African being.

Acknowledgements

We would like to thank Danielle Sandhu, JD, Osgoode Law School, University of Toronto, and Rukiya Mohamed, of the Department of Social Justice Education, Ontario Institute for Studies in Education of the University of Toronto (OISE/UT), for reading and commenting on an earlier draft of the chapter.

Notes

1. Email correspondence on April 11, 2020 discussing a CNNj report on Africans being abused in China during the COVID-19 pandemic.

References

Abdi, A. (2015). Re-culturing de-cultured education for inclusive social development in Africa. In E. Shiza & A. Abdi (Eds.), *Indigenous discourses on knowledge and development in Africa.* (pp. 63–77). Routledge.

Abdi, A., & Cleghorn, A. (Eds.). (2005). *Issues in African education: Sociological perspectives.* New York, NY: Palgrave Macmillan.

Abubakre, R. D., & Reichmuth, S. (1997). Arabic writing between global and local culture: Scholars and poets in Yorubaland. *Research in African Literatures, 28*(3), 183–209.

Adebisi, F. I. (2016). Decolonising education in Africa: Implementing the right to education by re-appropriating culture and indigeneity. *Northern Ireland Legal Quarterly, 67*(4), 433–451.

Ahenakew, C., de Oliveira Andreotti, V., Cooper, G., & Hireme, H. (2014). Beyond epistemic provincialism: De-provincializing Indigenous resistance. *Alternative, 10*(3), 216–231.

Akinwale, A. A. (2020). The role of Indigenous knowledge system in African development. In Information Resources Management Association (Ed.), *Indigenous studies: Breakthroughs in research and practice* (pp. 445–458). IGI Global.

Akporobaro, F. B. O., & Emovon, J. A. (1994). *Nigerian proverbs: Meanings and relevance today.* Department of Culture, Federal Ministry of Information and Culture.

Apple, M. (1993). *Official knowledge: Democratic education in a conservative age.* Routledge.

Apple, M. (1999). The absent presence of race in educational reform. *Race Ethnicity and Education, 2*(1), 9–16.

Apple, M., & Weiss, L. (1983). Ideology and practice in Schooling: A political and conceptual introduction. In M. Apple and L. Weis (Eds.), *Ideology and Practice in Schooling.* Temple University Press.

Asante, M. K. (2003) *Afrocentricity: The theory of social change.* Chicago, African American Images.

Assié-Lumumba, N. T. (2016a). Evolving African attitudes to European education: Resistance, pervert effects of the single system paradox, and the ubuntu framework for renewal. *International Review of Education—Journal of Lifelong Learning, 62*(1), 11–27.

Assié-Lumumba, N. T. (2016b). Harnessing the empowerment nexus of Afropolitanism and higher education: Purposeful fusion for Africa's social progress in the 21st century. *Journal of African Transformation, 1*(2), 51–76.

Biraimah, K. L. (2016). Moving beyond a destructive past to a decolonized and inclusive future: The role of ubuntu in providing culturally relevant pedagogy for Namibia. *International Review of Education, 62*(1), 45–62.

Boateng, F. (1990). African traditional education: A tool for intergenerational communication. In M. K. Asante & K. W. Asante (Eds.), *African culture: The rhythms of unity* (pp. 109–122). African World Press.

Bohan, D. M., van Wyk, N. C., Ekman, S., & Hogskola, B. T. (2009). Tradition in transition--intergenerational relations with focus on the aged and their family members in a South African context. *Scandinavian Journal of Caring Sciences, 23*(3), 446–455.

Brock-Utne, B. (2003). The language question in Africa in the light of globalisation, social justice and democracy. *International Journal of Peace Studies, 8*(2), 67–87.

Brock-Utne B. (2015). Language, literacy, power and democracy in Africa. *Education and Society, 33*(2), 5–24.

Burns-Ross, J. (2016). Indigenous intergenerational teachings: The transfer of culture, language, and knowledge in an intergenerational summer camp. *American Indian Quarterly, 40*(30), 216–250.

Cabral, A. (2000). National liberation and culture (return to the source). In E. C. Eze (Ed.), *African philosophy: An anthology* (pp. 260–266). Blackwell Publishers.

Cordoba, T. (2006). Aboriginal literacy and education: A wholistic perspective that embraces intergenerational knowledge. Retrieved from: http://citeseerx.ist.psu.edu/viewdoc/download?doi=10.1.1.540.7801&rep=rep1&type=pdf

Coulthard, G. S. (2014). *Red skin, White masks: Rejecting the colonial politics of recognition.* University of Minnesota Press.

Crate, S. A. (2006). Elder knowledge and sustainable livelihood in post-Soviet Russia: Finding dialogue across the generations. *Arctic Anthropology, 43*(1), 40–51.

d'Abdon, R. (2016). Teaching spoken word poetry as a tool for decolonizing and Africanizing the South African curricula and implementing "literocracy." *Scrutiny2, 21*(2), 44–62.

Dei, G. J. S. (1996). Basic principles of anti-racism education. In *Anti-racism education: Theory and practice* (pp. 25–49). Fernwood Publishing.

Dei, G. J. S. (1999). Knowledge and politics of social change: The implication of anti-racism. *British Journal of Sociology of Education, 20*(3), 395–409.

Dei, G. J. S. (2000). African development: The relevance and implications of "Indigenousness." In G. Dei, B. Hall, & D. G. Rosenberg (Eds.), *Indigenous knowledges in global contexts: Multiple readings of our world* (pp. 70–86). University of Toronto Press.

Dei, G. J. S. (2008). Equity and the economics of schooling in the context of a neo-liberal educational agenda. In B. Porfilio & C. Malott (Eds.), *International examination of urban education: The destructive path of neoliberalism* (pp. 195–210). Sense Publishers.

Dei, G. J. S. (2012). Suahunu: The trialectic space. *Journal of Black Studies, 43*(8), 823–846.

Dei, G. J. S. (2014a). African Indigenous proverbs and the instructional and pedagogic relevance for youth education: Lessons from the Kiembu of Kenya and Igbo of Nigeria. *Journal of Education and Training, 1*(1), 1–28.

Dei, G. J. S. (2014b). Indigenizing the school curriculum: The case of the African university. In G. Emeagwali & G. J. S. Dei (Eds.), *African Indigenous knowledge and the disciplines* (pp. 165–180). Sense Publishers.

Dei, G. J. S. (2018). Reframing Education through Indigenous, Anti-Colonial and Decolonial Prisms. In P. Mclaren and S. Soohoo (Eds.), *The radical imagine-nation* (pp. 214–235). New York: Peter Lang.

Dei, G. J. S. (2019). Neoliberalism as a new form of colonialism in education. In S. Chitpin & J. Portelli (Eds.), *Educational policy in neoliberal times: Issues, challenges and possibilities an international perspective* (pp. 40–58). Routledge.

Dei, G. J. S. (2020). Elders' cultural knowledges and African indigeneity. In J. Abidogun & T. Falola (Eds.), *Palgrave handbook of African education and Indigenous knowledge* (pp. 279–301). Palgrave Macmillan.

Dei, G. J. S., & Karanja, W. (2020). Indigeneity and the Black/African student: The benefits and challenges of a claim to indigeneity in enhancing educational outcomes for Black diasporic students. [Paper for Publication]

Dei, G. J. S., Mazzuca, J., McIsaac, E., & Zine, J. (1997). *Reconstructing 'dropout': A critical ethnography of the dynamics of Black students' disengagement from schools.* University of Toronto Press.

Dei, G. J. S., Odozor, E., & Vasquez, A. (Eds.). (2020). *Cartographies of Blackness and Black indigeneities.* Myers Educational Press.

Diop, C. A. (1974). *The African origin of civilization: Myth or reality* (M. Cook, Trans.). Lawrence Hill & Company.

Emeagwali, G., & Dei, G. J. S. (Eds.). (2014). *African Indigenous knowledge and the disciplines* (pp. 165–180). Sense Publishers.

Emeagwali, G., & Shizha, E. (2016). *African Indigenous knowledges and the science: Journeys into the past and present.* Sense Publishers.

Environmental Monitoring Alberta. (2016, December 15). *16| Keynote Address - Dr. Leroy Little Bear: Big thinking & rethinking: Blackfoot metaphysics* [Video]. YouTube. https://www.youtube.com/watch?v=DUDzK_Huq-s

Fals-Borda, O. (1980). *Science and the common people.* Yugoslavia.

Fanon, F. (1967). *Black skin, White masks.* Grove Press.

Freire, P. (1970). *Pedagogy of the oppressed.* Seabury Press.

Garcia, J., & Shirley, V. (2012). Performing decolonization: Lessons learned from Indigenous youth, teachers and leaders' engagement with critical Indigenous pedagogy. *Journal of Curriculum Theorizing, 28*(2), 76–91.

Gaudry, A., & Lorenz, D. (2018). Indigenization as inclusion, reconciliation, and decolonization: Navigating the different visions for indigenizing the Canadian Academy. *AlterNative: An International Journal of Indigenous Peoples, 14*(3), 218–227.

Giroux, H. (1981). *Ideology and culture and the process of schooling.* Temple University Press.

Glasson, G. E., & Evans, M. A. (2007, September 13–15). *Connecting community elders and schools in 422 Malawi using mobile phones and Web 2.0 technologies.* Paper presented at the Mid-Atlantic 423 Association for Science Teacher Education, Hawk's Nest, WV

Gudynas, E. (2011). Buen vivir: Today's tomorrow. *Development, 54*(4), 441–447.

Gumbo, M. T. (2016). A model for indigenising the university curriculum: A quest for educational relevance. In V. Msila & M. Gumbo (Eds.), *Africanising the curriculum: Indigenous perspectives and theories* (pp. 33–56). Sun Media.

Gumbo, M. T. (2017). Alternative knowledge systems. In J. Williams & K. Stables (Eds.), *Contemporary issues in technology education: Critique in design and technology education* (pp. 87–105). Springer.

Hewitt, J. (2016). Decolonizing and indigenizing: Some considerations for law schools. *Windsor Yearbook on Access to Justice, 33*(1), 65–84.

hooks, b (1992). Eating the other: Desire and resistance. In *Black looks: Race and representation,* (pp. 21–39). Boston: South End Press.

Karanja, W. (2018). An inconvenient truth: Centering land as the site of Indigenous knowledge protection. In G. J. Sefa Dei & M. Jajj (Eds.), *Knowledge and decolonial politics: A critical reader* (pp. 60–94). Brill | Sense Publishers.

Kazembe, L. (2018). "Listen to the blood": Du Bois, cultural memory, and the Black radical tradition in education. *Socialism and Democracy, 32*(3), 146–163.

Kithi, N. (2004). Elders warn of Mijikenda identity crisis. *Daily Nation.*

Kudadjie, J. N. (1996). *Ga and Dangme proverbs: For preaching and teaching.* Asempa Publishers.

Mamdani, M. (2007). *Scholars in the marketplace: The dilemmas of neo-liberal reform at Makerere University. 1989–2005.* Codesria.

Mawere, M. (2015). Indigenous knowledge and public education in sub-Saharan Africa. *Africa Spectrum, 50*(2), 57–71.

Mignolo, W. (2000). *Local histories/global designs: Coloniality, subaltern knowledges, and border thinking.* Princeton University Press.

Mpofu, V., Otulaja, F. S., & Mushayikwa, E. (2014). Towards culturally relevant classroom science: A theoretical framework focusing on traditional plant healing. *Cultural Studies of Science Education, 9*(1), 221–242.

Mundy, K. (2008). Global politics and local realities in the realization of the universal right to education. In S. Moor & R. Mitchell (Eds.), *Power, pedagogy and praxis: Social justice in the globalized classroom* (Routledge Adult and Professional Education Series, pp. 105–124). Routledge.

Mundy, K. E., Green, A, Lingard, B., & Verger, A. (Eds.) (2016). *The handbook of global education policy.* John Wiley & Sons.

Ndlovu-Gathsheni, S. J. (2015). Decolonization as the future of Africa. *History Compass, 13*(10), 485–496.

Ngulube, P. (Ed.). (2017). *Handbook of research on Indigenous knowledge systems in developing countries.* IGI Global.

Nkosi, D. A., & van Niekerk, C. (2017). Modern African classical drumming: Contemporary African drumming practice for a multicultural music curriculum. *Muziki, 14*(1), 123–139.

Nyamnjoh, F. (2012). 'Potted plants in greenhouses': A critical reflection on the resilience of colonial education in Africa. *Journal of Asian and African Studies.* Advanced online publication. https://journals.sagepub.com/doi/abs/10.1177/0021909611417240

O'Donoghue, R., Shava, S., & Zazu, C. (Eds.). (2013). *African heritage knowledge in the context of social innovation.* United Nations University–Institute of Advanced Studies (UNUIAS).

Odora-Hoppers, C. A. (2001). Indigenous knowledge systems and academic institutions in South Africa. *Perspectives in Education, 19*(1), 73–86.

Odora-Hoppers, C. A. (2002a). Indigenous knowledge and the integration of knowledge systems: Towards a conceptual and methodological framework. In C. A. Odora Hoppers (Ed.), *Indigenous knowledge and integration of knowledge systems towards philosophy of articulation* (pp. 139–143). New African Books Limited.

Odora-Hoppers, C. A. (Ed.). (2002b). *Indigenous knowledge and integration of knowledge systems towards philosophy of articulation.* South Africa: New African Books Limited.

Opoku, K. A. (1975). *Speak to the winds: Proverbs from Africa.* Northrop, Lee & Shepard Co.

Opoku, K. A. (1997). *Hearing and keeping. Akan proverbs.* Asempa Publishers.

Otulaja, F. S., & Ogunniyi, M. B. (2017). *The world of science education handbook of research in science education in sub-Saharan Africa.* Sense Publishers.

Phasha, N., Dikeledi M., & Dei, G. S (Eds.). (2017). *Inclusive education in African contexts.* Sense Publishers.

Republic of South Africa. (1996a). The Constitution of the Republic of South Africa, Act No. 108 of 1996. Government Printer.

Republic of South Africa. (1996b). The South African Schools Act No. 84 of 1996. Government Printer.

Semali, L., & Kincheloe, J. (Eds.). (1999). *What is Indigenous knowledge? Voices from the academy.* Falmer Press.

Sesanti, S. (2019). Decolonized and Afrocentric education: For centering African women in remembering, re-membering and the African renaissance. *Journal of Black Studies, 50*(5), 431–449.

Shava, S., O'Donoghue, R., Krasny, M. E., & Zazu, C. (2009). Traditional food crops as a source of community resilience in Zimbabwe. *International Journal of African Renaissance Studies—Multi-, Inter- and Transdisciplinary*, 4(1), 31–48.

Shizha, E. (2005). Reclaiming our memories: The education dilemma in postcolonial African school curricula. In A. Abdi & A. Cleghorn (Eds.), *Issues in African education: Sociological perspectives* (pp. 65–84). Palgrave Macmillan.

Shizha, E. (2014). Counter visioning contemporary African education: Indigenous science as a tool for African development. In Edward Shizha and A. Abdi (Eds.), *Indigenous discourses on Knowledge and Development in Africa* (pp. 78–93). New York: Routledge

Simpson, L. B. (2011). *Dancing on our turtle back: Stories of Nishnaabeg recreation, resurgence and a new emergence*. Arbeiter King Publishers.

Simpson, L. B. (2014). Land as pedagogy: Nishnaabeg intelligence and rebellious transformation. *Decolonization: Indigeneity, Education & Society*, 3(3), 1–25.

Smith, L. T., Tuck, E., & Yang, K. W. (Eds.). (2019). *Indigenous and decolonizing studies in education: Mapping the long view*. Routledge.

Styres, S. (2019). Literacies of land: Decolonizing narratives, storying, and literature. In L. T. Smith, E. Tuck, & K. W. Yang (Eds.), *Indigenous and decolonizing studies in education: Mapping the long view* (pp. 24–37). Routledge.

Taiaiake A., Mihesuah, D., & Cavender Wilson, A. (2004). *Indigenizing the academy: Transforming scholarship and empowering communities*. University of Nebraska Press.

Tedla, E. (1995). *Sankofa: African thought and education*. Peter Lang.

Teferra, D., & Altbach, P. (2004). African higher education: Challenges for the 21st century. *Higher Education*, 47(1), 21–50.

Verdon, S., Wong, S., & McLeod, S. (2015). Shared knowledge and mutual respect: Enhancing culturally competent practice through collaboration with families and communities. *Child Language Teaching and Therapy*, 32(2), 205–222.

Watts, V. (2013). Indigenous place-thought & agency amongst humans and non-humans (First Woman and Sky Woman go on a European world tour!). *Decolonization: Indigeneity, Education & Society*, 2(1), 20–34.

Wexler, L. (2011). Intergenerational dialogue exchange and action: Introducing a community-based participatory approach to connect youth, adults and elders in an Alaskan Native community. *International Journal of Qualitative Methods*, 10(3), 248–264.

Yankah, K. (2004). *Globalization and the African scholar*. Faculty of Arts University of Ghana Monograph.

CHAPTER 1

Decolonizing Knowledge in the Bosom of the "Marketplace": Makerere University Scholars in the Age of the National Resistance Movement's Neoliberal Policies (1989–2007)

Nakanyike Musisi

The National Resistance Movement (NRM) government's strategies to influence the commodification of knowledge production and its growing encroachment on academic freedom have become legendary. Seen as "carved in the belly" of neoliberal policies, commentators have accused Makerere University in Uganda of relinquishing its mission and the work of decolonization in particular. In this chapter, the NRM government's neoliberal policies are seen as representing a complex web of neocolonial relations that, like the political colonialism of the past century, are as destructive as they are generative, and they have tended to provoke comparable responses. Nonetheless, a neocolonial state such as Uganda, driven by neoliberal principles, is more than a set of power/commercial/economic relations; it is a system of exploitation and oppression that, since the 1980s, has turned universities across the globe into what Achille Mbembe (2016) calls "a springboard for global markets in an economy that is knowledge based, innovation based" (p. 38). Mbembe asks: "Can we fight against this?" Limiting myself to the period from 1989 to 2007—a time frame discussed in *Scholars in the Marketplace* (Mamdani, 2007, 2016)—and to a case study approach, I employ the cultural anthropologists' concept of "refusal," particularly as advanced by Audra Simpson (2014) in *Mohawk Interruptus*, to answer Mbembe's question in the affirmative.

To cultural anthropologists, "refusal" is not merely a "no"; it is a stance that connotes an end to something and beginning of something new—a way in which to produce and reproduce communities. It rejects hierarchical relationships in order to create different relationships. Within this understanding, refusal permits an alternative vision of not only "doom" but also a more optimistic future as it exemplifies both limits and possibilities. At the same time, refusal is strategic. It is not an accidental, random act but rather a premeditated, conscious, unhurried action/step toward one thing, belief, or practice. Although cultural anthropologists caution us not to see refusal as simply a response to authority or a revised/modernized version of resistance, it is as much about recognition and about the social as it is about the political. Above all, in Simpson's (2014) lexicon, it is about not authorizing others to define and determine the conditions of engagement. Ultimately, refusal is instead about individuals refusing identities, restrictive structures, and systems, as well as a gauge that indicates that a "limit" has been reached for things to continue in a certain way (Mcgranahan, 2016; Ortner, 1995; Redfield, 2013; Simpson, 2014).

For the task at hand, I find the concept of refusal attractive for it allows us to conceptually map a vast swath of decolonizing efforts at Makerere. Specifically, I use it in this chapter to do two things: first, to search for productive subversive elements that refused to submit to the ostensible "consultancy culture" that *Scholars in the Marketplace* (Mamdani, 2007) posits as having produced knowledge for capital and, second, to map out how these subversive elements navigated between different sites of knowledge production (communities, activists, or social movements) to advance knowledge and curricula that spoke/speaks to the histories of the subjugated and marginal. The intent is not to deny that the conditions described in *Scholars in the Marketplace* were real nor that the analysis of the book was faulty. *Scholars in the Marketplace* reflects major anxieties about the future of Makerere University and, by extension, African universities, in general, and the work they must continue to perform. I contend, however, that the use of the economistic analysis as a mono lens through which to view Makerere masks appreciation of the important work, however slim, many are doing to decolonize the institution, curricula, pedagogy, and the production of knowledge, challenging the system at its core.

Argument

There is no doubt that the Makerere of the time described in the *Scholars in the Marketplace* (1989–2005; Mamdani, 2007) was filled with tensions along many axes (political alignments, social groups, ethnicities, or issue-based coalitions) that were not always as stable as one would expect or assume. Nevertheless, Makerere and pockets in it were able to reignite the spirit of decolonization and emancipation that had almost been smothered out by 20 years of decay during and following the atrocious Idi Amin and Obote II regimes in the 1960s and 1970s (see Sicherman, 2005). I submit that, although conditions and the NRM's neoliberal policies produced unpalatable calamities so eloquently and in places melodramatically described in *Scholars in the Marketplace,* they also provided Makerere with a productive space for a process of ongoing decolonization. Elements of this decolonization not only survived that era but have also been replicated in the region. They cannot be simply written off patronizingly as some scholars have done.

I argue that the neoliberal quandary created a window for the ivory tower/development university to reimagine its role in the present and the future, positing a complex revaluation between theory and praxis. Far from being complacent with the NRM's neoliberal policies, progressive inquiry did not lose the spirit of decolonization and emancipation. Key to my argument is that this reignition often interrupted the colonial episteme by tampering with the very processes and mediums through which knowledge was/is produced while suggesting alternative solutions/critiques to old colonial problematics. Playing and engaging with the politics of refusal were key in these processes: refusal to be constrained by the neoliberal limits' to be defined by certain and often unattainable standards; to engage in "intellectual Olympics"; to teach in certain ways, the colonially inherited definitions of instructional time of 8 a.m. to 5 p.m.; to reject traditional forms of knowledge and ways of knowing; to continue entertaining historical discriminations on the basis of gender, class, ableism or sexual orientation; to be silenced—the list goes on and on.

In all these instances, Makerere was a pioneer in the region, and inexplicably, these instances took place between 1989 and 2007, the years covered in the *Scholars in the Marketplace* (Mamdani, 2007), which was the most difficult period but also the most productive in Makerere's history—a turning point. What was at stake was for Makerere to find itself beyond the colonial perimeters and privileges on which it had been founded (including doing away with giving "boom," a stipendiary allowance given to all university students by the government) and under whose tutelage it had long operated as well as often favorably been evaluated/imagined or even defended. Work done in various departments alongside feminist and lesbian, gay, bisexual, and transgender (LGBT) scholarship testifies to Makerere scholars' commitment to the spirit of decolonization, emancipation, and freedom. Among several exemplary scholars, I note here the late professor Moses Musazi, who, combining Indigenous knowledge and modern technology, invented papyrus sanitary towels (MakaPads). Musazi did not generate a fortune from his invention, nor could we say that his willingness, as a member of the faculty of engineering, to participate in multidisciplinary research with Women and Gender Studies and Education, was part of any agenda other than to address the issue of "how best to improve the retention of girls in school/curtail their dropout." I would have liked to bring to your attention the work of several units and scholars at Makerere, such as Associate Professor Jjuko from the Faculty of Law and partner of the dean of the School of Women and Gender Studies, Professor Consolanta Kabonessa; Abasi Kiyimba; Joe Oloka-Onyango (Sylvia Tamale's partner); Ruth Mukama; Joy Kwesiga; Deborah Kasente; and several others, but, in the interest of time, the discussion is limited to one department (psychiatry) and one individual (Sylvia Tamale) and leads into an exposé of one episode (Stella Nyanzi).

Psychiatry

The Department of Psychiatry at Makerere University was started in 1966 in spite of mental health care's long existence in Uganda since 1894. Although Ugandan and expatriate psychiatrists had acknowledged the importance of "Africanization"—cultural and traditional healers—in the profession's golden age (1962–1972), psychiatry continued to be taught in a manner in which Indigenous knowledge and practitioners were obscured and not given a central place in instruction and research. As Yolana Pringle (2013) narrates, the focus was more on the creation of modern psychiatry, given that many Ugandan psychiatric professors, such as Stephen Bbosa, feared the public would perceive them as "unscientific."

The atypical appointment of anthropologists and psychologists into the Department of Psychiatry signaled a change in the way the discipline would be taught, maladies approached (acknowledgment), and the nature of the research to be conducted. On one hand, this change unsettled deeply entrenched colonial presuppositions about the supposed superiority of Western ideas about mental health that denigrated African concepts, healing methods, and practices (Ovuga, Boardman, & Wasserman, 2006). On the other, it advanced and implemented the apprehensive aspirations of earlier years, particularly the early 1970s. The goal was to decolonize African concepts that deal with mental well-being, medicine, and traditional practitioners—concepts such as witchcraft, *mizimu, ddalu, ddogo, lubaale, kisamira, misambwa, ebyekikia,* and *kazoole*—and to bring them into the realm of the students' learning and ultimate praxis.

If the positioning of traditionalists' healing knowledge alongside Western psychiatric knowledge in the curriculum marked a departure from the previous teaching regimes in the department, it also called into question colonial normative assumptions about mental health—particularly its being linked to "modernity" and "detribalization" among Africans. Nonetheless, inasmuch as it embarked on a critique of earlier approaches, it did not completely toss them out. The current approach acknowledges the historical existence and treatment of mental illness that predate colonialism and draws from both systems to bring wellness to sufferers. As a result, Makerere's Department of Psychiatry is among the most rigorous and integrative on the continent. Its hallmark is sensitivity to Uganda's different cultural concepts/idioms and languages within which mental well-being is expressed and communities and the ragged history of war, violence, and

HIV/AIDS acknowledged (Abbo, Ekblad, et al., 2008; Abbo, Okello, et al., 2008; Abbo et al., 2009; Nakimuli-Mpungu et al., 2015; Okello & Musisi, 2006).

In the period following independence, as well as during the early 1970s, the medical school syllabus tended to mimic British medical schools. Although it was new for psychiatry to link with other departments (e.g., pediatrics and sociology), in a more definitive but quiet move to decolonize psychiatry, new courses were added to the curriculum that went beyond just forming links. These courses included Medical Anthropology, Cultural Psychiatry, Medical Sociology, HIV Psychiatry, Psycho-Trauma, and Old Age Psychiatry, which emphasized, for example, local Indigenous symptom expression and interpretations of mental well-being and illness, traditional healing practices in mental illness, the roles of traditional healers, culturally relevant and sensitive tools or test instruments, appreciating family structure and functions, sensitivity to the effects of war and conflict on mental health in communities, understanding the special psychological disorders of elderly people, and integrating culture in the treatment of the elderly (Ovuga, Boardman, & Oluka, 1999). A multidisciplinary approach was embraced.

The challenge the psychiatry faculty faced was how best to fuse the universality of disease with the particularity of context (between society, culture, politics, and mental illness) and the relationship among psychiatrists, their patients, and alternative Indigenous systems and healing practices (practitioners as expert knowledge custodians). Nonetheless, in an interview, the then head of the department noted that they also continued to teach "old" core subjects of psychiatry, for example, psychoses (such as schizophrenia) or the classic affective disorders (such as bipolar affective disorder, depression, or anxiety disorders). He also emphasized that they overhauled the curricula "to reduce stigma, to de-mystify stereotypes surrounding mental illness and to see that psychiatry made sense to the population and related it to their everyday lived experiences in their communities" (Seggane Musisi Interview, July 15, 2018). It was made clear that their project was not to reject Western traditions (a position shared by Sylvia Tamale—see the next section) but more so about rejecting the notion that there is only one source of psychiatric knowledge. African knowledge systems were brought into the center (wa Thiong'o, 1986) not as appendices to knowledge (content and curriculum reform) but in an open dialogue among equal but different epistemic traditions.

The intent of the decolonizing spark is to accommodate local ways of knowing and to ensure that teaching material has local relevance in the context of Uganda. This was a deliberate refusal of the earlier approaches, a moving away from a Eurocentric to an Africentric curriculum. As the head of the department stated, "using locally relevant material and examples other than 'normative' textbooks, makes the material relevant to students and to the instructors" (Seggane Musisi Interview, July 15, 2018). It "brings a different engagement as it increases students' agency. Students could see themselves at the center of and could directly relate to the knowledge being taught; [they] sometimes bring new and personal perspectives on cases being studied" (Seggane Musisi Interview, July 15, 2018). Such courses have contributed significantly to the Africanization/

Ugandanization of psychiatry in Uganda and have provided students with an accurate understanding of locally expressed symptoms, leading to correct diagnoses (Boardman & Ovuga, 1997). The courses have centered traditional healing practices, spirituality, and disease perception in the curricula; grounded psychotherapy HIV-related mental illnesses and counseling techniques work in local settings; and tailored family therapy training on local conditions (with an appreciation of family structures and local interventions, population displacements, child soldiers, rape, abductions, and the condition of being an orphan). This innovation was supported by a rigorous research agenda that prioritized cultural explanatory models of disease and health-seeking behaviors and pathways to care. It also examined why some patients preferred traditional forms of care to Western medicine, advocated group support psychotherapy (GSP) for a massively HIV-affected and war-traumatized population, and supported commitment to the development of locally suitable test or screening instruments for illiterate patients. Between 2002 and 2012 and beyond, in an activity that further contributed to the decolonization of the curriculum, the Department of Psychiatry carried out an unprecedented number of research studies on local issues that generated publications that were used in the classrooms.

Decolonizing the curricula increased students' agency; they could see themselves at the center of and directly relate to the knowledge being taught. These publications have changed students' viewpoints, particularly regarding the place of Indigenous knowledge in their profession. As one of the most prolific departments in the medical school in terms of research and publications, the psychiatry department's research began to influence health policy in the area of service delivery, for example, to integrate mental health care into HIV care and to institute mental health departments and wards in general hospitals. The team behind this work of decolonizing the curricula includes Drs. E. S. Okello, C. Abbo, E. Nakimuli, D. Akena, J. Nakigudde, W.W. Muhwezi, N. Nakasujja, D. Akena, and S. Musisi. Unlike the earlier generation of African/Ugandan psychiatrists, these practitioners do not denigrate or ridicule African/indigenous psychiatrists for their so-called lack of "scientific" training. In an interview, the then head of the department emphasized that

> we approached mental health work as "of the people, by the people and for the people." We detested and discouraged "hands off ivory tower" research. We worked within communities and gave back to the community through community involvement/participation including workshops, seminars and national conferences. The annual Psycho-trauma conferences were one example. We held these in various regions of the country and the capital cities of the Eastern Africa Region. We attracted [a] local and international audience. (Seggane Musisi Interview, July 15, 2018)

Much of the labor was nonetheless a continuation of the decolonizing initiatives undertaken in the late 1960s and early 1970s, such as group psychotherapy among selected patients (started in 1968) and the utilization of television (WBS TV and UBC TV) to sensitize and increase awareness in the population about mental illness. Above all, it was during this period that psychiatry became a mandatory university examinable subject in the College of Health Sciences. It had previously been taught as a "subject of interest" to which medical students were introduced; it was not a course unit with grade point average points. Failing it meant not being allowed to graduate. Other specialist medical disciplines, such as pediatrics, also made it mandatory. The graduate program encouraged students to do mental health research fieldwork in communities rather than in hospitals in an effort to identify community approaches to public mental health challenges. This strategic approach reverses the colonial and the immediate postcolonial practice of concentrating psychiatric research using patients in hospital settings. We must interpret what this department was able to achieve as ongoing decolonizing work (see Ndlovu-Gatsheni & Siphamandla, 2016; Parker, 2016). Although not an end in itself, it can be seen as on the continuum of a struggle to integrate Indigenous mental health knowledge on its own terms and in relation to other (Western) knowledge systems. This was a struggle about what is to be taught.

Sylvia Tamale

Often-noted consequences of neoliberalism are the destruction of commitment to liberatory politics, the institutional site of the university, and its teaching staff's detachment from the public and giving up the project of decolonization. This is a script that does not fit the character of Sylvia Tamale. She epitomizes the refusal to agree with or acquiesce to the neoliberal agenda and politics. The decolonization of her pedagogy, classrooms, and students, as well as herself, has been a long-term personal investment for Tamale. Her first act of refusal, and one that possibly prepared her for her future work of decolonizing knowledge, is revealed by the choices she made early in her education. Having obtained a Master of Law from Harvard University and a PhD in sociology and feminist studies from the University of Minnesota, Tamale returned to Uganda to take up her appointment in the faculty of law at Makerere.

In addition to espousing insurgent and radical ideas in the period covered by *Scholars in the Marketplace* (Mamdani, 2007), Tamale also became the first female dean of the faculty of law at Makerere (2004–2008). And, in later years, she founded the Law, Gender and Sexuality (LGS) Research Centre in the School of Law. At a time when many of her colleagues working in the realm of women's rights were afraid to be called "feminists," she purposely refused the popular assigned title of "gender activists," arguing that it lacked the "political punch" (Tamale, 2005). The terrain that Tamale traversed combined academia with activism and adopted a critical approach to the law, enriching students' transformative personal growth and agency. This often meant researching, teaching, and speaking the "unspoken"—uncovering silences and secrecies—particularly around sexuality and the body. This journey was not unproblematic; she was often the recipient of anonymous and vicious letters and called names such as "BITCH" in print and audio media, and she and her family members were often the targets of threats. In fact, in 2003, Tamale, along with the murderous Joseph Kony, was declared the "Worst Woman of the Year" by Uganda's largest and leading daily newspaper, the *New Vision*. Undeterred by this malevolence, Tamale made it a badge of honor which she wore "with a lot of pride and dignity!" (Tamale, 2016a).

Hate dispatches received by Tamale and aimed at Tamale's research, teaching, and labor of activism expose the ragged intellectual terrain scholars who do radical work traverse. Tamale's contribution to decolonizing university education was her fearless battle to couple the academy with society and politics and to operationalize theory and praxis, challenging not only embedded societal patriarchal values and consciousness but also their institutionalization within the education system (Desai & Sanya, 2016). This meant becoming a champion advocating for the inclusion of sexual minorities' voices, perspectives, and knowledge in the curriculum. Her work exemplifies a seamless coupling between the university, the women's movement, and sexual minorities' groups such as Sexual Minorities Group in Uganda. This was very important, especially in a hostile environment that made "many afraid to speak out publicly or to take activists action" (Tamale, 2007, p. 21). Tamale's pedagogy and standpoint were among the first to challenge and oppose the NRM government's neoliberal policies.

This was done on two grounds: first, because of its pretense about liberating women (women in politics) and, second, because of its dehumanizing and incriminating narratives about othered Ugandans on the basis of their sexual orientation. First, inasmuch as Tamale applauded the NRM's pro-women policies, particularly the introduction of affirmative action programs, such as reserving seats for women in the Parliament and local councils, she questioned whether a reformist state that shies away from dealing with structural problems underlying the system can deliver gender equality in politics in any meaningful way. Instead, Tamale advocated for women to advance a feminist political agenda outside the confines of state-led initiatives. She also reminded those women elected to high seats not to be complacent in their positions of power; they should not take their office as a privilege but rather should see it as their right and do all they can to use it as an opportunity to advance the emancipation of women in different aspects of their lives (Tamale, 1999, 2000). Tamale (2003, p. 4) was not afraid to denounce a fellow feminist who, as minister of gender, advised her fellow women activists to remove all references to "sexual orientation" in their recommendations to the Equal Opportunities Commission. The minister was afraid that this would badly "taint" women, and Tamale saw this as a betrayal refusing to acquiesce to such an outright denial of the rights of lesbians and gays.

Another important aspect of Tamale's decolonization work was her take on "culture" that she articulated as double-edged with a high potential to enhance women's access to justice. For her, short of cultural reductionism and an uncritical embrace and equipped with critical questions coupled with a realization that culture is shaped by agency, women activists should not be shy about speaking out in support of culture. She is convinced that

> for many African women the sustainable solutions to their oppression, exploitation and subordination hardly lie in vague, alien legal rights, but in a careful and creative deployment of the more familiar cultural norms and values.... our activism must begin from the assumption that bottom-up approaches anchored in local cultures and traditions are more likely to succeed than those working from without. (Tamale, 2008, p. 63)

Tamale denounced claims that she was doing anti-homosexual advocacy work for monetary gain. Insinuations that her campaign for homosexuality was Western-driven—another form of colonization—are castigated by Tamale, who sees them as "tired myths" aimed at derailing her. Seeing the rampant homophobia in Uganda and, indeed, in Africa in terms of gendered politics, she asserts that

> sexual activities that go against the grain of mainstream ones subvert conventional gendered relations and hierarchies. Sexuality therefore becomes a critical site for maintaining patriarchy and reproducing African women's oppression ... gendered dimensions of sexuality are very clear when considering the implicit erasure of lesbian identity (and the preoccupation with) male-on-male sex. Homosexuality presents a challenge to the deep-seated masculine power within African sexual relations and disrupts the core of heterosexist social order. (Tamale, 2007, p. 19)

Her work, therefore, seeks to interrogate and expose the various agendas (including patriarchy) and tools (including sexuality) aimed at sustaining the superiority and dominance of one group over another. In reclaiming the Indigeneity of homosexuality in Uganda, Tamale is engaging in a decolonizing project that claims from Africa, that which is African. The Africanization of the homosexuality discourse in Africa has gained immensely from Tamale's work; Tamale (2011), who inasmuch as she is open to Western concepts and theories, remains concerned about the language of colonialism in Western discourses. The act of refusal entails reclaiming one's position in academia (academic freedom). But it was more than this for Tamale. It became/was/is a way she demonstrated her allegiance to a community of activists that advanced rights for the sexually marginalized and refused sexual normativity. Tamale's politics of refusal is twinned with the politics of recognition of the multiplicity/plurality of sexualities in

Uganda. Yet, paradoxically, Tamale neither seeks recognition from her critics or detractors nor does she compete in the "intellectual Olympics." This is because she does not recognize detractors' recognition as the route through which independence from domination and subjugation should be sustained and legitimated.

Her decolonization work has been premised on political engagement, supported by a strong belief in a research agenda that "produces home-grown feminist theory and radicalism" (Tamale, 2005). Her decolonization work is not deterred by fear. Tamale wrote in 2005 that

> in our struggle we must be brave enough to tread where others fear to go. Many times, we are intimidated into avoiding controversial paths, our work is discredited and delegitimized by the dominant patriarchal forces, we are made to feel lonely, isolated, and unsupported like social outcasts. . . . We should not be ashamed to associate ourselves with stigmatizing terms such as "militant" and "radical" that are used to describe us, for it will only take radical and revolutionary actions to overthrow patriarchy. Patriarchy uses the age-old trick of divide and rule. (p. 41)

The important decolonization work Tamale continues to do at Makerere challenges institutional, as well as managerial, alienating cultures. Her Inaugural Lecture of October 2016, which she titled "Nudity, Protest and the Law in Uganda," was premised on reading the political body and used Stella Nyanzi's episode (Monday, April 18, 2016). Tamale concludes the lecture, which encapsulates who Tamale is in the decolonizing labor group, by stating that "naked bodies make strong political statements that challenge structures of domination or exclusion" (2016b, p. 31).

It is to be expected that this lecture received similar unwarranted contemptuous reviews, not from the media or the public but from a triad organized from within the Makerere Institute of Social Research (MISR). At times, the first member of this triad engaged in a calculated misreading of Tamale, accusing her of engaging in a "naïve exercise," having a "simplistic unidirectional analysis," not showing "awareness of current scholarly debates," and "misreading and misusing 'culture'" (Bezabeh et al., 2017, p. 3). Using lengthy jargon, the second member of the triad criticized Tamale for linking Nyanzi's nudity to powerlessness, "suggesting its complete disarticulation from any power" (Bezabeh et al., 2017, p. 7). Nyanzi chose the form within which to lodge her protest—a form that refuses clear-cut theorizing and academic jargon; it was in our face, and it was not meant for one individual to see. Otherwise, she could have waited for the director to arrive at the office to stage her protest. It was a public demonstration. Tamale was critiqued for neglecting to give the background to her action but to instead have staged her analysis with the act itself. The third member of the triad, who was the target of Nyanzi's wrath, accused Tamale of being silent on the "object of Nyanzi's protest" (Mamdani, 2017, p. 21). Asking "What was Stella Nyanzi's demand?" he concludes that it was tantamount to "a demand for privilege . . . constituting a claim to special and thus privileged treatment"; he emphasized: "In my view Nyanzi's act was not a protest against the denial of a right but a demand for privileged treatment" (Mamdani, 2017, pp. 21–22). Granted that the director may have a point here, one can query whether it was the first time that management had heard about Nyanzi's complaints. What is wrong in entertaining a dialogue on how a program might be run and the human resources deployed, other than the politics of refusal to entertain views from "juniors"—an autocratic, colonizing, despotic, and undemocratic style of management? Besides, is it not a "privilege" to be heading a prestigious institute when one is 74 years of age at a university where people generally retire at 60 and where un-/underemployment is abundant?

Considering Tamale's (2016b) Inaugural Lecture as an extension of her decolonizing work, however, it is easy to see that, in this instance, as in her work in general, she is not necessarily looking for consensus or approval but rather for a chance to move beyond the colonizing attitudes and narratives of self-righteousness where broad-minded counternarratives should inspire faculty (and administrators), as well as students, to act to bring about a more tolerant future. This leads to my analysis of the case study, known as the "incident."

An Incident: Stella Nyanzi

Rather than providing a description of the Nyanzi incident (as various versions of this story could be found in diverse media outlets and particularly in Uganda newspapers), I will be brief so as to return to the politics of refusal. Suffice to note we learn of how Nyanzi framed her protest from Sylvia Tamale, one of the first people to arrive on the scene just a few minutes after the event began. Tamale (2016b) writes:

> But as soon as she saw me she stripped again: "Sylvia, I didn't want to burden you with my problems, but I've had enough. I've complained to the authorities, written several letters but no action has been taken. They have left me with no choice; I've had enough of my boss's tyranny at this place. . . . She was yelling profanities, obscenities and vulgarities, waving her defiant fists in the air. (pp. 1–2)

Let me emphasize that what Nyanzi did was not new in the long history of decolonization in the region. What sets it apart from previous such actions and thus delivers it to the erroneous and injudicious accusation of "a demand for privilege" was

a. who she was—a highly educated, "very intelligent woman";
b. where it was done—Makerere University, the highest seat of intellectual labor;

c. who was protested against—a Guru, an internationally renowned scholar;
d. its potentiality to ruin at least something "good" happening at Makerere—some worried about funding to the MISR being cut off, as that mattered most, and not why she had staged the protest in the first place; and
e. the presence of media.

Indeed, privilege marked each of these factors. Let us for a moment revisit Marcel Mauss's (2016) *The Gift*, as translated by Jane Guyer. In this notable social science classic, we are given to understand that refusal breaks social relations and marks a compromise with the conditions of these bonds. After several failed attempts at negotiation to consider and enact a model that could allow for both teaching and research (in an institute whose original mandate is research) and tired of carrying the burden of being rebuffed, for Nyanzi, reality became articulated on the realization that the conditions of recognizing the MISR, as it was just then, had been built on their—the faculty's and the support staff's—erasure, thus denying them any contribution to the unfolding programs and governance of the institution (top-down management style). Any deviation from their prescribed role of docility was identified as a symptom of asking for a singular "privilege" (not to teach in the Graduate Program). Refusal shaped the way that both actors (the director and the faculty) understood themselves as subjects in opposition to each other's agenda. These signs of refusal (particularly the way they were deployed) divided the intellectual and civil communities.

Focusing on the "cultural shame" of the naked body and the implications of the act for the continuation of the funding for programs at the MISR resulted in neglecting/missing the origins of refusal and the obscured, multifaceted concealed privileges taken for granted. Just as Nyanzi's act could be read as refusal, refusal was also the politics played by the international community and the Makerere Council that suspended her. They refused to acknowledge Nyanzi's act as a signpost of deeper problems at the MISR, particularly the asymmetrical power relations and the upper-handedness of the government in dealing with the crisis. The government's politics of refusal was betrayed when the minister of ethics and integrity, Father Simon Lokodo, ordered Stella Nyanzi's arrest. Indeed, as Sylvia Tamale asked in her Inaugural Lecture: "How do we reconcile the fact that Lokodo's own people, the men and women of Karamoja, even today move around naked or semi-naked without sanction in public, with the fact that Lokodo is the same man who attempted to impose punishment for public nakedness?" (2016b, p. 3). Let me end by echoing Audra Simpson (2014), who reminds us that "refusal can be a powerful alternative to recognition" (Ashley, 2017) of the otherwise obvious.

Conclusion

There is no doubt that the Makerere of today, which continues to be highly rated among African universities, has been hard hit by President Museveni's neoliberal policies. Nevertheless, it is important to note that Makerere scholars have, for years, suffered debilitating psychological anguish in ways that might deflate energies away from the decolonizing work in the university. Audra Simpson (2014) cautions that "concepts have teeth" and that these teeth "bite through time" (p. 100). Rather than being limited and embarrassed by the spiteful debates (some of which do remain productive), we should ask, "How did Makerere survive and what productive lessons do we take from this onslaught, particularly in the ongoing fight to decolonize the African university?" As part of the country's neocolonial historical processes, the NRM government's neoliberal policies have no doubt structured all aspects of Uganda's life, including how academics produce and disseminate knowledge, to such an extent that some acts of refusal were otherwise read as a betrayal and a "sellout" to capitalism or even as irrational.

The case studies covered in this chapter demonstrate what was possible, even when in the bosom of the "marketplace." Faced with insurmountable challenges and compelled by circumstances not of its own making, evidence supports a rereading of Makerere scholars' and administrators' positions vis-à-vis the government's neoliberal politics. Makerere was a postcolonial institution reengaging the state in a manner different from the usual tactics of tools down. Drawing from anthropologists' framework of the politics of refusal, my starting point has been to position the actors' subjectivities not as mere desperados turned into "scholars in the marketplace" driven by a neoliberal agenda and disengaging but instead imagining new subjectivities and continuing the work of decolonizing knowledge production and their disciplines. Refusing to entertain other competing narratives is a failure to interrogate the dominant and normative "truth" regime of what a university should and should not do. Throughout the period covered in *Scholars in the Marketplace* (Mamdani, 2007), we see cases in which scholars "entrapped in the bosom of the marketplace" refused to play by the dictates of the market to produce knowledge for colonial enterprises. The work of decolonizing colonial institutions such as universities is not easy. Part of the challenge lies in the absence of a ready-made model to emulate, in addition to de-entrenching its foundational dreams and fantasies. The cases covered here give us a glimpse of what the building blocks of that model could look like.

References

Abbo, C., Ekblad, S., Waako, P., Okello, E., Muhwezi, W. & Musisi, S. (2008). Psychological distress and associated factors among the attendees of traditional healing practices in Jinja and

Iganga districts, Eastern Uganda: A cross-sectional study. *International Journal of Mental Health Systems, 2*(1), 16.

Abbo, C., Okello, E., Ekblad, S., Waako, P., & Musisi, S. (2008). Lay concepts of psychosis in Busoga, Eastern Uganda: A pilot study. *World Cultural Psychiatry Research Review, 3*, 132–145.

Abbo, C., Waako, P., Okello, E., & Musisi, S. (2009). The prevalence and severity of mental illnesses handled by traditional healers in two districts in Uganda. *African Health Sciences, 9*(Suppl. 1), 16–22.

Ashley, F. (2017). Audra Simpson's mohawk interruptus: A book review. *Medium*. Retrieved from https://medium.com/@florence.ashley/audra-simpsons-mohawk-interruptus-a-book-review-75cc6e5425cc

Bezabeh, S., Ossome, L., & Mamdani, M. (2017). *Commentaries on Professor Sylvia Tamale's inaugural lecture, "Nudity, Protest and the Law in Uganda"* (MISR Working Paper, No. 28). School of Law, Makerere University.

Boardman, J., & Ovuga, E. (1997). Rebuilding psychiatry in Uganda. *Psychiatric Bulletin, 21*(10), 649–655.

Desai, K., & Sanya, B. N. (2016). Towards decolonial praxis: Reconfiguring the human and the curriculum. *Gender and Education, 28*(6), 710–724.

Fanon, F. (1963). *The wretched of the earth.* (C. Farrington, Trans.). Grove Press.

Mamdani, M. (2007). *Scholars in the marketplace: The dilemmas of neo-liberal reform at Makerere University. 1989–2005*. Codesria.

Mamdani, M. (2016). Between the public intellectual and the scholar: Decolonization and some post-independence initiatives in African higher education. *Inter-Asia Cultural Studies, 17*(1), 68–83.

Mamdani, M. (February 2017). Comment on Sylvia Tamale, 'Nudity, Protest and the Law in Uganda,' Inaugural Professorial Lecture, October 28, 2016. MISR Working Paper No. 28, pp. 17–23. Makarere Institute of Social Research.

Mauss, M. (2016). *The gift.* (J. I. Guyer, Trans.). Hau Books.

Mbembe, A. (2016). Decolonizing the university: New directions. *Arts and Humanities in Higher Education, 15*(1), 29–45.

Mcgranahan, C. (2016). Theorizing refusal: An introduction. *Cultural Anthropology, 31*(3), 319–325.

Musisi, S. (July 15, 2018). Interview. Entebbe, Uganda.

Nakimuli-Mpungu E., Kizito, W., Okello J., Alderman, S., Odokonyero, R., Mojtabai, R., Mills, E. J., Kanters, S., Nachega, J. B., & Musisi, S. (2015). Group support psychotherapy for depression treatment in people with HIV/AIDS in northern Uganda: A single-centre randomised controlled trial. *Lancet HIV, 2*(5), e190–e199.

Ndlovu-Gatsheni, S. J. & Siphamandla Z. (2016). *Decolonizing the university, knowledge systems, and disciplines in Africa.* Durham, Carolina Academic Press.

Nyanzi, S. (2016) Nudity, Protest and the Law in Uganda. In Feminist Africa, 22 2016 pp. 52–86.

Okello, E. S., & Musisi, S. (2006). Depression as a clan illness (eByekika): An indigenous model of psychotic depression among the Baganda of Uganda. *World Cultural Psychiatry Research Review, 1*, 60–73.

Ortner, S. B. (1995). Resistance and the problem of ethnographic refusal. *Comparative Studies in Society and History, 37*(1), 173–193.

Ovuga, E., Boardman, J., & Oluka, E. G. A. O. (1999). Traditional healers and mental illness in Uganda. *The Psychiatrist, 23*(5), 276–279.

Ovuga, E., Boardman, J., & Wasserman, D. (2006). Undergraduate student mental health at Makerere University, Uganda. *World Psychiatry, 5*(1), 51–52.

Parker, K. R. (2016). Introduction: Decolonizing the university: A battle for the African mind. *CLA Journal, 60*(2), 164–171.

Pringle, Y. (2013). *Psychiatry's 'golden age': making sense of mental health care in Uganda, 1894-1972* [PhD thesis]. Oxford University, UK.

Redfield, P. (2013). *Life in crisis: The ethical journey of Doctors Without Borders.* University of California Press.

Sicherman, C. (2005). *Becoming an African university: Makerere, 1922–2000.* Africa World Press.

Simpson, A. (2014). *Mohawk interruptus: Political life across the borders of settler states.* Duke University Press.

Tamale, S. (1999). *When hens begin to crow: Gender and parliamentary politics in Uganda.* Westview Press.

Tamale, S. (2000). 'Point of order, Mr. Speaker': African women claiming their space in parliament. *Gender and Development, 8*(3), 8–15.

Tamale, S. (2003). Out of the closet: Unveiling sexuality discourses in Uganda. *Feminist Africa,* (2), 1–6.

Tamale, S. (2005, October 29) African feminism: How should we change? *The Association for Women's Rights in Development Forum.*

Tamale, S. (2007). Out of the closet: Unveiling sexuality discourses in Uganda. In C. M. Cole, T. Manuh, & S. F. Miescher (Eds.), *Africa after gender?* (pp. 17–30). Indiana University Press.

Tamale, S. (2008). "The Right to Culture and the Culture of Rights: A Critical Perspective on Women's Sexual Rights in Africa," Feminist Legal Studies 16: 47–69.

Tamale, S. (Ed.). (2011). *African sexualities: A reader.* Oxford, Pambazuka Press.

Tamale, S. (2016a). *African Feminist Forum.* Retrieved from http://www.africanfeministforum.com/sylvia-tamale-2/

Tamale, S. (2016b). Nudity, protest and the law in Uganda. *Feminist Africa, 22,* 52–86.

wa Thiong'o. N. (1986). *Decolonising the mind: The politics of language in African literature.* J. Currey.

CHAPTER 2

An Antiracist Education Critique of Curriculum Policy Reform in Postapartheid South Africa

Samiera Zafar

The democratically elected government led by the African National Congress (ANC) in post-1994 South Africa rapidly integrated a racially segregated public education system and implemented a new outcomes-based school curriculum (Curriculum 2005), signaling a rupture with the apartheid-era education system. As part of a raft of education policies, Curriculum 2005 gave expression to the values in the new constitution (Republic of South Africa [RSA], 1996a) and international human rights instruments. The new education policies and curriculum reform also honored the lives and aspirations of Black learners who spearheaded the "Soweto Uprising" in 1976. The Soweto Uprising, as it became known, began as a peaceful student protest against a new language policy and the introduction of Afrikaans as a medium of instruction for some subjects at the secondary school level. Police opened fire on the student protestors and some youth lost their lives (Pampallis, 2007, p. 16). In the aftermath of this uprising, the Congress of South African Students (COSAS) was formed in 1979 to take forward the students' struggle. These students expressed their opposition to the racism embedded in schooling as follows:

> The education we receive is meant to keep the South African people apart from one another, to breed suspicion, hatred and violence, and to keep us backward.

> Education is formulated so as to reproduce this society of racism and exploitation. (Christie, 1985, p. 14)

To counter this logic of White supremacy that underpinned apartheid-era schooling, the democratically elected government in 1994 guaranteed the right to education for all children to realize their potential, to live in freedom, and to participate as engaged citizens, aligned to the new constitutional values. These values, among others, are human dignity, equality, the advancement of human rights and freedoms, nonracism, and nonsexism (RSA, 1996a; 1996b). The ANC-led government also considered the provision of free, quality, inclusive basic education for all learners in Section 29 of the Constitution as important for South Africa's long-term development and future prosperity. Therefore, in addition to incorporating these constitutional values, the new Curriculum 2005 policy also aimed to develop critical, engaged citizens with education and training skills for the 21st century. However, the efficacy of Curriculum 2005 was the subject of heated national debates (Maodzwa-Taruvinga & Cross, 2012). Nevertheless, Curriculum 2005 offers a unique opportunity to critique school curriculum policy in a postconflict African context. A more compelling reason to review this curriculum reform process through an antiracism education lens is to shed light on the significant disparities in achievement for "African" learners. To date, the historic disparities in learner achievement across these groups persist, as reported in *The Sowetan*:

> The 2016 Progress in International Reading Literacy Study (PIRLS), an international comparative reading assessment among some 50 countries across the world, . . . found that 78% of South African Grade 4 learners that were tested could read for meaning. . . . Of the 78%, 93% of Grade 4 learners tested for reading in Sepedi, 90% in Setswana, 89% in Tshivenda, 88% in isiXhosa, 88% in Xitsonga, 87% in isiZulu and 87% in isiNdebele, could not do so competently and with understanding. . . . The crisis [for learning outcomes in this public schooling system] is therefore more acute with African children to this day. Needless to add that South Africa came out last of the 50 countries surveyed. (Mashile-Nkosi, 2019, para. 7–9).

This leads me to the following questions related to the 1994 political transition and school curriculum reform: Why did policy makers give importance to political gestures over improvements in teaching and learning in the curriculum reform process? Why, 25 years later, despite substantial investments in public education, are the inequities for African learners so different from that of other groups? How can the current school curriculum ensure a firmer articulation and implementation of antiracism education, inclusive of decolonial approaches? Other broader questions relate to the convergence and divergence of school curriculum reform in South Africa, the wider African context, and the North American contexts.

In the first section of the chapter, I set out working definitions for the use of concepts, such as antiracism, antiracism education, and race, based on the literature and position myself as the writer. In the second part of this chapter, I highlight the barriers presented by apartheid-era public education for post-1994 racial integration of schools and the implementation of Curriculum 2005 (Vally & Dalamba, 1999). I then comment on the "political symbolism," drawing on Jansen (2002) and the human rights discourse that framed education policy and curriculum reform in the post-1994 political moment. I conclude by suggesting how antiracism education and decolonial approaches in the curriculum can support more socially just outcomes for all learners, based on emerging practice in South Africa. In doing so, I suggest a wider relevance for policy makers, teachers, learners, parents, and communities in other African contexts and in "multicultural" contexts such as Canada and the United States of America. For the purposes of this chapter, the following section provides working definitions of antiracism education, antiracism education practice, and race.

Race Is Salient in a "Multiplex of Oppressions"

Although this chapter focuses on historic and systemic racial injustice as salient in the South African education system, it keeps sight of the multiple and intersectional sites and experiences of oppression. My use of the terms *antiracism* and *antiracism education* and my antiracism education praxis align with the working definitions proposed by Dei (1996). According to Dei (1996),

> anti-racism explicitly names the issues of "race" and social difference as issues of power and equity rather than as matters of cultural or ethnic variety. . . . Anti-racism education is an action-oriented strategy for institutional systemic change *to address racism and the interlocking systems of social oppression*. (p. 25, emphasis added)

These interlocking systems of oppression include class, gender, sexual orientation, ethnicity, religious affiliation, and place of residence. As argued by Dei (1996) antiracism education should be done through an engagement with "a politics of difference" that is part of a "politics of transformation" and through collective action for social change (p. 38).

Given the preceding, it is vital to counter the postracial illusion accompanied by the notion of color-blindness incubated in the United States and circulated in the global/transnational context. Proponents of these narratives believe that race is inconsequential in a society where all are equal before the law. Success in the postracial worldview is based on merit and available for those who seize an opportunity and work hard. None of these assumptions hold up as explanations for random police carding of Black youth in Canada; the criminalization by law enforcement of Black youth; the shooting of innocent, unarmed Black males by police in the United States; and repeated patterns of underachievement of Black learners in public education in the United States, the United Kingdom, Canada, and South Africa. If this were a postracial world, why has COVID-19, a global pandemic, become a racial justice issue with larger numbers of Black and African people disproportionately being affected by this pandemic (Washington, 2020)? Why has COVID-19 resulted in anti-Asian racism and xenophobia in many parts of the world? Clearly, the postracial worldview is dishonest. It appears subtly, but it is brutal in its impacts. It also effectively reinscribes Whiteness, screening out the daily suffering of those who experience racial injustice and other forms of discrimination based on a range of intersecting identities. It also makes a case for antiracism work to be vocal and visible.

I have drawn on Ladson-Billings (1998), Omi and Winant (1993), Lopez (2013), Faegin and Elias (2013), Dei (1996, 2013, 2014, 2017) and others to inform my use of *race* in this chapter. Based on their work in the United States, Omi and Winant (1993) argue that "race is neither ideological nor objective" (p. 4). Instead, they advance a social ontology of race through the racial formation theory. This theory provides one viewpoint on how different groups produce racial meanings (i.e., self-definitions as well as definitions of other groups that can shift over time). Whiteness is formed and sustained in the "racial formation" process, much like other group identities. White groups are known to construct and reconstruct their group identity as the norm; therefore, White groups position their individual and group identity as the hegemonic frame of reference for all other groups. Omi and Winant also point out that race cannot be reduced to ethnicity or class but "is an autonomous field of social conflict, political organisation and cultural/ideological meaning" (1993, p. 48). In summary, Omi and Winant conclude that race as a social construct is an intrinsic part of the social fabric and intersects with a range of social identities, including gender, sexual orientation, and disability.

Because of these social processes, race is made real and material with consequences for the body of racialized people. In my view, the "race as a social formation" argument is helpful but inadequate as it fails to capture the oppressive cultural, structural, and systemic components of race and its historicity. Instead, Faegin and Elias's (2013) systemic racism theory is more relevant. In their critique of Omi and Winant's (1993) model, Faegin and Elias point out that although racial formation theory considers both the role of social groups (micro-level) and "the role of the state" (macro-level) in shaping racial meanings, it needs to extend beyond these sites. Faegin and Elias use systemic racism theory to extend beyond social formations theory's analysis of "'ethnicity/assimilation,' class/stratification and nation/colonialism approaches to explicating 'race' in the USA" (2013, pp. 932–933). Faegin and Elias draw on the theoretical traditions of Black studies to provide an analysis of the power and structural realities of racism. In other words, they focus on the role played by Whites and White supremacy in shaping the racial hierarchy and the dominant beliefs and practices of social, economic, and cultural institutions, including larger governance structures (Gilborn, 2007). Like Omi and Winant, they base their theory on the analysis of race and racism in the United States, but it can be applied to other contexts.

Faegin and Elias argue that a powerful "White racial frame" has been established by the White elite, based on centuries-long systemic racism in the United States. They define this dominant White racial frame as

> materially and ideationally embodied and created to rationalize and buttress the oppressive hierarchy and related societal structures of systemic racism. The white frame is socially constructed, a meta-structure shaping and *pervading not only the "state" but also the "economy" and "civil society."* It involves *much more than racial prejudices and discrimination – the conventional concepts of mainstream social science.* (Faegin & Elias, 2013, p. 937, emphasis added)

In addition to the insights gleaned from Faegin and Elias (2013), I find Lopez's (2013) response to racial formations theory helpful. Lopez deepens the social construction of race by arguing that shifts in meanings are attributable to a complex interplay between wider historical, socioeconomic, and colonial forces, including slavery. Lopez grounds this thesis in *Hudgins v. Wright* in 1806, in which the status of a daughter, a mother, and a grandmother "to be free" or to be "deemed as slaves" was decided by the law based on ancestry and appearance. Thus, Lopez (2013, pp. 238–239) implicates the law in the construction and reinforcement of racial subordination.

For Lopez (2013), race is not only socially formed and structurally anchored; race is also manufactured and can change to take on many forms. In other words, "Social meanings connect our faces to our souls" (Lopez, 2013, p. 240). In addition, Lopez introduced the concept of "racial fabrication" as opposed to "racial formation" to capture the idea of the ability of dominant groups to hold power over other subordinated groups. As Lopez states, "Fabrication implies the workings of human hands and suggests the possible intention to deceive" (2013, p. 243). Therefore, based on these and other theorists, I use the term *race* in this chapter as a sociohistoric and political construct that has its roots in slavery and colonialism and with real and material consequences for racialized individuals. The White racial frame, with its accompanying cultural and economic logics, circulates globally and can mutate and embed in contextual specificities and micro-narratives. Ladson-Billings (1998, p. 18) quotes Swartz (1992) to demonstrate how the White racial frame regulates education through the curriculum:

> Master scripting silences multiple voices and perspectives, primarily legitimizing dominant, white, upper class, male voicings as the "standard" knowledge students need to know. All other accounts and perspectives are omitted from the master script unless they can be disempowered through misrepresentation. Thus, content that does not reflect the dominant voice must be brought under

> control, mastered, and then reshaped before it can become a part of the master script. (Swartz, 1992, p. 341)

Using critical race theory, Ladson-Billings (1998, p. 11) emphasizes the importance of voice and storytelling by students of color as a form of resistance and healing to their exclusion in the curriculum. This brings me to the next section in which I similarly locate myself prior to reflecting on antiracism education and Curriculum 2005.

Locating the Self: Entangled, Complicit, and Reflexive

One may ask the following questions: Why revisit a curriculum reform effort from 25 years ago in my home country? Why reflect on my nascent school-based racial integration research in that context to deepen current antiracism education efforts? These are valid questions. Moving back in my mind's eye to my home country, as I know and remember it, is both seamless and visceral. I ground my identity as a racialized woman born on African soil and as a South African citizen of South Asian descent. In these identities and in the South African context, I am both embraced and entangled. As such, I am both the product of apartheid-era education and the transitional subject and activist in the post-1994 political moment. I am the product of the very issues I critique and that I seek to change. I draw on this deep sense of belonging and lived experience to engage my authentic voice and to orient my work. In many ways, being rooted in this context supports me to better navigate the theory–practice divide. There are caveats. I am very aware of where I fall in the interlocking oppressions, multiplex oppressions and prism of identities (Dei, 2014). I therefore subscribe to the idea that "oppressions are best understood 'and/with' rather than 'either/or'" (Dei, 2014, p. 18). In addition, I take seriously Dei's (2014, citing Lorde, 1984) assertion that "we must always maintain a critical gaze on the oppressions and the oppressive possibilities within ourselves" (p. 18). Thus, I am mindful of my relative privilege and careful not to flatten differences or to claim to know anti-Black racism or appropriate the associated injury.

In Canada, I embody the "racialized immigrant" identity. More pertinently, I am complicit in a settler-colonial project that challenges my antiracism education analytical standpoint and praxis. In this regard, the advice of Lawrence and Dua (2005) and Tuck and Yang (2012) has been instructive for my locatedness in Canada. Indeed, the presence, role, and impacts of racialized immigrants, such as myself, inside of Canada's colonial project, must be problematized. Furthermore, although I am in "solidarity" with Canadian Indigenous struggles, this solidarity has to be negotiated as "there are parts of the decolonization project that are not easily absorbed by human rights or civil rights-based approaches to educational equity" (Tuck & Yang, 2012, p. 3). For example, central to Canadian Indigenous struggles is the right to self-determination and the issue of land, which must be respected. Thus, there is a need on my part to un-/relearn how to engage with Indigeneity and decoloniality in antiracism education work. I bring this orientation to future antiracism education work. Prior to applying the theoretical issues and positionality of self as writer and reviewer of Curriculum 2005, I sketch one example of colonial and apartheid-era schooling that predated the 1994 political moment and curriculum reform to provide more context.

Segregated Schooling and a Colonial Legacy

As Mignolo and Walsh (2018) point out, "There is no colonialism without all kinds of violence (physical, psychological, racist, sexist) and without the arrogance of the colonizer" (p. 232). In South Africa, colonialism lasted roughly 300 years, and it was sustained in the latter years by a White minority government that functioned as an "internal colonizer." All forms of colonial rule, whether by the Dutch in 1962, the British in 1806, or the Afrikaner "internal colonizer" in 1961, took steps to segregate schools. Coverage of this long and expansive process tied to coercive forms of labor and linked to racial capitalism is beyond the scope of this chapter. Instead, Soudien's (2019) incisive account on how various types of missionary schools attended by children of all race groups in the Cape were gradually "Whitened" will suffice. Soudien uses this example to explain how racial segregation was inscribed in public education in the Cape in legal and judicial terms with the passing of the School Boards Act of 1905. Such regionalized school segregation processes in education were cemented on a national scale when the then ruling National Party passed the draconian Bantu Education Act in 1953 (Act No. 47 of 1953). The primary objective of this law was to enforce racially separated educational facilities across the country. This finds echoes in Lopez's (2013) assertion that the law is complicit in the construction and reinforcement of racial subordination. As stated earlier, mandatory segregation in education in South Africa only ended roughly four decades later with the passing of the South African Schools Act (SASA) in 1996 (RSA, 1996b) by the new ANC-led government. The SASA also paved the way for Curriculum 2005 implementation into a unified public education system. Nevertheless, despite the stated policy intentions of SASA on paper, class and racial inequities remain embedded in the unified education system.

Post-1994 Education Policy Making and Curriculum Reform From an Antiracist Lens

Class and Race Cohere to Sustain Inequity in Public Education

As outlined in the introduction to this chapter, education policy making and curriculum reform post-1994 aligned with the constitutional goals, the nation-building project, and the dominant global human rights discourse. In earlier work (Zafar, 2007, citing Wilson, 2001, p. 6), I noted how the human rights language prior to 1994 was sufficiently "broad and indeterminate" to support the consensus that framed the negotiated political settlement. However, this rights-based framing invariably led to contradictions in the schooling system. An example was the political negotiations on the status of Model C schools. (Just prior to the constitutional negotiations, the apartheid government developed the "Class Models," i.e., models for school governance that catered to White parents having a say in the management of "White only" schools. Model C schools, a form of semiautonomous public school, were among these options.) As part of the "negotiated settlement" between the ruling National Party and the ANC, Model C schools were able to retain their original status post-1994, with parents having a significant say in the management, admission, and language policies of these schools, provided these school-based policies were not based on racial exclusion.

Soudien (1994) reflected on the political negotiations over the status of Model C schools and identified this as a form of interest convergence between the ANC and the White middle class. In this scenario, the ANC was keen to retain the participation of the White and Black middle classes in public education and to prevent "middle-class flight." White middle-class parents, in turn, conceded to an ANC-led government provided they could retain control over the schools attended by their children and have a say in the school admission policies. Once these terms were negotiated, the governing bodies at these schools, largely composed of White parents, maintained the exorbitant user fee rates; in doing so, they ensured that these schools were largely attended by White and racialized middle-class learners. In addition, many racialized middle-class families moved into the former White suburbs to ensure their children could attend these schools.

The sustained presence of Model C schools within the public education system in South Africa is an example of the "plasticity of race" (Lopez, 2013) as these schools were able to retain their space (and White identity), despite the transformative antiracist intentions of the post-1994 education policies. Despite the policy efforts to unify the national public education system, Model C schools effectively divided public education into a two-tier system. Based on the prior inequitable apartheid-era funding, these former "Whites only" schools were fully equipped with science laboratories and facilities such as swimming pools, soccer, and cricket fields, which catered to a range of extracurricular activities. In contrast to Model C schools, township (residential areas zoned under apartheid for Africans) schools remain racially homogenous and relatively under-resourced. The teaching staff across the public education system also remain racially homogenous, with some exceptions. As outlined in the Curriculum 2005 Review Report (Review Committee on Curriculum 2005, 2000) the curriculum was implemented with greater ease in the well-resourced Model C schools. As such, the post-1994 rights-based education policy framework and Curriculum 2005 failed to address the historical, structural, and systemic racialized features of the public education system.

Curriculum 2005: An Overly Designed Curriculum With Unspecified Content

As stated in the Curriculum 2005 Review Committee Report (Review Committee on Curriculum 2005, 2000), Curriculum 2005 aimed to address the legacy of apartheid-era schools and a future for education aligned to the rights-based constitutional goals of social justice, equity, personal, and social development and skills for the 21st century (Lebeloane, 2017). To address these goals, the curriculum policy was based on "learner centredness" outcomes-based approach with and a nondisciplinary division of knowledge (Review Committee on Curriculum 2005, 2000, p. 28). All three of these curriculum influences sought to develop learners who were critical and independent thinkers and democratic citizens with skills for the 21st-century economy. The objective to develop globally benchmarked economic skills was aligned to the strong neoliberal trajectory in the economic policies of the ANC-led government. However, the newly integrated public education system was not able to cope with these onerous demands. These demands made by the new curriculum deepened the cracks in the education system, prompting the ministry to commission a full review of Curriculum 2005.

Curriculum 2005 positioned teachers as facilitators of the curriculum to signal a transformative approach to pedagogy. To fulfill this role, teachers were required to design individual tasks, group work, group projects, and experiential learning opportunities to support learning outcomes. Teachers were also required to complete elaborate assessment rubrics to map learner progress. There was minimal to no provision of textbooks to support the implementation of this curriculum. Instead, teachers were expected to develop outcomes-based teaching and learning material to support learners to meet the stated outcomes. This expectation was placed on all teachers across the education system from Model C schools to historically disadvantaged and the highly under resourced township and rural and remote areas. Teachers were not provided with in-service training, nor was there a coordinated national teacher development strategy to support teachers to meet these implementation requirements (Department of Education, 1995, 2002). These and other curriculum design features led Jansen (2010), an esteemed academic and public intellectual, to reflect on the legacy and human costs of Curriculum 2005 in the national media as follows:

> Children already disadvantaged were exposed to a curriculum that made a fragile learning environment worse. Instead of learning those vital competencies of reading, writing and calculating, they were exposed to highbrow constructivist theories that kept many of them illiterate. Those effects not only forced many to leave the school system, they pushed weaker and weaker students into universities where they again struggled to succeed. (para. 13)

Much of the failure of Curriculum 2005 was also attributed to the policy borrowing from the Australian school curriculum model. In my view, these failures also speak to the theory–practice divide on the part of policy makers who were not familiar with the needs in the classroom. Jansen (2002), on the other hand, provides a far more incisive critique to explain the Curriculum 2005 policy failure. Jansen asserts that education policy change and curriculum reform during the 1994 political moment was driven by "political symbolism" instead of a rigorous attempt to address the teaching and learning needs in the classroom. Jansen's political symbolism thesis is that curriculum policy reform in 1994 was, in large measure, driven by the need for the new democracy to gain global legitimacy—a political priority that short-changed the learning needs of some of the most vulnerable learners in the country.

Apart from the design flaws outlined earlier, the knowledge base of Curriculum 2005 is also questionable. In assessing Curriculum 2005 against the typologies of knowledge presented by Banks (1993), I noted that Curriculum 2005 did not adequately incorporate "transformative academic knowledge" as defined by Banks. To quote Banks (1993), "transformative academic knowledge positions "all knowledge forms as reflective of power and social relationships within society" (p. 9). Importantly, Banks argues that transformative academic knowledge "questions mainstream knowledge forms and can contribute to social change" (1993, p. 9). Thus, in my view, the absence of transformative academic content in Curriculum 2005 was a missed opportunity to address the history of slavery, colonialism, and apartheid in South Africa and to bring the diverse groups of learners in the classroom to new understandings of the history of race and other inequities in South Africa. On the contrary, under the outcomes-based approach, the inclusion of Africentric content and Indigenous knowledges were left to the discretion of individual teachers. As a result, one can conclude that racialized learners in public schools were by default required to fit into a Western and Eurocentric episteme. Furthermore, Maodzwa-Taruvinga and Cross (2012) point out that the guidelines for the respective learning areas in Curriculum 2005 were "silent on specific values relating the need to fight sexism and racism" (p. 137). Furthermore, Maodzwa-Taruvinga and Cross assert that failure to specify content (in essence leaving this to individual schools and teachers) catered for both "continuities and discontinuities with apartheid-era curriculum" (2012, p. 137). In my view, this omission also contributed to the erasure of the diverse knowledge and histories of the learners in the postapartheid South African classroom.

Inside the Racially Integrated Classroom

Soudien (1994) undertook a school-based study to understand the role of teachers in the newly integrated classroom at the cusp of the political transition. He noted at that point that little was known about how "race" is tackled in teaching and learning in the South African classroom and pointed to the need for more dedicated and micro-level research focused on the racially integrated classroom. Based on his exploratory study,

Soudien refers to a "racial inexplicitness" in the content of what was being taught and noted that racism was discussed historically rather than how it impacted the lives of the learners in the classroom. I, too, came across a similar trend in case study research in 1996 conducted in a newly integrated school (Zafar, 1996, p. 88). Some teachers I interviewed indicated that they choose not to discuss race or racism directly as they did not wish to polarize the students. Others shared that they did not address the topic of race directly as they did not want to be misunderstood by their students as being racist. Yet others shared that they preferred to select learning material that emphasized the universality of values across cultures. All of these strategies clearly pointed to how teachers avoided engaging the issue of race and racism in the curriculum, despite the abiding presence of these issues in their classrooms. Soudien (1994) draws on Stuart Hall's (1980, p. 3) advice to teachers in England to explain why and how race should be addressed in the classroom:

> To understand the strong emotional ideological commitments people have towards race . . . you have to create an atmosphere that allows people to say unpopular things. What I am talking about are the problems about handling the time bomb and doing so adequately so that it connects with our student's experience. The experience has to surface in the classroom even if it is pretty horrendous to hear—better to hear it than to not hear it, because what you don't hear you don't engage with. . . . It matters crucially [how you set up the teaching situation]. (p. 286)

Makoelle (2017) reiterates Soudien's call made early in 1994 for more attention to race work in the South African classroom. In a recent school-based study by Makoelle, research findings reveal that the underlying cause of racial tendencies in schools can be attributed to apartheid-era racial attitudes that still make their way into the classroom. Clearly, race is the elephant in the room in the South African classroom that is calling for attention.

Across the school-based studies conducted in South Africa (Naidoo, 1996; Samuel & Sayed, 2003; Soudien, 1994), including in my own exploratory work (Zafar, 1996), White and racialized teachers spoke in assimilationist and multicultural terms with respect to the African learners in their classrooms. For example, Black learner needs, with respect to English-language competency in the school where I conducted research, were described as a challenge that individual learners faced, a barrier that learners should attempt to address to increase their English language competency. Ladson-Billings (1998) reminds us of the risks to learners of individualizing such barriers to learning and the importance of institutional responses to address these and other learning needs of diverse groups of learners. Shifting the burden for English-language proficiency onto Black learners for whom English is a second language as noted in my case study research is a form of "symbolic violence." Tomlinson et al. (2018) draw on Bourdieu's conceptual framework and explain symbolic violence as "the imposition of specific modes of cultural and institutional practice by dominant cultural groups subsequently accepted by less dominant groups" (p. 3). Interestingly, the implementation of Curriculum 2005 in racially integrated and multilingual classes placed no obligation on White and racialized teachers to attain even the minimum levels of competency in any of the Indigenous languages spoken by African learners in their classrooms. Neither did the national department of education create any incentive or provide support for teachers to do so.

The overall response by the progressive teacher unions to Curriculum 2005, at the time of political transition, is also worth noting. Despite the onerous demands placed on teachers to implement Curriculum 2005 and its obvious design flaws (which led to its demise), the progressive teacher education unions did not voice overt and/or public criticism. This is yet another example of interest convergence during the 1994 political transition where the progressive teacher unions demonstrated support for the nation-building project and the underlying global human rights discourse framing the curriculum reform policy. Their response had very little to do with the merits/demerits of the curriculum policy or the challenges they faced to implement this curriculum in their classrooms or the learning challenges that Curriculum 2005 presented for learners.

In summary, the gains made in this curriculum reform process must be placed in context. Chief among the gains made was the removal of racist apartheid-era textbooks and rote learning from the public education system. Other gains included the commitment to developing critical thinking and 21st-century skills for South African learners. The introduction of creative learning pedagogies that included both independent and group work was also transformative as compared to apartheid-era schooling chalk-and-talk teaching strategies in apartheid-era schools for racialized groups. As well, the challenges related to Curriculum 2005 resulted in a public debate on the efficacy of the public school curriculum that included parents and South Africans from all walks of life. Despite these gains, the embedded racial inequities in this curriculum and school curricula more broadly are a cause for concern and point to the need for dedicated antiracism education efforts.

Antiracism Education Futures and Decolonial Approaches in Curriculum Reform

For this section of the chapter, I have drawn on the knowledge production and praxis related to decoloniality in South Africa. This body of work on decoloniality is largely based on hands-on research and scholarly thought by academics and academic activists in higher education. Furthermore, a renewed focus on decoloniality in higher education has reemerged since the nationwide 2015 #FeesMustFall protests by higher education students. Decolonizing university curricula was a large part of their call to action (Jansen, 2017). In my view, this work should fuel and ignite anti-racism education and decoloniality approaches in the school curriculum. I also want to emphasize that decoloniality is a highly complex concept and that the following suggestions must be considered as an initial exploration of how decolonial approaches can address the racism in the curriculum.

Ndlovu-Gatsheni (2013, 2015) has led the theoretical trajectory on decoloniality in higher education in South Africa. Of relevance to the school curriculum is Ndlovu- Gatsheni assertion that "decoloniality works to de-centre the colonial hold on 'power, knowledge and being' given Western-centric hierarchies reproduce themselves in these areas of struggle " (2013, pp. 10–11). Some examples of these Western-centric colonial hierarchies that operate in the school curriculum and elaborated on by Grosfoguel (2007) include "a global racial/ethnic hierarchy privileging European people; a global gender hierarchy; an epistemic hierarchy privileging Western knowledge and cosmology; a linguistic and cultural hierarchy privileging European languages" (cited in Christie & McKinney, 2017, p. 5). Keet (2014), in his work on decoloniality and higher education, points out that, among other related arguments on knowledge forms and power, Western-centric hierarchies are embedded in the various knowledge disciplines (or subjects/knowledge areas). Keet argues that this can lead to "epistemic injustice" and "epistemic othering" of students in the case of higher education. Following this thread in his broader argument about knowledge forms and power, one can conclude that Western-centric knowledge forms can have similar effects for learners in schooling. In particular, learners who are not White and/or positioned elsewhere in the "multiplex and prism of identities" that Dei (2014) speaks of.

The key question is, How can the "epistemic injustice" and "epistemic othering" that Keet (2014) highlights be addressed in the school curriculum through decoloniality approaches? One overarching strategy that Mignolo and Walsh (2018) posit is to focus on how "the decoloniality project and praxis *takes form in and contributes to the fissures of the dominant order, also noting that these are present throughout the world including in the Global North*" (p. 24, emphasis added). Drawing on their argument, one can therefore argue that decolonizing the (school) curriculum is not simply a case of replacing the Western episteme with Indigenous or Africentric knowledge systems. Christie and McKinney (2017) cite earlier work by Mignolo and draw on his proposed pluriversalist approach as a suggested way forward. Christie and McKinney explain that Mignolo's pluriversalist approach "recognises that different cosmologies exist in complex and entangled power relations in the present" (Mignolo, 2013, cited in Christie & McKinney, 2017, p. 6).

In practice, policy makers and curriculum developers can draw on Mignolo's pluriversalist approach to engage school-based stakeholders, for example, parents to source and include Indigenous, Africentric, and other forms of knowledge in the curriculum. In doing so, African and Indigenous epistemologies, traditions, and ways of being can be integrated beyond the curriculum on paper into the life of the school. Thus, these knowledge forms can become situated in the school–community context and not through superficial cultural evenings, parent–teacher consultation nights, and tokenized representation of racialized parents in extracurricular committees. Pluriversality should be used to decenter Whiteness in all aspects of the curriculum. For example, Whiteness can be uncovered and challenged through archaic school traditions as many of these are often positioned as sentimental and innocent practices. Many school traditions are often exclusionary and serve to maintain racial, cultural, and power hierarchies embedded in a White racial frame. Linked to the inclusion of Indigenous and other forms of knowledge in the school curriculum is the need to address the hegemonic status of English. In my view, shifts in the language policies and practices in a plurilingual society such as South Africa should be an essential part of any antiracist curriculum reform.

Conclusion

In conclusion, antiracism education work, including decolonial approaches, requires a deep understanding of the transactions between teachers and learners. An education system that is committed to antiracism education must support teachers in an ongoing way to embrace a critical pedagogy. Class discussions should include a strong recognition of the multiplicity of oppressions and identity at the intersections of race, ethnicity, gender, sexual orientation, and place of residence, among others. What teachers could do to draw on decolonial approaches is to work with existing teaching and learning material but cater to different conceptual starting points for learners. For example, teachers can engage with issues and pose questions to encourage learners to draw on their respective sociohistoric and cultural locations and knowledges other than colonial depictions. Such approaches can result in classrooms that are more inclusive for learners who sit outside the White racial frame. Central to these and other antiracist education and decolonial approaches is the need for learners to have a substantive voice in all aspects of the curriculum and education, such that all learners can come to know and enjoy their full potential as human beings of equal worth. To achieve this outcome, education policy making and curriculum reform initiatives should place the needs of all learners and in equal measure at the front and center of education systems (Apple, 1999). Learner interests should not be sacrificed to achieve wider political objectives.

References

Apple, M. (1999). The absent presence of race in educational reform. *Race Ethnicity and Education, 2*(1), 9–16. doi:10.1080/1361332990020102

Banks, J. A. (1993). The canon debate, knowledge construction and multicultural education. *Educational Researcher, 22*(5), 4–14. doi:10.2307/1176946

Christie, P., & McKinney, C. (2017). Decoloniality and "Model C" schools: Ethos, language and the protests of 2016. *Education as Change, 21*(3). http://dx.doi.org/10.17159/1947-9417/2017/2332

Christie, P. (1985). *The right to learn: The struggle for education in South Africa*. Ravan Press.

Dei, G. J. S. (1996). Basic principles of anti-racism education. In *Anti-racism education: Theory and practice* (pp. 25–49). Fernwood Publishing.

Dei, G. J. S. (2013). Reframing critical anti-racist theory (CART) for contemporary times. In G. J. S. Dei & M. Lordan (Eds.), *Contemporary issues in the sociology of race and ethnicity: A critical reader* (pp. 1–9). Peter Lang.

Dei, G. J. S. (2014). A prism of educational research and policy: Anti-racism and multiplex oppressions. In G. J. S. Dei & M. McDermott (Eds.), *Politics of anti-racism education: In search of strategies for transformative learning* (pp. 15–28). Springer.

Dei, G. J. S. (2017). The foundations of transformative anti-racism: A conversation. *Canadian Education, 57*(3), 50–52.

Department of Education. (1995, March 15). *Education and training in a democratic South Africa: First steps to develop a new system* (White Paper, Government Gazette, No. 16312). Government Printers.

Department of Education. (2002). *Revised national curriculum statement for general education and training*. Government Printers.

Faegin, J., & Elias, S. (2013). Rethinking racial formation: A systemic critique. *Ethnic and Racial Studies, 36*(6), 931–960.

Gilborn, D. (2007). Education policy as an act of White supremacy: Whiteness, critical race theory and education reform. *Journal of Education Policy, 20*(4), 485–505.

Grosfoguel, R. (2007). The epistemic decolonial turn. *Cultural Studies, 21*(2–3), 211–223. doi:10.1080/09502380601162514

Hall, S. (1980). Teaching race. *Multiracial Education, 9*(1), 3–13.

Jansen, J. D. (2002). Political symbolism as policy craft: Explaining non reform in South African education after apartheid. *Journal of Education Policy, 17*(2), 199–215. doi:10.1080/02680930110116534

Jansen, J. D. (2010, July 22). The enduring legacy of OBE. *Times Live*. https://www.timeslive.co.za/ideas/2010-07-21-jonathan-jansen-the-enduring-legacy-of-obe/

Jansen, J. D. (2017). Introduction – Part II. Decolonizing the university curriculum given a dysfunctional school system? *Journal of Education, 68*(i), 4–13.

Keet, A. (2014). Epistemic 'othering' and the decolonisation of knowledge. *Africa Insight, 44*(1) 23 37.

Ladson-Billings, G. (1998). Just what is critical race theory and what's it doing in a 'nice' field like education? *International Journal of Qualitative Studies in Education, 11*(1), 7–24.

Lawrence, B., & Dua, A. (2005). Decolonizing antiracism. *Social Justice, 32*(4), 120–143.

Lebeloane, L. (2017). Decolonizing the school curriculum for equity and social justice in South Africa. *KOERS—Bulletin for Christian Scholarship, 82*(3). doi:10.19108/KOERS.82.3.2333

Lopez, I. J. (2013). The social construction of race. In R. Delgado (Ed.), *Critical race theory: The cutting edge* (pp. 163–177). Temple University Press.

Makoelle, T. M. (2017). Race and inclusion in South African education. Analysis of Black African learners' perceptions in previously advantaged White schools. *Mediterranean Journal of Social Sciences, 5*(14), 283–290.

Maodzwa-Taruvinga M., & Cross, M. (2012). Jonathan Jansen and the curriculum debate in South Africa: An essay review of Jansen's writing between 1999–2009. *Curriculum Inquiry, 42*(1), 126–152.

Mashile-Nkosi, D. (2019, December 18). Re-examination of our schooling system needed. *Sowetan*. https://www.sowetanlive.co.za/opinion/2019-12-18-south-african-education-in-the-doldrums-study/

Mignolo, W. D. (2013). *On pluriversality.* Retrieved from https://scholar.google.ca/scholar?cluster=9617876796951623154

Mignolo, W. D., & Walsh, C. E. (2018). *On decoloniality, concepts, analytics and praxis.* Duke University Press.

Naidoo, J. P. (1996). *Racial integration of public schools in South Africa – A study of practices, attitudes and trends.* Education Policy Unit, University of Natal, Durban.

Ndlovu-Gatsheni, S. J. (2013). Why decoloniality in the 21C? *The Thinker, 48*(10), 10–15.

Ndlovu-Gatsheni, S. J. (2015). Decoloniality as the future of Africa. *History Compass, 13*(10), 485–496.

Omi, M., & Winant, H. (1993). On the theoretical concept of race. In C. McCarthy & W. Crichlow (Eds.), *Race, identity and representation in education* (pp. 3–10). Routledge.

Pampallis, J. (2007). The establishment and transformation of a repressive system: A historical perspective on educational change in South Africa. In C. Odora-Hoppers, B. Gustavsson, & J. Pampallis (Eds.), *Democracy and human rights in education and society: Explorations from South Africa and Sweden* (pp. 15–40). Orebro University.

Republic of South Africa. (1953). Bantu Education Act No. 47 of 1953. Pretoria: Government Printers

Republic of South Africa. (1996a). The Constitution of the Republic of South Africa, Act No. 108 of 1996. Government Printer.

Republic of South African. (1996b). The South African Schools Act No. 84 of 1996. Government Printer.

Review Committee on Curriculum 2005. (2000, May 31). *A South African curriculum for the 21st century: Report of the Review Committee on Curriculum 2005.* https://pmg.org.za/committee-meeting/3204/

Samuel, M., & Sayed, Y. (2003). Inside and outside the school gates. Exploring marginalisation in Kwa-Zulu Natal in South Africa. *IDS Bulletin, 34*(1), 90–95.

Soudien. C. (1994). Dealing with race, laying down patterns for multiculturalism in South Africa. *Interchange, 25*(3), 281–294.

Soudien, C. (2019). Institutionalising racial segregation in the South African school: The School Board Act, 1905. *Paedagogica Historica, 55*(1), 21–37.

Swartz, E. (1992). Emancipatory narratives: Rewriting the master script in the school curriculum. *Journal of Negro Education, 61*(3), 341–355.

Tomlinson, M., Enders, J., & Naidoo, R. (2018). The Teaching Excellence Framework: Symbolic violence and the measured market in higher education. *Critical Studies in Education.* Advanced online publication. https://doi.org/10.1080/17508487.2018.1553793

Tuck, E., & Yang, K. W. (2012). Decolonization is not a metaphor. *Decolonization: Indigeneity, Education & Society, 1*(1), 1–40.

Vally, S., & Dalamba, Y. (1999, February). *Racism, 'racial integration' and desegregation in South Africa public Secondary School: A report on a study by the South African Human Rights Commission.* South African Human Rights Commission.

Washington, K. (2020, April 8). 'It's a racial justice issue': Black Americans are dying in greater numbers from Covid-19. *The Guardian.* https://www.theguardian.com/world/2020/apr/08/its-a-racial-justice-issue-black-americans-are-dying-in-greater-numbers-from-covid-19

Zafar, S. (1996). *Racial and linguistic differences between Indian teachers and African students at P.R. Pather Secondary School* [Unpublished Master's thesis]. University of KwaZulu Natal.

Zafar, S. (2007). A critique of Millennium Development Goals 2 and 3: Framing basic education in South Africa. In C. Odora-Hoppers, B. Gustavsson, & J. Pampallis (Eds.), *Democracy and human rights in education and society: Explorations from South Africa and Sweden* (pp. 181–197). Orebro University.

CHAPTER 3

Africanizing the Ghanaian Education System: Learning Through the Prism of an Africentric System of Thought

Patrick Radebe

THE GHANAIAN PUBLIC education system faces several challenges. After 62 years of national independence, it continues to function under ad hoc government policies, for example, increasing and reducing, by turn, the number of years required to complete secondary school from three to four, depending on which political party is in office. Problems, including shortages of textbooks, especially those with an Africentric or critical orientation; antiquated libraries; teacher shortages; uncertified and overworked teachers; and overcrowded classrooms and truancy, have crippled the education system, rendering it incapable of graduating students who take pride in their heritage and who are grounded in the nation's history.

In this chapter, I use Kwame Nkrumah's anticolonial theoretical framework and Paolo Freire's liberation pedagogy to examine the negative impact of neocolonial education on Ghanaian students and the implications for the country's political, social, and economic development. Also addressed is a question that should be, but isn't, uppermost in the minds of the country's educators: What steps would be required to "Africanize" Ghana's education system with a view to reforming an institutional culture fundamentally opposed to the intellectual liberation of students? This chapter has four objectives. First, I provide a working definition of anticolonial theory. Second, drawing on Kwame Nkrumah's anticolonial theoretical framework and Paolo Freire's liberation pedagogy,

I problematize neocolonial education using the Ghanaian experience as a case study. Next, I discuss the consequences and implications of neocolonial education for Ghana's social, political, and economic development. Finally, I propose a remedy based on the Africanization of the school curriculum as one of the ways and means of reforming an educational culture that remains in many respects neocolonial and thus wholly inadequate to fostering the kind of critical thinking required of students to liberate themselves intellectually and, ultimately, free their country from the yoke of Western domination.

Anticolonial Theory: A Working Definition

Anticolonial theory embodies a system of thought that challenges neocolonialism in all its forms. It seeks to free the oppressed of the third world, in this case Ghanaian students, from oppression, and it spawns counternarratives that challenge the status quo. Nowhere can this theory be put to better use than in African public education systems, viewed here as political sites wherein students are indoctrinated, however subtly, in ways that promote neocolonialism and impede the development of intellectual agency.

Anticolonial theory draws attention to a Western neocolonial project that, while racist and oppressive, is often signified as a remedy for the wretched condition of those it subordinates and marginalizes. It empowers the oppressed to question neocolonial ideations, narratives, and representations that diminish the history, culture, and capabilities of colonized bodies (Dei & Asgharzadeh, 2001). It further rejects the notion that civilization/modernity, as broadly defined, is a European project to be bequeathed to grateful and subservient colonial subjects. It reveals the European account of African history and anthropology to be an "instrument of . . . oppressi[on] (Nkrumah, 1964, p. 62) and provides the oppressed "alternative, oppositional paradigms" (Dei & Asgharzadeh, 2001, p. 301) with which to challenge colonial accounts that present Africans as insignificant actors in human affairs. In the context of public education, it fosters among Ghanaian students the courage to articulate their history on their own terms.

Kwame Nkrumah: Impact

Kwame Nkrumah (1962, 1964) provides key insights regarding Ghanaian students' appropriation of the English language and a lack of knowledge of their nation's history and government policies. The current education system, which is modeled on its British counterpart, is very much European-oriented, with the aim of promoting knowledge and English literacy as a ticket to power and a better life. In his critique of neocolonial education, Nkrumah asserts that it was designed not to foster critical thinking or intellectual curiosity but, rather, to equip students with a European education that would enable them to serve the colonial enterprise. In a speech delivered at the Ecole Coloniale in 1923, Albert Sarraut, France's colonial secretary asserted, "What is the use of painting the truth? Nkrumah lays bare the nefarious goals of neocolonial education." According to Sarraut, "[Neocolonial education] was not an act of civilization; [it] was not a desire to civilize. It was an act of force motivated by interests" (Sarraut, cited in Nkrumah, 1962, p. 3). In other words, for the French colonial secretary, neocolonial education aimed to compel Africans to oppose everything African and to "think White." His words reaffirm Nkrumah's belief that neocolonial education falls far short of providing Ghanaian students with the prerequisite knowledge and language skills required to think outside the neocolonial box (Nkrumah, 1962).

A key part of the project to arrest the intellectual development of Ghanaian students lies in stripping them of their language; indeed, colonial policy stipulated that in some schools this was to be rigorously enforced. Even today, the nation's educational elite subscribes to academic guidelines and benchmarks that are European-oriented. For example, the Basic Education Examination is conducted primarily in English, and within the classroom, teachers measure academic performance based on a student's ability to express themselves in the English language. The nullification of Ghana's Indigenous languages and the erosion of knowledge of the country's history and political leadership by the public school system demonstrate a conscious effort to promote Western languages and a Western historical perspective (Boykin, 1986; Gordon, 1993).

Freire's Theory of Critical Pedagogy

Critical pedagogy was born in the 1960s in northwestern Brazil. Its origins lie in the work of Paolo Freire (Kincheloe, 2012). The theory was informed by the austere conditions in which the poor resided and drew its inspiration from liberation theory and critical theory. Founded on a revolutionary ethos, it lays bare, among other things, the impact of dominant education on the oppressed. It charges teachers, whom it deems to be on the front line of the fight against illiteracy, to challenge public education systems with a view to reconstituting them as neutral sites for the cultivation of ideas (Kincheloe, 2012).

An educational model of the people, by the people, and in the service of the people, critical pedagogy is premised on the belief that lived experiences can serve as a fortress standing firm against the insidious influence of dominant education and, in so doing, can foster unity among students, teachers, and their allies committed to reforming public education systems. Fortified by a plurality of thought, critical pedagogy counters dominant narratives often packaged as science and claiming to embody the truth (Kincheloe, 2012). Ultimately, it fosters among the oppressed the agency to resist constructs that threaten their existence and freedom. Freire contends that neocolonial education, whatever the context, aims at conditioning the minds of colonized populations. He characterizes it as an intellectual virus seeking to destroy the intellectual capabilities of the colonized (Freire, 1970). In his introduction to the 2000 edition of Freire's *Pedagogy of the Oppressed,* Macedo argues that what was intended to educate the oppressed instead transformed them into androids. He posits that neocolonial education maintains "subordination through imposed assimilation policy" (Macedo, as cited in Freire, 2000, p. 12).

Linguistic Hybridism: An Emerging Practice Among Ghanaian Students

A primary objective of Ghana's education system is to promote the use of and to maintain the purity of the country's many Indigenous languages as a way to preserve the social cohesion and cultural identity of its people. Whether it is up to the task is a matter of debate, however. In this chapter, I use anecdotes collected during my many encounters with Ghanaian students to elucidate what is the growing practice of "linguistic hybridism" (adulterating local vernaculars with English words). Whereas most of the senior high school students I interviewed in Accra dismissed this practice as the "latest fashion in town," others saw it as a way to improve their English vocabulary and still others as a status symbol. And for some, pronouncing English words with an Afro-American accent was a mere affectation. Why would a people once thought to be so proud of their cultural identity want to contaminate their Indigenous languages?

In the largely working-class district where I was residing, it was commonplace to hear children, even as young as 6, struggling to converse in English with parents whose grasp of the language was tenuous at best. Although these anecdotes would strike the average Ghanaian as hardly noteworthy, in my view, they signify a disturbing trend, namely, a reversion to a colonial culture with all the negative implications for preserving Indigenous languages.

Neocolonial Education: Consequences and Implications for Ghana's Social, Political, and Economic Development

Ghana's inability to formulate education policies informed by the national experience and the country's real needs has grave implications. In particular, the standard use of the English language by teachers and students is not without consequences. According to Abdi (2012), the overuse of English at the expense of Indigenous languages renders the latter "essentially useless" (p. 13). Privileging English as the medium of instruction reinforces the belief, however subtle, that local languages are inferior to their European counterparts, which has the effect of eroding the linguistic heritage of students. Prohibiting the use of Indigenous languages in the classroom, which is the norm at some schools, also acculturates students to Western mores. It conditions them to "speak and think White" and to act in ways that perpetuate White supremacy, further diminishing their interest in Indigenous languages. According to Ngugi, the importance of African languages extends well beyond mere verbal expression:

> In our native [African] language[s], we have learnt to value words for their meaning and nuances. Language [is for us] not a mere string of words. It ha[s] a suggestive power well beyond the immediate and logical meanings.... [Our] language, through images and symbols, g[i]ve[s] us a [unique] view of the world.... [It serves as an earthwork against European] domination, [Black] alienation and disenfranchisement. (as cited in Abdi, 2012, p. 21)

This analysis suggests that Ghanaian languages provide students with a sense of who they are, without which they can hardly be expected to excel academically. Stripped of their native tongue, they can no longer speak with conviction to the nation's struggles. Effectively, they become "adjuncts" (Nyerere, 1968, p. 270) of the neocolonial project.

Privileging English as the medium of instruction and the standard against which indigenous languages are measured has grave implication(s) for the Ghanaian nation, in general, and students, in particular, with the latter "bec[o]m[ing more] prone to accept [the English language] as universal" (Nkrumah, 1964, p. 3). Not only does this serve to promote White preeminence, but it also provides the colonizers and the Indigenous teachers who serve them free rein to deny students the ability to think and speak for themselves in the native languages in which they have cultural capital. Put another way, it programs students to view their heritage as worthless. The predominance of English in the Ghanaian school system reveals it to be predicated on what Freire (1997, 2000) calls a "banking" system. According to this model, the students are treated as empty vessels to be filled with prescribed knowledge (Freire, 2000). It denies the nation the intellectual talent and technical know-how it needs to develop.

According to Fanon (1967), neocolonial education informed by an assimilative philosophy has one principal goal: to obliterate a Black identity. This requires, among other things, that students supplant local languages with English to demonstrate to kinfolk that they have transcended the barbarity and parochialism of Ghanaian culture. Including in the curriculum a token number of Indigenous language courses creates the impression that the public school system is committed to promoting local languages. This tactic circumvents charges of elitism—that the school system functions to promote the use of English—and, relatedly, instills Western values. Moreover, requiring students to limit their use of local languages and focus on mastering English, the idiom in which exams and classes are conducted and careers forged, results in their loss of fluency in the Indigenous vernacular(s). Those who lack English-language proficiency are ultimately viewed as uneducated and are ostracized accordingly.

Neocolonial education also fragments Ghanaian society by creating an elite social stratum differentiated from the common people by virtue of its monopoly on knowledge and appropriation of the English language. This fosters on the part of the nation's students a sense of preeminence manifest in their "intellectual arrogance and intense individualism" (Nyerere, 1968, p. 275). Confident in their assumed superiority, they adopt the mannerisms and self-centeredness of their former colonial masters, thereby undermining efforts to build a cohesive nation. They also come to perceive indigenous languages as primitive and therefore as obstacles to creating a civilized nation. For them, speaking even broken English is preferable to using an Indigenous language they perceive as backward. However, addressing their base in English or in the local vernacular, albeit strewn with English words, exacts a heavy price: Much of the intent and rhetorical power of their words is lost. So why then do these political elites and the students who aspire to join their ranks subscribe to neocolonial education and the language practices it inculcates? The answer is simple: It is the one way, however odious, to graft themselves onto the neocolonial enterprise that butters their bread (Blauner, 1969).

Thus, the unwillingness of policymakers to reform the existing school system can be explained by the material benefits it provides them. According to Nkrumah (1962), neocolonial education, whatever its "noble" intentions, works to bind resource-rich Ghana to the "mother country," thus allowing its natural and human resources to be exploited by the colonial center to meet economic, security, and military requirements. This pattern of exploitation is manifest across the entire African continent.

Neocolonial education works to indoctrinate Ghanaian students with a colonial ideology and worldview (Nkrumah, 1964) such that as political leaders they "welcome with open arms the very [enemy] . . . [the founding fathers of the country] sought to destroy at [the] cost of terrible suffering" (p. 103). Nkrumah's presentiment of what might befall Ghana should it fail to adopt an anticolonial policy, namely, the loss of sovereignty and ownership of natural resources, has come to pass as evinced by the frequent flights by state officials to Western capitals, and more recently Beijing, to beg for foreign investment at a prohibitive cost to the nation, including exorbitant terms of debt repayment. Foreign companies have been allowed to deplete the country's gold, timber, and oil reserves at unimaginable speed and using crude methods of extraction to generate the foreign exchange so desperately needed for national development, resulting in the wholesale destruction of the natural environment. The price paid for Western and, more recently, Chinese foreign aid is political influence and access to the country's markets and natural resources (Nkrumah, 1962, 1964). Moreover, in adopting neoliberal economic policies, Ghana has descended ever deeper into the pit of economic colonialism as evinced by growing levels of poverty, violent crime, unemployment, and prostitution. While Kenneth Clark has written on the impact of internal and economic colonialism in Black America, his subsequent analysis of the impact of neoliberalism on colonial subjects anticipated conditions in Ghana following the introduction of neoliberal policies in the early 1980s. Clark asserts that

> [Ghanaian poverty is] the consequence of the imposition of external power and the institutionalization of powerlessness. . . . [It is] in fact social political, educational, and above all—economic. [Conditions in present-day Ghana] can best be described in terms of . . . [the country's] power[lessness]. Its political leadership is divided . . . short-sighted. . . . Its [educational system is] . . . precarious and dependent upon . . . support outside the [country]. Under a [neocolonial] system of centralization, [the nation's] schools are controlled by forces outside the [country]. (cited in Blauner, 1969, pp. 396–397)

During the course of my conversations with Ghanaian students, I also became aware of their appalling ignorance of the country's history. They struggled to answer to questions bearing on, for example, the significance of Ghanaian independence or the importance of providing state-funded education at the senior high school level. Even basic facts such as the name of the country's first prime minister, Kwame Nkrumah, were beyond their keen. Although their knowledge and interest in the country's history and government policies left much to be desired, these students proved surprisingly well informed about foreign corporate superstars such as Mark Zuckerberg and Jeff Bezos, the chief executive officers of Facebook and Amazon, respectively. What explains their disinterest and/or ignorance? The answer lies, I believe, with the education system.

According to Nkrumah, the full-spectrum domination of neocolonial education lies in its ability to valorize European history as authentic and universal knowledge to be learned dutifully and its merits emulated without question. While privileging European history, neocolonial education signifies African history as static and Africans as lacking agency. Nkrumah (1964) asserts that

> the history of Africa, as presented by European scholars, has been encumbered with malicious myths. It was even denied that [Africans, especially their leadership, have the capacity to think for themselves]. It was said that whereas other continents had shaped history, and determined its course, [colonial Africa] had stood still, held down by inertia; that [it] was only propelled into history by European [colonization]. [African history] was therefore presented as an extension of European history. . . . In presenting the history of [Africa] as the history of the collapse of traditional societies in the presence of the European advent, colonialism and imperialism employed their account of [its] history and anthropology as an instrument of their oppressive ideology. (p. 62)

Fed a steady diet of Eurocentric historiography, Ghanaian students may be forgiven for embracing everything that is Western while either ignoring or denigrating their own past and its contributions to African civilization.

Africanizing the Ghanaian Education System: Making Students Think and Act Ghanaian

Educating students to embrace Ghana's history and its Indigenous languages will entail, first and foremost, Africanizing the country's education system. By this I mean privileging its history and culture vis-à-vis that of the West and replacing English as the idiom of instruction with Indigenous vernaculars. Disabused of the notion that Western knowledge and English-language fluency are the sole measures of success, students will come to take pride in their own past, which, in turn, will instill the confidence required to excel in all areas of life.

The approach to Africanizing the education system envisioned here requires root-and-branch change rather than piecemeal reform. That said, as space limitations preclude so comprehensive a treatment, I shall focus instead on Africanizing the curriculum, which is in my view the single most important corrective to a dysfunctional, some might even say toxic, school system. As a first step, it is essential to expose students to literature that chronicles the struggles of the pan-African family and, more important, provides strategies for resisting neocolonialism and challenging the racist and classist ideologies that sustain it. Reintroducing into the curriculum the "African Writers Series" would serve this purpose well, as would major works such as *The Beautyful Ones Are Not Born* by Ayi Kwei Armah (1968), *Things Fall Apart* by Chenua Achebe (1964), and books by Kwame Nkrumah, for example, *Consciencism, Philosophy and Ideology for Decolonization and Development With Particular Reference to the African Revolution* (1964), *Neo-Colonialism: The Last Stage of Imperialism* (1966), *I Speak of Freedom: A Statement of the African Ideology* (1961), and others. Also required are accounts of Ghanaian/African history that illuminate what Black societies have achieved in politics, the arts, and sciences, thus cultivating among students a sense of pride in their cultural heritage.

Ghanaian/African folklore must also be included in the curriculum. For Ghanaians in particular, folklore brings history and culture alive (Asante, 2003) and, in the process, dispels neocolonial stereotypes of Black men and women. These counternarratives have four functions:

> They . . . build [a sense of] community among those at the margins of society; . . . challenge the perceived wisdom of [elites] . . . by providing a context to understand and transform established belief systems; . . . open new windows into the reality of those at the margins of society by [revealing] . . . possibilities beyond the ones they live and demonstrating that they are not alone in their position; and . . . teach others that by combining elements from both the story and the current reality, one can construct another world that is richer than either the story or the reality alone. (Solorzano & Yosso, 2001, p. 475)

Having students share these stories in the vernacular will provide them with a voice and the confidence to claim ownership of their history without fearing their contribution will be judged unworthy of attention. Black feminist scholar bell hooks (1989) goes so far as to contend that denying students the right to tell stories makes "creativity [and transformative learning] impossible" (p. 8). As part of Africanizing the curriculum, I propose that classical Ghanaian songs be included in the syllabus. For example, *Yen ara asaase ni*, "Ghana our homeland" (Harmonious Chorale—Ghana, 2017), by Ephraim Amu, chronicles the sacrifices made to free the nation from the colonial yoke and exhorts the people to preserve the nation while warning that greed and self-interest may undo all that the country has achieved. It enjoins us to be each other's keeper, ethnic, class, cultural, and political affiliations notwithstanding. Amu's *Tete wo bi ka*, "Let's learn from history" (The Voltarian, 2018), challenges the present generation to walk in the footsteps of its forebears—presumably the leaders of the anticolonial movement.

The Ghanaian public education system should also promote religious/spiritual diversity by, to take but one example, teaching students about Christianity, Islam, and Judaism and permitting the adherents of these faiths to pray during the course of the school day. However, this kind of ecumenical initiative should not be purchased at the expense of denying students their African spirituality. Promoting the latter, and, in particular, an African cosmology, would serve to awaken in them, or perhaps more accurately "reawaken," a sense of the connection between the human, natural, and spiritual worlds. Thus will dawn a new age of spirituality. Dillard (2006) speaks eloquently to what Africans have always known in this regard, namely, that "we are all spirit, connected by the Creator's energy of breath. As spirit, we are engage[d] in a human journey for as long as we have the energy of breath: When it is no longer ours, the human journey ends" (p. 68).

African spirituality also offers an alternative to Western individualism and a competitive ethos that have uprooted social relations. Under the aegis of neoliberalism, neocolonial education fosters rational and independent thought, along with materialism, which is antithetical to both an African spirituality and, relatedly, a sense of social cohesion (Dei, 2008). The individual is everything, the community nothing; power and wealth are the sole measures of success. An African spirituality turns all this on its head. From a very early age, the young are taught the importance of community of which even ancestors are a part; indeed, they play a key role in maintaining social cohesion. African spirituality connects the living with the dead and with the unborn, who are believed to be reincarnated ancestors. Although "physically dead[, one's forbearers are believed] to be alive in the memory of those who knew [them] ... as well as ... in the world of the spirit" (Mbiti, cited in Sindima, 1990, p. 198). This spiritual community of the living and the dead provides the former with a " sense of solidarity and security[,] ... [as the latter] are believed to mediate between God and man[,] and ... [steer the community toward] virtues [they] define [as constituting the] morally good life" (Dickson, as cited in Sindima, 1990, p. 198). In a truly profound way, incorporating African spirituality into the curriculum would lead students to become their brothers' and sisters' keepers. African spirituality, as I understand it, would preclude their engaging in the kind of thought and behavior that might endanger their well-being and that of the collective (Schiele, 1994).

Africanizing the curriculum would require moving beyond the current racist and neocolonial pedagogic practice of signifying Ghanaian languages as lacking in the sophistication required to express modern concepts and therefore useless for communicating in a globalized world. To this end, educators should encourage students to view fluency in Indigenous languages as a sine qua non for "speaking truth to power." Integrating Indigenous languages and African knowledge systems into the syllabus would help students "see and interpret the world through [their] own eyes, rather than through those of the 'other'" (Dei, 1996, p. 180). In speaking this truth to power, African-centered schooling facilitates equipping students with the requisite knowledge systems to counter neocolonial narratives (Levine-Rasky, 2014).

Africanizing the curriculum calls for revisiting the work of Marcus Garvey (August 17, 1887–June 10, 1940), Wilmot Edward Burghardt Du Bois (February 23, 1868–August 27, 1963), Albert Memmi (December 15, 1920–present), and other seminal thinkers of the African anticolonial movement (1880–present). This will ensure that students come to perceive Blackness as a continuum transcending all borders and to understand that we are one people and that our strength lies in unity (Dei, 1996). It is no coincidence that the philosophy informing Nkrumah's anticolonial campaign drew heavily on the thought of Marcus Garvey (Carter, 2002). Ghana's first president readily admitted that, but for Garvey, the decolonization of the continent would not have been possible. It was this august figure that charged the pan-anticolonial movement with rejecting the "degradation . . . [of Africans and fighting] for . . . national and racial equality" (Jacques-Garvey, as cited in Lewis, 2011, p. 481).

African-centered schooling would require political elites to set aside ideological sophistries that work to dismiss or minimize Nkrumah's contribution to African independence and the African American cause, such as the civil rights movement of the 1960s. Permitting African writers to present views opposing Nkrumah's vision for an Africa free from colonial oppression would introduce into public discourse multiple perspectives on the struggles of Ghana and Africa—struggles too often recounted through a White/neocolonial lens (Asante, 2012; Botwe-Asamoah, 2013; Motlanthe, 2014; Poe, 2003). In addition, the Ghana Education Service would do well to provide schools with videos chronicling Nkrumah's efforts during the anticolonial period, his tenure as prime minister and then president, and his years in exile following a coup d'état on February 24, 1966. All this would, I believe, provide students with insight into the immediate prehistory and formative years of the nation while revealing the motives and ambitions of a great leader whose vision for his nation and for the African continent is more relevant today, I would argue, than in his own time. His is a vision that continues to inspire Africans, and in particular youth, to work to liberate their respective countries from the neocolonial yoke.

Africanizing the curriculum would also require showcasing the contributions of Ghanaian/African women to the cause of Black liberation. These have largely been ignored or examined after a cursory fashion, reflecting a gender bias endemic within Ghanaian/African education systems. This is not to suggest that such contributions be inflated or romanticized but to urge that they receive the recognition they warrant, just as those of White feminist scholars have. To this end, school curricula might feature accounts of, for example, great female warriors such as Nana Yaa Asantewaa, Queen of Ejisu, who fought the British in an ill-fated attempt to preserve the Asante Kingdom or the "women of Aba in Eastern Nigeria [who took to the streets to protest] against high taxes and low prices of Nigerian exports" (Gbowee, 2009, p. 50; also see Abaraonye, 1998; Onwuteka, 1965; Van Allen, 1975.) Their conduct is a testimony to the capability of African women to equal their male counterparts when afforded the requisite opportunity and support. Their exploits, along with those of other African women, would, I believe, inspire students to challenge misogynistic narratives that consign the outstanding contributions of Black women to footnotes in history books (Boahen, 2000; Brempong, 2000; Obeng, 2000). By Africanizing the curriculum, what has so often been signified by European historians as merely a "riot," with a view to representing African women as atavistic, impulsive, and violent, could be reframed as a "war" against British colonial rule (Abaraonye, 1998). An Africanized curriculum would also highlight such models of leadership as Winnie Mandela, an anti-apartheid shero, Ellen Sirleaf Johnson, the first African woman to serve as president of Liberia (2006-2018); and Nana Konadu Rawlings, a Ghanaian and politician. Africanizing the curriculum by celebrating such gender role models would inspire the present generation of young Africans, and especially the students among them, to fight for gender equality in all spheres of national life.

Conclusion

When the Union Jack was lowered for the last time in Accra's main square on March 6, 1957, it signaled not the end of colonialism but the transfer of power to an educated elite enamored with British culture and institutions, among which the British public education system was held in especially high esteem. Modeled on the latter, Ghanaian public education has, over the course of more than 60 years, persevered in "miseducating" the nation's youth, largely by privileging the English language at the expense of Indigenous vernaculars and ensuring that students learned as little as possible about the country's history. Entrenched as the problem is, the solution is at hand in the form of educational policies aimed at Africanizing the curriculum with a view to reconnecting students with their cultural roots through reviving Indigenous languages and reacquainting them with their rich past. One thing is certain: Whatever is left of a Ghanaian cultural identity will be irretrievably lost should the public school system fail in this crucial mission.

I shall conclude with a time-honored African adage: *The villager who is oblivious to the sound of the village chief's trumpet is likely to become the victim of the ensuing chaos.*

References

Abaraonye, F. I. (1998). The women's war of 1929 in south-eastern Nigeria. In M. L. Diamond (Ed.), *Women and revolution: Global expressions* (pp. 109–132). Kluwer Academic Publishers.

Achebe, C. (1964). *Things fall apart*. Heinemann.

Abdi, A. A. (2012). Eurocentric discourses and African philosophies and epistemologies of education: Counter-hegemonic analyses and responses. In H. K. Wright & A. A. Abdi (Eds.), *The dialectics of African education and Western discourses: Counter-hegemonic perspectives* (Vol. 21, pp. 12–26). Peter Lang.

Armah, A. K. (1968). *The beautyful ones are not yet born*. Houghton Mifflin.

Asante, M. K. (2003). *Afrocentricity: The theory of social change*. African American Images.

Asante, M. K. (2012). The character of Kwame Nkrumah's united African vision. *Journal of Pan African Studies, 4*(10), 12–24.

Blauner, R. (1969). Internal colonialism and ghetto revolt. *Social Problems, 16*(4), 393–408.

Boahen, A. A. (2000). Yaa Asantewaa in the Yaa Asantewaa War of 1900: Military leader or symbolic head? *Ghana Studies, 3*(1), 111–135.

Botwe-Asamoah, K. (2013). *Kwame Nkrumah's politico-cultural thought: An African-centered paradigm for the second phase of the African revolution*. Routledge.

Boykin, A. W. (1986). The triple quandary and the schooling of Afro-American children. In U. Neisser (Ed.), *The school achievement of minority children: New perspectives* (pp. 57–92). Lawrence Erlbaum.

Brempong, A. (2000). The role of Nana Yaa Asantewaa in the 1900 Asante War of Resistance. *Le Griot, 8*, 97–110.

Carter, S. (2002). The economic philosophy of Marcus Garvey. *Western Journal of Black Studies, 26*(1), 1–5.

Dei, G. J. S. (1996). The role of Afrocentricity in inclusive curriculum in Canadian schools. *Canadian Journal of Education, 21*(2), 170–186.

Dei, G. J. S. (2008). Schooling as a community: Race, schooling, and the education of African. youth. *Journal of Black Studies, 38*(3), 346–366.

Dei, G. J. S., & Asgharzadeh, A. (2001). The power of social theory: The anti-colonial discursive framework. *Journal of Educational Thought, 35*(3), 297–323.

Dillard, C. (2006). When the music changes, so should the dance: Cultural and spiritual considerations in paradigm proliferation. *International Journal of Qualitative Studies in Education, 19*(1), pp. 59–76.

Fanon, F. (1967). *Black skin, White masks*. Grove Press.

Freire, P. (1970). *Pedagogy of the oppressed* (M. Ramos, Trans.). The Seabury Press.

Freire, P. (2000). *Pedagogy of the oppressed* (3rd ed.; M. Bergman Ramos, Trans.). Continuum.

Gbowee, L. (2009). Effecting change through women's activism in Liberia. *IDS Bulletin, 40*(2), 50–53.

Gordon, B. (1993). African-American cultural knowledge and liberatory education. In M. J. Shujaa (Ed.), *Too much schooling, too little education: The paradox of Black life in White societies* (pp. 13–36). African World Press.

Harmonious Chorale—Ghana. (2017, February 17). *Yen ara asaase ni* [Video]. YouTube. https://www.youtube.com/watch?v=K90Lmbpd5PQ

hooks, b. (1989). *Talking Black: Thinking feminist, thinking Black*. South End.

Kincheloe, J. (2012). Critical pedagogy in the twenty-first century: Evolution for survival. *Counterpoint, 422*, 147–183.

Levine-Rasky, C. (2014). White fear: Analyzing public objection to Toronto's Africentric school. *Race, Ethnicity & Education, 17*(2), 202–218.

Lewis, R. (2011). Marcus Garvey: The remapping of Africa and its diaspora. *Critical Art, 25*(4), 473–483.

Motlanthe, K. (2014). The role of the African intelligentsia in post-Mandela Africa. *The Thinker, 60*, 19–23.

Nkrumah, K. (1961). *I speak of freedom: A statement of the African ideology*. Praeger.

Nkrumah, K. (1962). *Towards colonial freedom: African in the struggle against world imperialism*. Heinemann.

Nkrumah, K. (1964). *Consciencism: Philosophy and ideology for decolonization and development with particular reference to the African revolution*. Heinemann.

Nkrumah, K. (1966). *Neo-colonialism: The last stage of imperialism*. International Publishers.

Nyerere, J. K. (1968). *Freedom and socialism: Uhuru na ujamaa; a selection of writings and speeches, 1965–1967*. Oxford University Press.

Obeng, P. (2000). Yaa Asantewaa's war of independence: Honoring and ratifying an historic pledge. *Ghana Studies, 3*(1), 137–152.

Onwuteka, C. C. (1965). The Aba riot of 1929 and its relation to the system of indirect rule. *Nigerian Journal of Economic and Social Studies, 7*(3), 273–282.

Poe, D. Z. (2003). *Kwame Nkrumah's contribution to the pan-African agency: An Afrocentric analysis*. Routledge.

Schiele, J. H. (1994). Afrocentricity: Implications for higher education. *Journal of Black Studies, 25*(2), 150–169.

Sindima, H. (1990). Liberalism and African culture. *Journal of Black Studies, 21*(2), 190–209.

Solorzano, D. G., & Yosso, T. (2001). Critical race and LatCrit theory and method: Counter-storytelling. *Qualitative Studies in Education, 14*(4), 471–495.

The Voltarian. (2018, March 9). *Tete wo bi ka* [Video]. YouTube. https://www.youtube.com/watch?v=bf4tm2Jt9Ls

Van Allen, J. (1975). Aba riots or the Igbo women's war? - Ideology, stratification and the invisibility of women. *Journal of African Studies, 6*(1), 11–39.

CHAPTER 4

Decolonized Curriculum in Colonized Contexts: Assessing Ghanaian Public Schools' Role in the Decolonization Agenda

Richardson Addai-Mununkum and
Nyuiemedi Agordzo Edoh-Torgah

POSTCOLONIAL AFRICA HAS witnessed significant reforms aimed at reversing colonial philosophies that led to cultural repression, misrepresentations, misinterpretations, and devaluation of indigenous culture (Shizha, 2013). This agenda has been carried out through education generally and the school curriculum specifically. This is because "the school curriculum communicates what we choose to remember about our past, what we believe about the present, what we hope for the future" (Pinar, 2004, p. 20). The founding fathers of African liberation thus invested heavily in education. Expanding access and overhauling school curricula to make them instruments for the reconstruction of African cultures and identities—most of which had been decentered/dislocated and disrupted by colonization (Ashanti, 2003). In the words of Halagao (2010), "Educators have begun to look at developing curriculum and pedagogy with a decolonization framework with the aim to emancipate students from ignorance and ignite a commitment to social change" (p. 495). Having reviewed several pieces of literature about the curricula of Namibia and Zimbabwe, Jensen (2003) summarizes his thoughts about inherited "colonial curriculum" as

> racist because it was founded on an ideology that extolled the belief in inherent differences between the races, and because it portrayed Whites as heroes and Blacks as savages. The colonial curriculum was described as Eurocentric because it was dominated by a history of European ideas and events to the exclusion of African history, ideas, and movements. It was denounced as divisive and demeaning because it justified social, economic, and political segregation among the races in favor of White minority rule. It was dismissed as exploitative and unjust because it portrayed the capitalist system as the only viable economic system for African development, thereby denying the history of communal socialism of precolonial times. (p. 472)

It therefore comes as no surprise that countries around Africa have at some point in their history reworked their curricula towards decolonization. Botswana revised its philosophy of education after independence and outlined four principles, which included democracy, development, self-reliance, and unity. Later, the Africentric principle of *Botho* (compassion) was added. As one of the tenets of African culture, Botho "is the concept of a person who has a well-rounded character, who is well-mannered, courteous and disciplined, and realizes his or her full potential both as an individual and as a part of the community to which he or she belongs" (Pandey & Moorad, 2003, p. 153).

Since independence, Kenya's education reforms have focused on curriculum reconstruction "to reflect diverse indigenous ways of knowing, and to promote social change and the empowerment of Kenyans" (Shizha, 2013, p. 11). Similarly, Nigeria phased out colonial education, which was characterized as theoretical and not able to make a meaningful impact on the life of its people (Shizha, 2013). Inspired by the agenda of *Education for Self-Reliance*, President Julius Nyerere of Tanzania instituted curricular reforms in the 1970s in a way to indigenize the education system. Such reforms were seen as part of his concept of *Ujamaa*, or the villagization program (Shizha, 2013, p. 10).

Ghana, the torchbearer of African independence, charted this course by taking radical steps soon after independence to Africanize the educational system. Significant among these were curricular reforms that made space for Indigenous knowledge, which was conspicuously missing in colonial education. In the Education Act of 1961, mission schools were made public schools, which amounted to missionaries no longer holding control of education, and by extension, the curriculum of pre-tertiary education. Since then, successive reforms have attempted, in piecemeal, to introduce subjects and curricular forms that seek to reignite Africentrism in the younger generation. In 1987, for instance, a school subject called Cultural Studies was developed, which, among other things, supported educating students in the appreciation and championship of Ghanaian cultural identity. Quite recently, the promulgation of the National Language Policy legalized the use of local language as the medium of instruction in Grades 1 to 3 (Owu-Ewie, 2006) due to the growing use of the English language and the neglect of local languages. This policy aimed in part to legitimize local languages that were threatened in various fronts by the vestiges of colonialism and Western imperialism (wa Thiong'o, 1994).

Regardless of the perceived strides in decolonizing the education system, emerging research suggests that Ghanaian youth are heavily subjective to neocolonial influences (Quist, 2001) in areas of fashion (Ofori et al., 2014) language preferences (Anyidoho & Dakubu, 2008), sports (Darby, 2013), and music (Salm & Falola, 2002). In fashion, the perception of looking good is earned by the wearing of "international dress(s) of success"—suit and tie (De Witte, 2005). It is therefore not too surprising that professionals in positions to be promoted often lose the opportunity because they fail to wear this colonial suit (Addai-Mununkum et al., 2020). Furthermore, there is a general preference for the English language over local ones, as "its usage has come to be associated with literacy and academic intelligence" (Mfum-Mensah, 2005, p. 84). The inability to communicate in English is perceived as disgraceful, but to the contrary, incompetence in reading Indigenous languages remains acceptable.

With sports, Halabi-Ahma (2013) observes that a greater number of football enthusiasts are more frequent watchers of foreign matches than of local games. So pervasive is this practice that a Christian Thanksgiving service was organized when football team Chelsea won the Premier League in 2017 (BBC News, 2017). Local supporters of Chelsea wore their jerseys to the Living Streams International Church where the pastor led them to sing the Chelsea FC anthem and cut a celebratory cake. Similarly, in a comparative survey of youth music preferences, Quist (2001) reports that "85% of people who attended nightclubs in Ghana, as compared to 74% in Côte d'Ivoire, indicated their strong interest in and preference for Western music" (p. 309). It is clear from the foregoing that Ghanaians have acquired tastes for Western products in ways that exemplify the binary logic of imperialism—elevate Western products while rendering inferior products and ideas of indigenous origin (Matemba & Addai-Mununkum, 2017). Colonial patronage is in full force as calls abound in the local media for the youth to value and reembrace Ghanaian identity (Ghana News Agency, 2014).

It has long been established that public education is the most potent institution to carry out ideological reorientation and value education (Coe, 2005). This is because school curriculum translates societies' goals into programs of instruction by capturing and making provision for the passing on of relevant and valuable aspects of culture. This is the case in Ghana, where parts of the social education curriculum aim at "develop[ing] a sense of national consciousness and national identity," (Ghana Education Service, 2008, p. iii) "as Ghanaians and Africans with a heritage worthy of pride, preservation and improvement" (Ghana Education Service, 2010). With such an African-centered curriculum, students will be socialized to appreciate the history of Ghana's development and identify their own contributions to the writing of new histories.

In light of the foregoing descriptions of the existing curriculum, it is a wonder why graduates of public education continue to bow to colonial patronage. Although a significant number of scholars on decolonization of African education have focused on a descriptive assessment of the presence or absence of efforts to decolonize curriculum, little research has examined the impact of such reforms on attitudinal change. Questions relating to the effect of such reforms on the outcomes and products of schools remain largely unanswered. Specifically, in the case of Ghana, sociopolitical commentators have at various fora raised questions about the potency of the Ghanaian school curriculum in achieving the promise of educating for civic consciousness. Due to the dearth of research in this area, we challenged ourselves to pursue a study that asks the following:

a. How successful has the Ghanaian basic school curriculum been in inspiring Africentrism in students?
b. What are the challenges of the Ghanaian basic school curriculum to live up to its promise of inculcating Africentrism in students?
c. How might we explain the presence of the challenges that impede the success of the decolonization agenda within Ghana?

Answers to these questions are crucial because without an evaluation and deepened understanding of the process of decolonization, we run the risk of doing the same things and expecting different results. By effectively interrogating these questions related to successes, challenges, and their reasons, we can obtain a nuanced understanding of the present obstacles and offer appropriate solutions that will make our schools more responsive toward the decolonization agenda. Our use of the concept "curriculum" is in line with the school of thought that explains curriculum beyond what is taught in the classroom. Consequently, our use of the term is in its broadest sense synonymous with that of John Dewey (1933), who defines it to include content, instruction, overt and covert learning subsumed within the school's social environment, altogether influencing the learning outcomes of students. Inspired by this thinking, we define *curriculum* as varied experiences provided and guided by the school for learners' acquisition of socially valued knowledge, the practice of useful skills, and the development of socioculturally appropriate attitudes.

Theory

To fully explore this, we draw on the postcolonial concept of decolonization. Defined as "the process of revealing and dismantling colonialist power in all its forms" (Ashcroft et al., 1998, p. 62), decolonization is a complex and continuing process. In the words of Ngugi wa Thiong'o (1994), it is "the search for a liberating perspective within which to see ourselves clearly in relationship to ourselves and to other selves in the universe" (p. 87). The complexity of the decolonization process is that hidden aspects of institutional and cultural forms that maintained colonialist power remain deep-rooted, demanding a continuous reawakening of African consciousness to gradually transition from a state of blindness to becoming present (Mbembe, 2015). It is for this that calls have been made for a decolonized curriculum (Dei, 2012, 2014; Shizha, 2012).

Laenui (2000) proposes five phases of decolonization: rediscovery and recovery, mourning, dreaming, commitment, and action. In the foundation stage of rediscovery and recovery, people live in constant reminders of the superiority of colonial society over Indigenous ones. The second stage is mourning—a time when people are able to lament their victimization. The challenge at this stage is the possibility of people getting stuck in the awfulization of their victimhood, finding sufficient satisfaction in long-term grumbling. However, if they are able to progress, they get to the dreaming stage, where a full panorama of possibilities is expressed through consultations and debates aimed at laying the foundation for the creation of a new social order. The commitment stage comes next, during which people release themselves from the shackles of colonial patriotism to wade through the cult of personalities and family histories as a means of building consensus around statements of unified direction. The final stage of action is a derivative of consensus and commitment reached in the fourth stage. Action at this stage is a proactive step toward the creation of a new social order. With the appreciation of decolonization as a process, we implore Laenui's theory here as an assessment tool. Sixty years since the end of political colonization, we assess how far the Ghanaian basic school curriculum has advanced in the decolonization process.

Methodology

This chapter arises out of a bigger study we undertook that examined African indigeneity in public schools in Ghana. We designed and used a qualitative case study to consider decolonization in six junior high (middle) schools in Ghana. We designed the multiple case instrumental research to explore multiple bounded systems (Creswell, 2007; Stake, 1994) in order to assess the successes and failures of the curriculum in the decolonization agenda. By choosing a multiple case study, we were afforded the opportunity to explore differences within and between the cases (Baxter & Jack, 2008). Such differences and similarities will help deepen our understanding of how public schools in Ghana are engaging with decolonization—an instrumental use of case study (Stake, 1994). We purposefully selected different schools for their unique characteristics: (a) a Catholic school with the majority of students being Christians, (b) an Islamic school with a majority of Muslims, (c) a Seventh-Day Adventist school with a majority of students being Christians, and (d) three wholly public schools. We involved three principals, six teachers, and 34 students. Whereas a census was used in the case of the principals, teacher participants were selected by volunteer and snowball sampling. For every school we selected, the principal became an automatic choice for participation and was invited while seeking permission to undertake the study. For teachers, we explained the study to them and invited them to participate, with those who showed interest being selected. In some instances, the first set of teachers referred us to other colleagues who they thought were passionate about decolonization, thereby snowballing an opportunity for them to be added.

The methods of data collection included interviews, observations, document analysis, and focus group discussions. We researched the schools for one school term of 3 months, during which in- and out-of-classroom activities were observed. We observed cocurricular activities such as school assemblies, worship services, and other routines, in addition to physical artifacts. The teachers chosen for this study had varied years of teaching experience ranging from 2 to 25. They were interviewed for an average of three 30-minute sessions at their own convenience of time and venue. Student participants were engaged in focus group discussions in their schools. Following the discussions, those with strong opinions were selected for individual interviews, which was meant to provide them with a conducive atmosphere to confide in the researchers about views they could not share with the larger group.

Although the bigger study was structured as case study, for this chapter, we analyzed our data thematically in the likeness of phenomenology (see Creswell, 2007; Denzin & Lincoln, 2011). Data generated for the study included observation notes, documents, and several hours of audio recordings of interviews and focus group discussions. The audio recordings were first transcribed into text with the aid of computer software—F4. We then began a process of open coding (Strauss & Corbin, 1990). We read through texts and listened to audio recordings repeatedly, looking out for data that spoke to cultural identity, nationalism, and Africanism. From these codes, we generated themes that pointed to hope and disappointment in the curriculum in relation to decolonization. An iterative process of recoding, regrouping, and realigning resulted in the emergence of broader themes of successes and challenges of the curriculum. Our findings along the lines of these themes are presented in the subsequent sessions, with our commentary.

Findings

Decolonized Curriculum

We observed from our study that educational reforms carried out in 1987 and 2008 made significant attempts at decolonization in the curriculum. A new subject introduced—cultural studies, which later found space in social studies—consciously attempted to place Ghanaian pride as a key component of the curriculum. For instance, the social studies syllabus requires students to "explain how colonization retards progress in Ghana" and "give suggestions of how to correct our negative attitudes and values as a result of colonization" (Ghana Education Service, 2008, p. 8). Although we expected to see more of such explicit content about colonization to run through the entire syllabus, it appears that only a few learning areas actually make space for it. Besides social studies, other subjects, such as religious and moral education and Ghanaian language and culture, contain implicit content that seeks to reignite Africentrism in students. Content such as African traditional beliefs, traditional festivals, puberty rites, and others offer opportunities for learners to know, understand, and appreciate Indigenous culture as unique and crucial to our identity as Ghanaians. It was clear from our analysis, however, that some of this content was presented superficially and that their connection to decolonization is not clearly expressed. That notwithstanding, the attempt to include such content is a step in the right direction toward "seeing ourselves clearly" (wa Thiong'o, 1994).

Besides the formal curriculum, the cocurriculum of schools allows for cultural performances that are showcased at periodic interschool festivals. During our study, one of our schools had just won a district completion and was feverishly rehearsing for a regional competition. We witnessed students learn and dance Adowa, Kpalogo, and Boborbor. In contrast to other studies that report students scorn at some traditional practices (Coe, 2005), we witnessed students demonstrate enthusiasm and a penchant quest to claim their heritage through these traditional dances.

We also witnessed students sing songs on different occasions, the lyrics of which inspired nationalism and *Ghanaianess* in students. One such song is by Ephraim Amu (1929):

Yɛn ara asase ni	This is our land
Ɛyɛ aboɔ denden ma yɛn	It is precious to us
Mogya a nananom hwie gu	Our forefathers shed their blood
nya ne too hɔ ma yɛn	to keep it for us
Aduru me ne wo nso	It is our turn now to continue
so sɛ yɛbɛyɛ bi atoa so	from where they left
Nimdeɛ ntoaso nkotokrane ne	Pride, cheating and selfishness
pɛsɛmenkomenya	has scared our character and diminished
Adi yɛn bra me dɛm ama y'asase yi	our affection for our land
dɔ atɔmu sɛ	
Ɔman yi sɛ ɛbɛyɛ yie oo	Whether or not this nation prospers
Ɔman yi sɛ ɛnnyɛ yie oo	depends on the character of citizens
Ayɛ nsɛmnnahɔ sɛ	
Ɔmanfo bra na ɛkyerɛ	

This song has been characterized as an informal national anthem, and it is sung at national functions. In the schools we visited, students sing it daily, either in the morning or before closing. The lyrics are very patriotic and inspire a sense of ownership of the country, placing the responsibility on learners to contribute toward the development of the country. This and other such inspirational songs, such as "Ɛnyɛ obi ara o me ara" (What Is to Be Done Is for Me to Do and Not Anyone Else), "Ma Ɔman ho nhia wo" (Cherish Your Country Ghana), and "Arise Ghana Youth for Your Country," promote a sense of liberation and have been instrumental in the quest for educated students with decolonized civic consciousness. Undoubtedly, the public school, through its formal and informal curriculum, is providing opportunities for students to be educated as a pan-Africanist will expect.

Colonized Contexts

As with many attempts at educational reform, the abovementioned efforts by the schools were routinely hampered. Regardless of the injection of Africentrism in the curriculum, the vestiges of colonization are still very present and enacted mostly through the hidden curricula of public schools. During one of our school visits, students marched to a song that we saw to be intriguing:

Yɛn nananom	(our forefathers)
Yɛn nananom	(our forefathers)
Yɛn nananom som abosom (abosom keseɛ)	(our forefathers worshipped big idols)
Na yɛn deɛ	(but for us)
Na yɛn deɛ	(but for us)
Na yɛn deɛ yɛbɛsom Yehowa	(but for us we would worship Jehovah)

Songs such as these are Christian by all accounts, which is problematic. It is even more worrying to observe that it attacks the very essence of Africentrism. Prior to colonization, our cherished ancestors practiced Indigenous religions that venerate gods and ancestors as mediums for communicating with God (Awolalu, 1975). Thus, describing our forefathers as idol worshippers is factually inaccurate. Again, the pervasive nature of Indigenous religions in the lives of precolonial persons makes it near inseparable from the cultural fabric of society (Mbiti, 1969). By denigrating our forefathers as "idol worshippers" all their deeds (including patriotic ones) are smeared with religious colorizations, thus making emulating their examples a matter of choice rather than an imperative. We also observed educators whose religious biases influenced their pedagogical actions, countering efforts at decolonization. One such person is Mary (pseudonym), who remarked in an interview:

> We are so blessed to have had the Whiteman introduce God to us. It is what has sustained us through the ages. . . . That is why we say, "if you are going to church and you meet a Whiteman, return home because you have met Jesus."

As insiders, such statements are not surprising to hear, but for it to have come from a professionally trained teacher is most worrisome. Besides the factual inaccuracy of a White man introducing God, her equating of the White man to God propels colonial dependency. The White man is seen as God because he is projected as a more benevolent creature on whom we can depend to supply our basic needs. If such statements and impressions are finding spaces in curriculum enactment, it must be a serious concern.

Even more disturbing is the content of textbooks used in public schools. With the inability of the state to supply adequate textbooks (Okyere et al., 1997), private publishers have cashed in on the demand and supply versions of textbooks with little to no regulation. In one such textbook widely used in our study area, we observed on one of its pages a section that explores the "Positive Effects of Colonization on Ghana." Within this section is a topic that read:

> Colonial rule brought Christianity. . . . Before Christianity, Ghanaians practiced traditional religion which allowed practices such as human sacrifice, slavery and other uncivilized methods of worship. The introduction of Christianity put a stop to those wicked practices. (Okyere, 2013, p. 46)

This content is not only factually inaccurate, but it is also cunningly recolonizing. Edward Said (1979) has said that the Occident's representation of the other is not maintained in myths but in the conscious creation of knowledge used to legitimize such depictions—depictions, in this case, that have found space in textbooks. Evidently, its cancerous effect is enough to derail all the attempts at intellectual decolonization.

Perhaps the most significant, which somewhat influences all the other factors identified, is religion. I follow the lead of Comaroff and Comaroff (1991) to explain Western religions, particularly Christianity, as more than just a religion but as "part of the historical anthropology of colonialism and consciousness, culture and power" (p. 11). In Ghana, missions still manage over 70% of basic public schools owing to a long history of educational partnership. By this arrangement, some religious practices are permitted as part of the co-curriculum, a situation that allows for curricular conflicts. During our research, two school administrators said they would not allow resource persons who identified as traditional worshippers to their schools. Neither would they admit any teacher who self-identified as a Rastafarian to teach in their schools. Their reason was to maintain the purity of their schools' religious ethos. If Indigenous religion, which undergirds culture, is being denied space in public schools, where lies the authenticity of content being transmitted in classroom discourse? In sum, religion appears to be erecting obstructions to educationally appropriate activities that could support decolonization.

Discussion

We see from our study parallels of Laenui's (2000) first stage of decolonization, where educators' and students' "elevation of form over substance [and] dealing with traditional culture from the perspective of a foreign culture" (p. 153) characterizes curriculum enactment in the schools. Having been so long separated from the practice and appreciation of their culture, Indigenes can abuse their own culture by perceiving it from the perspective of foreign ones. As our findings suggest, students demonstrated excitement at their participation in cultural competitions yet did not demonstrate any appreciation for why they do them. Laenui warns that such theatrics, although they may make good media clips, should not be mistaken for substance because they just dramatize the foreigner's concept of the Indigenous person.

Throughout the research, there was no evidence we gathered that suggested Ghanaian students in a state of mourning (Laenui's, 2000, second stage). Students did not see themselves (and forefathers) as victims in the colonization that happened centuries ago. They recounted it as part of the Ghanaian history without any reflective sense of how things could have been different in the absence of colonization. In fact, students held positive perceptions of colonization in ways similar to the content of the textbook. With some textbooks presenting Indigenous religions as the cause of barbaric cultural practices, such as human sacrifice and the like, the obvious stance for students is to rupture ties with tradition and embrace a "civilization" as espoused by the Western world.

What this study teaches us is that our school curriculum is miles away from energizing students to action. Going by Laenui's (2000) stages, our students are not in a position to dream about other possibilities beyond acting in neocolonial ways. Indeed, we did not see in our research the sense of commitment to the African course among the students. Neither did we observe action on the part of students to rewrite the script of development. Students, and, to a large extent, teachers, did not see anything wrong with colonial patronage. To the contrary, they were quick to justify their preference for foreign goods and services, citing reasons such as inferior Indigenous products as rationalizations. They condemned anything Ghanaian and adored foreign materials. It therefore comes as no surprise to us that Africentrism is at its lowest ebb in the consciousness of the average Ghanaian.

Recommendations

In spite of such discouraging observations, there are still opportunities to reinvigorate the school curriculum to make it more impactful in the process of decolonization. One of the ways we suggest is to reorganize teacher education to infuse African-centered practices in the next generation of teachers. With the present curriculum, student teachers, at least at the university, enroll in African-themed liberal courses; however, we believe this should be scaled up significantly. Perhaps the approach of designating a course for this agenda might not be enough. African-centered education should be made a crosscutting issue that permeates the entire teacher training curriculum in a bid to make the next generation of teachers conscious of their identities and use their teaching to champion an African course.

The current state–mission partnership in the provision of education is great, but clearer lines ought to be drawn. The state, through its ministry and agency, needs to engage missions about religious inclusion and build consensus around religious-themed activities and professional conducts. As we observed, missions still consider schools as their own and are less likely to make concessions about tolerance. If we seek to restore African-centered practices through school curricula, missions should be encouraged to reflect and concede to certain practices that denigrate and demean indigenous traditions and practices.

For the current crop of students, we need to act fast by introducing intervention programs that will foster a greater appreciation for the African continent. Through school guidance and counseling programs, orientation, information, remedial, and follow-up services should be provided for educators to meet students individually and as larger groups. Such meetings formal or informal could be used to make students reflect on their own identities as Africans and what they can become. For example, orientation services for students should not only be geared toward appreciating their new environments and understanding the acclimatization process, but they should also be provided opportunities to recognize that social deviance is not just a moral problem but one that is contrary to the Africentric practice of *Ubuntu*—I am because we are. Therefore, any act by an individual that negatively affects the communal interest takes away from our African identity and heritage. It is by the transmission of such positive messages that other Africentric principles and practices such as wearing traditional clothing in school will make sense to students.

Conclusion

Whereas we would have wished that African-centered schooling is the defining ethos, we witnessed schools that are caught in a milieu of postcolonial ambivalence, where actors are simultaneously attracted to, and repulsed by indigenous culture (Ashcroft et al., 1998). Efforts by the state to implement, an Africentric curriculum in public schools were visible in our research. Yet the contexts within which such curricula are implemented are themselves centers of complex interrelationships among personal faiths, institutional ideology, religious ethos, and official knowledge. Colonial patronage in the area of religion has had an enduring effect to the extent that the support some educators have for a decolonized curriculum is questionable. It is such complexities that we wish to bring to the forefront, courting scholarship attention to and seeking answers to better ways of empowering public schools to enact curriculum that will awaken Africentric consciousness.

References

Addai-Mununkum, R., Amos, P., & Ofosu-Dwamena, E. (2020). Assessing the counselling needs of Ghanaian teachers due for promotion. *International Journal of Psychology and Education, 14*(1). Kumasi: PA Publishers.

Amu, Ephraim. (1932). Twenty Five African Songs. London: Sheldon Press.

Anyidoho, A., & Dakubu, M. K. (2008). Ghana: Indigenous languages, English, and an emerging national identity. In A. Simpson (Ed.), *Language and national identity in Africa* (pp. 141–157). Oxford University Press.

Ashanti, K. (2003, November 23). Leaders in African-centered education. *The Initiative Anthology.* http://www.units.miamioh.edu/eduleadership/anthology/rci/com03005.pdf

Ashcroft, B., Griffiths, G., & Tiffin, H. (1998). *Key concepts in post-colonial studies.* Psychology Press.

Awolalu, J. O. (1975). What is African traditional religion? *Studies in Comparative Religion, 9*(1). http://www.studiesincomparativereligion.com/Public/articles/What_is_African_Traditional_Religion-by_Joseph_Omosade_Awolalu.aspx

Baxter, P., & Jack, S. (2008). Qualitative case study methodology: Study design and implementation for novice researchers. *The Qualitative Report, 13*(4), 544–559.

BBC News. (2017, June 5). *Ghana church gives thanks for Chelsea.* BBC Africa. https://www.bbc.co.uk/news/world-africa-40164369

Coe, C. (2005). *Dilemmas of culture in African schools: Youth, nationalism, and the transformation of knowledge.* University of Chicago Press.

Comaroff, J., & Comaroff, J. L. (1991). *Of Revelation and Revolution, Volume 1: Christianity, colonialism, and consciousness in South Africa.* University of Chicago Press.

Creswell, J. W. (2007). *Qualitative inquiry and research design: Choosing among five traditions.* Sage Publications.

Darby, P. (2013). Moving players, traversing perspectives: Global value chains, production networks and Ghanaian football labour migration. *Geoforum, 50*(1), 43–53.

De Witte, M. (2005). The spectacular and the spirits: Charismatics and neo-traditionalists on Ghanaian television. *Material Religion, 1*(3), 314–334.

Dei, G. J. S. (2012). Reclaiming our Africanness in the diasporized context: The challenge of asserting a critical African personality. *Journal of Pan African Studies, 4*(10), 42–57.

Dei, G. J. S. (2014). Indigenizing the school curriculum. In G. Emeagwali & G. J. S. Dei (Eds.), *African Indigenous knowledge and the disciplines* (pp. 165–180). Brill.

Denzin, N. K., & Lincoln, Y. S. (2011). *The SAGE handbook of qualitative research.* Sage Publications.

Dewey, J. (1933). *How do we think: A restatement of the relation of reflective thinking to the educative process.* D.C. Heath.

Ghana Education Service. (2008). *Teaching syllabus for social studies (JHS 1–3).*

Ghana Education Service. (2010). *Teaching syllabus for history.*

Ghana News Agency. (2014, April 29). *Ghanaian traditional and cultural values eroding - David Dontoh.* http://www.ghananewsagency.org/social/ghanaian-traditional-and-cultural-values-eroding-david-dontoh-74204

Halabi-Ahma, O. (2013). *An investigation into the reasons for low attendance at Glo Premier League matches in Ghana: A focus on Accra Sports Stadium* [PhD thesis]. Ashesi University.

Halagao, P. E. (2010). Liberating Filipino Americans through decolonizing curriculum. *Race, Ethnicity, and Education, 13*(4), 495–512.

Jensen, J. D. (2003). What education scholars write about curriculum in Namibia and Zimbabwe. In W. F. Pinar (Ed.), *International handbook of curriculum research* (pp. 484-490). Taylor & Francis.

Laenui, P. (2000). Processes of decolonization. In M. Battiste (Ed.), *Reclaiming Indigenous voice and vision* (pp. 150–160). UBC Press.

Matemba, Y., & Addai-Mununkum, R. (2017). 'These religions are no good – they're nothing but idol worship': (Mis)representation of religion in Religious Education at school in Malawi and Ghana. *British Journal of Religious Education, 41*(2), 1–19.

Mbembe, A. (2015). *Decolonizing knowledge and the question of the archive.* Retrieved from https://wiser.wits.ac.za/system/files/Achille%20Mbembe%20%20Decolonizing%20Knowledge%20and%20the%20Question%20of%20the%20Archive.pdf

Mbiti, J. S. (1969). *African religions and philosophy* (2nd ed.). Heinemann.

Mfum-Mensah, O. (2005). The impact of colonial and postcolonial Ghanaian language policies on vernacular use in schools in two northern Ghanaian communities. *Comparative Education, 41*(1), 71–85.

Ofori, I., Mensah, A., Amenakpor, F., & Gablah, P. G. (2014). Perceptions of University of Ghana students towards campus female fashion. *Arts and Design Studies, 25*(1), 19–25.

Okyere, B. A. (2013). *Social studies for junior high schools.* New Golden Publications.

Okyere, B., Mensah, A., Kugbey, H., & Harris, A. (1997). *What happens to the textbooks?* Arlington, VA: Institute or International Research. Retrieved from http://www.ieq.org/pdf/textbooks.pdf

Owu-Ewie, C. (2006). The language policy of education in Ghana: A critical look at the English-only language policy of education. In J. Mugane et al. (Eds.), *Selected proceedings of the 35th Annual Conference on African Linguistics* (pp. 76–85). Cascadilla Proceedings Project.

Pandey, S. N., & Moorad, F. R. (2003). The decolonization of curriculum in Botswana. In W. F. Pinar (Ed.), *International handbook of curriculum research* (pp. 143–170). Taylor & Francis.

Pinar, W. (2004). *What is curriculum theory?* Lawrence Erlbaum.

Quist, H. O. (2001). Cultural issues in secondary education development in West Africa: Away from colonial survivals, towards neocolonial influences? *Comparative Education, 37*(3), 297–314.

Said, E. W. (1979). *Orientalism.* Random House.

Salm, S. J., & Falola, T. (2002). *Culture and customs of Ghana.* Greenwood Publishing Group.

Shizha, E. (2012). Are we there yet? Theorizing a decolonizing science education for development in Africa. In A. A. Abdi (Ed.), *Decolonizing philosophies of education* (pp. 163–176). Sense Publishers.

Shizha, E. (2013). Reclaiming our Indigenous voices: The problem with postcolonial sub-Saharan African school curriculum. *Journal of Indigenous Social Development, 2*(1). Retrieved from https://scholarspace.manoa.hawaii.edu/bitstream/10125/29818/v2i1_06shizha.pdf

Stake, R. E. (1994). Case studies. In N. K. Denzin & Y. S. Lincoln (Eds.), *Handbook of qualitative research* (pp. 236–247). Sage Publications.

Strauss, A., & Corbin, J. (1990). *Basics of qualitative research. Grounded theory procedures and techniques.* Sage Publications.

wa Thiong'o, N. (1994). *Decolonising the mind: The politics of language in African literature.* Heinemann.

CHAPTER 5

Indigenous African Philosophies as a Critical Thinking Pedagogical Tool for Schooling and Education

Isaac Nortey Darko, Paul Banahene Adjei, and Chloe Weir

EDUCATION IN THE 21st century calls for new ways of teaching and learning in higher education, particularly with meaningful and effective pedagogical practices borrowed from and informed by various knowledge systems, values, and worldviews. This chapter contributes to the critical education needs of students. Critical thinking is integral to the everyday discourse of higher education. It is one of the important pillars on which the academy, especially higher education, prides itself and its process and encourages educators and learners to vigorously pursue. It is common to find the concept at least appearing once in a course outline or a syllabus used by most departments and faculties in the academy. The phrase is easily and commonly accentuated in many discourses and academic conversations. Teaching and learning will become incomplete if this phrase is not often evoked to remind students and teachers alike the essence of education. Critical thinking has thus become the buzzword in the academy, but questions still exist on what is meant when the phrase is used.

The essence of this chapter is to interrogate, navigate, and try to understand the idea of critical thinking by engaging Indigenous philosophies. Many scholars have given guidelines and processes for which students and the academy may consider or follow to exemplify their critical thinking abilities. To this effect, the primary aims of this chapter are to explore the act of critical thinking by asking fundamental questions that explore the extent to which the process and phenomenon of critical thinking continue to be influenced by the Eurocentric understanding of the world (Elder, 2007; Paul & Elder, 2008). Some of these questions include the following:

a. When and how do we identify a critical thinker or the process of thinking critically?
b. What role does spirituality have on conversations around engagement and social consciousness? Should all engagement be rationally based to become useful to the community? What about spirituality and intuition?
c. To what extent have notions around critical thinking ignored other forms of knowledges that may have a different ontological understanding of knowledge or that may be a counter-discourse to the understanding of knowledge and its production in the academy?
d. How do language and presentation feed into the discourse of critical thinking?

In asking these questions, we seek to discuss the process of validating and hierarchizing knowledge systems in the academy. In this respect, the chapter seeks to ask the extent to which Indigenous knowledge systems, especially proverbs and folk stories, provide an alternative discourse to the quest of ensuring knowledge production. Specifically, this chapter examines the structure, use, and purpose of African proverbs, riddles, music, games, and folk stories among the Akans of Ghana and their pedagogic, instructional, and communicative values for critical thinking education in postsecondary education and how their formulation and use represent a valid understanding of how to engage the mind and body to work toward societal challenges.

Indigenous Knowledge in Context

We are following on the definitional works of Agrawal (1995), Dei et al. (2000), Semali and Kincheloe (1999), Battiste and Henderson (2000), Smith (1999), and Castellano (2000) in conceptualizing Indigenous knowledge as a body of knowledge associated with the long-term occupancy of a certain place. It is the knowledge that informs, shapes, guides, organizes, and regulates how people come to know about themselves, their worlds, and their place within their world. Indigenous knowledge emerges from the collective voices, experiences, history, cultures, and worldview of local people over generations as a result of the sustained occupation of or attachments to a place. In conceptualizing "Indigenous knowledge," we must move the discourse away from an essentialized, narrow, circumscribed, and bounded definition of *Indigenous* to recognize difference and the multiple and diverse experiences of Indigenous peoples not only in the limited sense of Canada but also across the globe (Dei, 2010). Marie Battiste (2002), in her definition of Indigenous knowledge, places particular emphasis on orality and the importance of language. She sees Indigenous knowledges as comprising "the complex set of technologies sustained by Indigenous civilizations. Often oral and symbolic, it is transmitted through the structure of Indigenous languages and passed on to the next generation through modeling, practice, and animation, rather than through the written word" (Battiste, 2002, p. 2).

Such a body of knowledge exhibits a great degree of sophistication, complexity, and abstract conceptual thinking and knowing. Scholars such as Abdi (2008), Eze (1998), Gyekye (1995), Mudimbe (1998), Osei (1971) and Wiredu (1996) insist Indigenous knowledge is a form of philosophy because it elicits deep critical reflections about the world and humans' place in it. Indeed, Aboriginal scholars such as Raven Sinclair and Marie Battiste have uncovered the ability of Indigenous knowledge to help learners develop critical consciousness and moral values (Battiste, 2002; Sinclair, 2002, 2004). Johnson's works (1993, 2003) among the Ojibway people of Canada reveal how Indigenous mythologies contain rich, complex, and dense philosophical thinking. Similarly, Qwul'sih'yah'maht Robinna Anne Thomas (2005) speaks about the wisdom in Indigenous storytelling. As a child, she resisted any opportunity to listen to stories from her grandmother—what she saw as "idle chat" (Thomas, 2005, p. 237). Today, as an adult, she has come to appreciate the ingenuity and wisdom of Indigenous stories to carry coded messages of survival, resistance, a sense of purpose, pride, and guidance to the younger generations.

Similarly, in an African context, Chinua Achebe (1966), Ayi Kwei Armah (1969), and Ngugi wa Thiong'o (1965, 1986), through their literary works, have demonstrated the importance of Indigenous African philosophies to carry the wisdom, histories, values, and cultural knowledge of society. Bascom (1965) long ago argued that for Indigenous people, philosophical expressions such as proverbs afford them a means of psychological, cultural, and emotional release through "venting socially impermissible expressions that are permissible only through folkloric or proverbial cloak" (p. 279). In contemporary times, Dei et al. (2018), Adjei (2018), and Asimeng-Boahene and Baffoe (2018) have shown how Indigenous proverbs, symbols, music, poetry, rituals, legends, and mythologies are critical literary expressions that carry the values, cultural generalizations, and philosophical precepts of traditional Africans. In effect, this body of knowledge constitutes collective traditional philosophies that cannot be conveniently dismissed.

Drawing on such bodies of knowledge can enhance critical thinking education in postsecondary education in Canada. We employ *critical thinking* in line with the earlier definition of Kurfiss (1989) as

> the process of figuring out what to believe or not about a situation, phenomenon, problem or controversy for which no single definitive answer or solution exists. The term implies a diligent, open-minded search for understanding, rather than for discovery of a necessary conclusion. (p. 42)

The purpose of accentuating critical thinking in postsecondary education is to influence and encourage a way of knowing that provides complex readings of societal problems (Freire, 2007; Gibbons & Gray, 2004). Such an understanding of critical thinking lies well with Indigenous philosophies. This chapter examines the structure, use, and purpose of Indigenous philosophies, in particular how their formulations and uses offer a valid understanding of how one can engage the mind and the body in complex and nuanced ways.

There is a saying among the Akan people of Ghana that "when one hangs at a cliff, any step backward is progress." The Akan people understand this proverb to mean that sometimes the most effective way to look for answers in the seemingly "unsolvable" situation is to pause, step back, and critically reflect on one's actions as well as one's thinking. The politics of indigenizing postsecondary education may require that critical educators pause, step backward, and rethink new and varied ways of creating spaces that allow for multiple knowledge systems, in particular those emerging from non-Western epistemologies. The inclusion of Indigenous knowledges in the academy reinforces the epistemic saliency of Indigenous peoples whose epistemologies and voices are often devalued or negated in postsecondary education. This chapter provides important decolonized lessons on how postsecondary educators can draw on Indigenous knowledge as a useful communicative tool to impart critical invaluable lessons about the world as seen through the eyes of Indigenous peoples. It provides rich data that can guide even non-Indigenous educators to teach Indigenous knowledge in postsecondary schools.

Toward Anticolonial Theorization of Indigeneity

Dei and Asgharzadeh (2001) remind us that any exercise to decolonize the academy must start from the knowledge that the academy accedes a false status by granting power, privilege, and discursive authority to the European system of thought while devaluing, delegitimizing, and misrepresenting Indigenous knowledge as something not worthy of intellectual engagement. The Native American scholar Vine Deloria (1997) calls it the "White lies" rooted in European colonization and racist cultural supremacy. What then are the consequences for Indigenous voices when the politics of identification, representation, and knowledge legitimation work to dissipate the collective histories, values, knowledge, and worldviews within academic spaces? Dei (2010) speaks of a wounded existence for Indigenous learners as they are being forced to seclude their cultural knowledge, values, and worldviews from the open arena of intellectual and public discourses. This has resulted in sometimes disturbing "imitative agenda" through which some Indigenous learners attempt to mimic and uncritically accept dominant paradigms to gain legitimacy from dominant scholars on Indigenous matters of which Indigenous learners are "unquestionably the best authority" (Yankah, 2004, p. 12). The approach is to adopt an anticolonial theoretical framework to challenge this epistemic violence in the academy and to reassert Indigenous knowledge, culture, values, and worldviews as legitimate forms of knowing (see Dei & Kempf, 2006; Grosfoguel, 2007; Kuokkanen, 2008).

Elsewhere in Dei (2002), he argues that the anticolonial theory is an epistemology of the colonized, anchored in the Indigenous sense of collective and common colonial consciousness. It, therefore, allows for the celebration of indigeneity that opposes the dominant knowledge system, hence the use of Indigenous philosophies for critical thinking pedagogy is a way of re-centering local voices in the academy. As a critical framework, anticolonial theory challenges Western paradigms that guide today's education systems and social diversity by agitating for knowledge, values, and worldviews that are more inclusive in the process of knowledge production, validation, and dissemination. Anticolonial theory allows critical educators to understand how these colonial remnants are being challenged, reproduced, or transformed in educational systems in contemporary times (Dei, 2010; Dei & Asgharzadeh, 2001). In a way, when Prah (1997) said local people feel insulted when others suggest they know and understand their problems better than they (local people) know themselves, he was alluding to the colonial tendencies to assign authorial control and discursive integrity to Western knowledge system over that of local knowledge.

Anticolonial theory acknowledges the importance of using voices emanating from local people in creating an understanding of social issues. The framework equally recognizes the importance of locally produced knowledge emanating from cultural history and daily human experiences and social interactions of local people. It accepts and legitimates the oral, visual, textual, political, and material resistances of colonized groups, which is a shift away from the sole preoccupation with victimization. It offers critiques of the wholesale degradation, and disparagement and discards of "tradition" and culture in the interest of "modernity" and the "global space" (Dei, 2002, 2010; Dei & Asgharzadeh, 2001). We align ourselves with Dei's (2002) thinking that only when Indigenous people are accorded discursive integrity to their accounts of histories, cultures, and worldviews that colonial imperialist projects can be destabilized and actual decolonization attained. By providing important lessons on how postsecondary educators can draw on Indigenous knowledge as a useful communicative tool to impart critical invaluable lessons about the world as seen through the eyes of Indigenous peoples, we are creating a multicentric educational environment where Indigenous knowledges, values, and worldviews are privileged and honored in the academy.

Identity and Critical Thinking

Interest in identity has taken center stage in most discussions in the social sciences and humanities. As a concept, identity has underpinned and informed several studies involving human subjects that seek to understand the relationship between people within a particular context. Thus, identity as a concept has been identified in several subject areas such as cultural studies, political science, social studies, history, education, language studies, psychology, sociology, and several others. As the role of the individual continues to grow in modern societies, identity becomes an important factor in determining interaction as the historical and cultural identities of people determine to a large extent how they relate to society and how to navigate the complexities within society (Fearon, 1999).

The enigma associated with "identity" can be succinctly expressed in the Akan proverb *Kokromoti a yensani ne ho mbo po*, literally translated to mean the thumb cannot be avoided if one wants to tie a knot. *Identity* is a powerful word and used often in daily discourse, but many do not understand the various intersections that make an identity. Even though the meaning of the term has undergone a drastic change since its initial use in the early 1950s by the famous psychologist Erik Erikson, it has come to represent one of the most complicated and vague concepts that nonetheless plays a significant role in social science studies. In earlier studies in the 1920s, Erikson had discussed the psychosocial development of humans and had noted the significant role of childhood experiences in personality development, as well the crisis in the socialization process that must be carefully resolved to produce a better person for the society. He argued on the paramountcy of culture and later life experiences in shaping personality during the socialization process. Furthermore, as mentioned by Fearon (1999),

> identity refers to either (a) a social category, defined by membership rules and (alleged) characteristic attributes or expected behaviors, or (b) socially distinguishing features that a person takes a special pride in our views as unchangeable but socially consequential (or (a) and (b) at once). (p. ii)

This definition establishes a relation among identity, the individual, and the society. At the same time, it refers to the social categories and is the source of an individual's self-respect or dignity. This means that one's culture or one's total understanding of the world to a large extent determines their ability to think through solutions, thus bringing up questions such as, How does an individual's identity, experience, and knowledge affect how critical thinking is engaged? To what extent do past and present experiences affect how individuals engage words and actions? Does thinking critical have a limitation on the thinking process of the individual? Can someone think critically outside their experience, knowledge, and self-embodiments? Is critical thinking a natural process of human thinking, or it is a special type of thinking devoid of the individual experiences or engaging in the act? How should critical thinking be accessed and evaluated? Are all the agents and agencies involved in critical thinking the same or similar irrespective of one's experiences and culture? Is the idea of critically thinking connected to the self-worth and values placed on an individual's perspectives? What role has colonization played in creating the elitist assumption that critical thinking is the preserve of the few educated? And how can we decolonize the idea of critical thinking and recognize the value of Indigenous philosophical knowledge in aspiring critical thinking?

In the remaining section, we share some of the processes, forms, ways, and methods Indigenous African philosophical knowledge can serve as critical thinking pedagogical tools for postsecondary education. The idea is to establish the significant value inherent in these outlooks and how they can encourage acceptance and knowledge pluralism.

African Proverbs, Storytelling, and Riddles

Proverbs

Proverbs are not limited to the African or Indigenous communities around the world. Historically, all civilizations at a point in the cycle used one form or the other to communicate information to the community. While some proverbs are regionally specific and may require some form of background information to appreciate their value, the power of proverbs to carry wisdom and philosophical thinking irrespective of geographical locations is very telling. In short, proverbs are wise sayings engaged in articulating direct or indirect messages in conversations. Proverbs are usually developed through life experiences, histories, values, and worldviews, and they are used to impart knowledge, wisdom, moral values, and teachings to younger generations. They are communally owned knowledge and serve both the orator and the listener as they force a process of engaging wisdom, knowledge and experience, and responsibilities.

Historically, proverbs have been an integral part of traditional education or socialization among many African and Indigenous communities. Proverbs have served as critical thinking tools as both the means and the end in itself. By engaging proverbs, we are interested in the implications they have on education and cognitive development as well as their implications for metacognitive knowledge development. How do proverbs promote self-assessment, peer assessment, and community assessment? How do students come to own their knowledge by using proverbs? How do proverbs encourage students to validate the knowledges they own? How does the use of proverbs improve self-image and self-awareness among students, especially of African or Indigenous backgrounds? By engaging the following proverbs, we hope to show that the knowledge they produce can validly provide a ground for engaging society's problems in equal ways as any other knowledge system.

Proverb 1: Nyansa tese baobab dua; nipa biako nsa ntumi twa ho nhyia

Literal translation: Knowledge is like a baobab tree; no one can encompass it with their hands. As a society, we are stronger and can solve any challenges if we bring our minds, strengths, and skills together. In unity, we are better at solving society's problems. Once we work together and use each other's wisdom, we can solve all problems.

Proverb 2: Woforo dua pa a na yepia wo

Literal translation: You only get a push when you are climbing a good tree. This proverb relates an interesting rule in many communities. Community members only support those efforts that are productive and seek the well-being of all community members. A selfish agenda will not be supported by the community, especially the elders. If an individual wants the support of the community, then their actions and what is engaged must be good and profitable to the whole community.

Proverb 3: Yɛsoma oba nyansafo, ɛnyɛ anamɔntenten

Literal translation: We send a wise person, not one with long legs. This proverb echoes the importance of sending the person who has the ability to communicate properly and the strengths to match the needs of the community. As much as a person with long legs may reach a destination faster, that individual may not be in a position to relay information appropriately.

Storytelling

In her book *The Circle Works: Transforming Eurocentric Consciousness,* Fyre Jean Graveline (1998) recounts how storytelling forms an important teaching practice for Aboriginal people of Canada: "Until recently, every Athapaskan learned from either direct experience or verbal description or instruction" (p. 64). For Graveline, storytelling is central to Aboriginal intellectual traditions and provides the core values for Indigenous education. According to Cruikshank (1992), "an ultimate value of oral tradition was to recreate a situation for someone who had not lived through it so that the listener could benefit directly from the narrator's experience" (p. 339). In the opinion of Allen Gunn (1986), storytelling constitutes one of the major and important ways of maintaining Aboriginal identity:

> Since the coming of the Anglo-Europeans beginning in the fifteenth century, the fragile web of identity that long-held tribal people secure has gradually been weakened and torn. But oral tradition has prevented the destruction of the web, the ultimate disruption of tribal ways. Oral tradition is vital; it heals itself and the tribal web by adapting to the flow of the present while never relinquishing

> its connection to the past. Its adaptability has always been required, as many generations have experienced. (p. 45)

Like Indigenous people of Canada, among Indigenous Africans, storytelling is one of the means of passing traditions, codes of behavior, values, worldviews, and beliefs from one generation to the other. For instance, the Indigenous Akans of Ghana use storytelling as a core traditional method in educating the younger generations.

The Akans of Ghana regard storytelling as *Anansesem* (spider tales). Ananse (Spider), in most stories, is depicted as a cunning individual who almost always plans and orchestrates evil things in the community. Thus, Ananse is always vilified in every spider tale and is shown as an example of a character that one ought to shun in any law-abiding society. Ananse, in the Akan story, has a wife named Okonore Yaa, an elder son called Ntikuma (Small Head), and two other children known as Naakonwhia (Lean Legs) and Afodohwedohwe (Big Stomach). We are yet to come across any oral or written literature that explains why Ananse's children were given names after these human body parts. However, given that it may only be a malnourished child that is likely to have a small head, big stomach, and lean legs, Akan storytellers might have adopted these body parts and described them this way to further depict Ananse as a greedy father who does not take care of his children. The greediness of Ananse knows no bound. This is depicted in several Ananse stories in which Ananse is always willing to sacrifice the welfare of his family for his greed.

Spider tales may well describe a potential or an actual happening but not necessarily a true story. Although there is no documented account or oral tradition that explains the origin of Anansesem (spider tales), we are, however, inclined to argue that, probably, storytelling was named Anansesem to acknowledge and celebrate the creative ways in which the spider weaves its web. Thus, if storytelling requires creative imagination and ingenuity, then it is only a person as blessed as the spider who can perform such exceptional arts.

According to Okrah (2003), in the realm of the Akans' oral literature, storytelling stands paramount as performing a direct pedagogical function in socializing young ones into society. In his essay "African Oral Artistry and the New Social Order," Boadu (1985) argues that the art of storytelling is a form of pedagogic role performed in traditional African society. An elderly person tells stories to young ones around the courtyard in the moonlight. The storyteller does not perform this act because there is a financial or material reward but, rather, sees it as a communal responsibility in ensuring that children are taught the moral values and sociocultural background of their society (see Boadu, 1985). The spider tale offers a relevant lesson for any discussion in how the Akans of Ghana approach knowledge production. The Akans understand that the source of knowledge is very large, that no one can claim to know everything. According to Dzobo (1992), the Akan approach knowledge production with the understanding that there is a limit to what any individual can know; hence, any individuals who boast of knowing everything are often viewed as knowing nothing. The following are examples of Indigenous African folklores and their pedagogic relevance for schooling and education:

Exploring Storytelling: Story 1—Community and Responsibility

> Once upon a time, three friends— a tortoise, a bird, and a twig—were living together in a forest near Life-is-hard village. The bird is notorious for singing at the slightest opportunity. On many occasions, the tortoise has asked the twig to advise the bird against singing at all times, warning that such behavior has the danger of bringing attention to the group. In each case, the twig responded that what the bird does should be of no concern to anyone. One afternoon, a hunter returning from hunting without a game heard the birds singing. The hunter took his gun and shot the bird. The bird fell exactly where the tortoise was sleeping. Satisfied that he, at least, has something to show his family, the hunter gladly took the tortoise alongside the bird. To make things easier for him to carry, the hunter cut the twig to tie both the bird and the tortoise. The action of the bird caused the life of the tortoise and the twig.

Meaning and Pedagogical Implications

This story speaks to how humans are connected. Whatever one does or fails to do may have direct implications on others. The story shows the need for an individual to strive for the collective good of society rather than the individual, selfish ambitions that have become prevalent in contemporary social relations. The story reminds us that when we act without thinking of the interest of others, we endanger the existence of the whole community. The bird acted in selfishness and, in the process, placed the twig and the tortoise at risk. The moral lesson from this story is that we all need to be considerate and mindful of the presence and interest of others. Within the African concept of *Ubuntu,* I am because we are, the "I" is intertwined with the "we." They are both inseparable and are connected in many ways. If we are connected, then each action has consequences for all. The tortoise was wise to have warned the twig.

This story also reminds us of our responsibilities as members that share the earth with other beings. To what extent do we act responsibly to protect others and ourselves? Our actions and inactions have direct implications on what happens to nature and the community as a whole. We share the earth with the living, the dead, and even the unborn. Our very survival as people is dependent on how we act in the collective interest of the community, and this is the lesson from this story.

Exploring Storytelling: Story 2—Power, Location, Subjectivity, and Voice

> Democracy used to be cherished and respected in the animal kingdom. In those days, all animals had the same rights to exercise free speech in every public gathering. In one such meeting, the antelope was seated beside the lion. Any time the antelope raised its hands to speak to any issue at the meeting, the lion stared angrily at it. Knowing the lion and the danger it presents to any animal that crosses its path, the antelope had to place its hand down. After several efforts to speak, albeit, the same reaction from the lion, the antelope realized that unless something is done about the current seating arrangement, it will leave the meeting without sharing its opinion. Thus, an important issue on the agenda was tabled for discussion; the antelope stood up and moved a motion to end the meeting on the ground that the sitting arrangement does not favour some of the animals. Since all the animals saw what was going on between the lion and the antelope, they seconded the motion and voted for the meeting to adjourn.

The Meaning and Pedagogical Implications

This story is about power and voice. It is important to know in any democratic setting who has the power to speak and also the power to refuse to listen to others. For the antelope, there was no place for it to speak—it was rendered voiceless because of where it was seated in the meeting and the body it occupied within the space. Within the education system, similar processes of silencing voices occur with curricular programming and the pedagogical practices used within classrooms. Dei et al. (1997, 2000) talk about disengaged and disenfranchised learners in the education system in Canada. These are learners who feel the education curricula do not speak to their history, culture, experience, and identity. Like the antelope, these learners feel voiceless in a democratic space where everybody is expected to speak freely. Yet, what has not become apparent is the passion of the lion to silence the antelope at all costs. We argue that perhaps it is not so much of an existing history but so much about sheer abuse of power by the lion to prevent the antelope from contributing to the discussions at the meeting. In our democratic environment, our focus should not only be about those who have been denied a voice to speak but also about those who have used their power to silence others from speaking. Our task, as critical educators, is to help the rest of the world hear the silenced and discriminated voices. Although what others have to say may sometimes feel discomforting and irritating, part of the democratic process is to leave room for even the "ugly noises."

We also noticed that even at the threat at his very existence, the antelope managed to express his voice of displeasure. Although recognizing the risk, the antelope still spoke knowing that its very survival and freedom depended on it. The ultimate lesson here is that although challenging dominant voices poses its own risks, there is greater danger when silence is chosen. Marginalized bodies cannot afford to play victims in the face of a threat to their existence.

Exploring Storytelling: Story 3—Identity and the Politics of Identity

> The bat was once considered a cunning species because of its ability to make convincing arguments over any issue. In those days, the birds' and the mammals' kingdom had different planting and harvesting seasons. Usually, the mammals harvest their crops at the time the birds are planting. Similarly, the birds have their harvesting at the same time the mammals are planting. The bat, realizing the two different seasons that existed between these two kingdoms, decided to explore the situation to its advantage.
>
> During the harvest season of the mammals, the bat convinced them that it cannot be a bird because it is warm-blooded and gives birth to young ones that are not hatched from eggs. It also has teeth; something that is not known with the members of birds' kingdom. Although it acknowledged that it has wings, it doesn't have feathers and therefore they cannot be used to disqualify it from becoming part of the mammals' kingdom. The bat was gladly accepted into the mammals' family and spent the whole harvesting season with them. Immediately, the harvest season ended with the planting season about to begin, so the bat left the mammals' kingdom to the birds' kingdom. Over there, the bat insisted that its fellowship with the mammals was a regrettable mistake since it is so different from mammals. The bat insisted that it has wings, and unlike, the "flying squirrel" and gliding possum—mammals that glide for short distances but cannot flap their wings—it can flap and fly for long distances. Therefore, this distinct characteristic makes it more of a bird than a mammal. The birds accepted the bat as one of them and shared their whole harvest with it.
>
> Once the harvesting ended for the birds, the bat went to the mammals again with the old argument. Unfortunately, luck had run out for the bat since its game was now known to the mammals. The mammals drove the bat way and warned it never to show its face in the mammals' kingdom again. After its rejection at the mammals' kingdom, the bat went to the birds' kingdom. At that time, the birds, who also heard of the bat's conniving ways, also rejected the bat. Having been rejected by the mammals and the birds, the bat was left hanging between the sky and the earth with no place to claim as its own. This explains why the bat is always seen hanging on trees.

Meaning and Pedagogical Implications

This story speaks to the complexity and fluidity of identity. No one is *one* thing. Thus, one cannot be tagged with only one form of identity. In the case of the bat, it possesses elements that can qualify it as both a mammal and a bird. Thus, the issue here is not about the rights of the bat to choose to be a mammal or a bird but its unwillingness to account for its identity. In the postmodernist era of so much claim of fluidity and multiplicity of identity, perhaps, the argument about identity should not be so much about "who we claim to be," but it should be "what it means to claim any particular identity." Addressing this issue is quite important because to claim a particular identity is also to be willing to embrace that the accountability and responsibility that comes with claiming a particular identity. In the story, it became obvious that the bat chose to be a mammal and then a bird to access certain privileges yet denied both identities when it was time to account for them.

The bat's story reminds us that we cannot claim the privileges and benefits that come with a particular identity and refuse to participate in the struggles that come with embodying that identity. In our educational experiences, we have encountered bodies that claim certain identities because of the material and cultural benefits that come with those identities, yet those same people are never seen when the struggles of their "communities" are tabled for discussions. The bat's story reminds us of a conversation that happened between one of the authors of this chapter and a colleague at the University of Toronto. A colleague, a Black female, was trying to justify why she does not "do race" in her scholarship. The colleague's argument was that race, racism, and Whiteness scholarship are controversial enough that those who do such works are often the target of institutional sanctions and discrimination. To avoid getting herself involved in such "a messy politics," she chooses not to engage in the scholarship of race, racism, and Whiteness. What is instructive and quite intriguing in the case of this colleague was her willingness to use her Black identity to seek equitable treatment in jobs targeting racialized people.

Elsewhere in Adjei and Gill (2013), they argued that speaking about race, racism, and Whiteness brings so much tension, anxiety, and anger that people often avoid them when even legitimate issues are tabled for discussion. Yet Dei et al. (2004) remind us that the discomfort of speaking about race should not inspire anybody to avoid race in any conversation. For authors of this present chapter, we ask, Is there redemption for racialized souls who refuse to talk about race, racism, and Whiteness yet use their racialized identity to seek opportunities reserved for racialized people? We cannot enjoy our privileges and deny responsibilities that come with them. Similarly, dominant bodies cannot maintain their privileges while claiming innocence. Fellows and Razack (1998) noted that when confronted with White racial superiority, many White women deny their dominance by retreating to a position of subordination with an argument that "since we are oppressed as women, we cannot be oppressors of women of colour" (p. 14).

The discourse of White victimhood not only acts to obscure the experiences of racialized bodies but also further reinforces barriers to dominant bodies' inability to acknowledge their own racial identity as members of the dominant or privileged group (Chesler et al., 2003, p. 226). Ultimately, what the story of the bat shows us is that privileges cannot be openly claimed while denying accountability.

Exploring Games and Songs

Traditional Game-Songs: The Hawk and the Hen

Traditional game-songs are used to encourage and develop active listening and multitasking in Indigenous education. They are intended to entertain, teach, educate, and impart virtues and moral lessons. One such song was composed of a friendship between the hawk and the hen that turned sour. According to legends, the hawk and the hen were good friends. A misunderstanding ensued between them because the hen was seen as greedy and lazy and was always trying to abuse its friendship with the hawk. This abuse of friendship reached such a disturbing point that it destroyed the great relationship between the hawk and the hen. The legend continues that the chief in the village intervened in the situation and resolved the problem. Things were improved, and the hen and the hawk became good friends again. However, after the death of both the hen and the hawk, the only child of the hawk decided to rekindle the conflict. This time, it decided to hunt and prey on chickens as retaliation for what the hen did to its mother (the hawk). This continued until one day, the hawk hunted three chickens belonging to the village hunter. The hunter, enraged by the behavior of the hawk, shot and killed it. In the song, the hawk is accused of being lazy and being a bully. Instead of working, it had been preying on chickens. The song goes like this:

Sansa Kroma	(roaming hawk)
Ne na wuo	(its mother is dead)
ɔkye kye nkokɔmba	(it snatches/preys on chicks)
ɔse ɔnnkɔ ye edwuma	(it says he won't find a real job)
Ne na wuo	(its mother is dead)
ɔkye kye nkokɔmba	(it snatches/preys on chicks)
ɔe kyin kyin, e kyin kyin, e kyin kyin	(it roams, and roams, and roams)
ɔse ɔnnkɔ ye edwuma	(it says he won't find a real job)
Ne na wuo ooo	(its mother is dead)
Ne gya wuo ooo	(its father is dead)
Sansa Kroma	(roaming hawk)
Ne na wuo	(its mother is dead)
ɔkye kye nkokɔmba	(it snatches/preys on chicks)

The song is sung during a game of passing objects from one person to the next in a circle—like the game musical chairs in North America. Any player that misses the rhythm of passing the object and misses its turn is eliminated from the game. The song and the game are done for not only moral education and virtue of hardworking but also for improving children's ability to focus and concentrate on multiple tasks.

Riddles and Their Meaning

Riddles among Indigenous people also provide a critical environment for learners and educators to have meaningful engagement. Like proverbs, riddles are used to address specific issues and concerns but with the ultimate goal of helping listeners to use their inherent abilities to solve or think through situations. It is a way of introducing learners to intellectual discourse in a relaxing and mostly humorous way. Riddles encourage participants to work their brains and provide critical insights into a conversation. In most communities, learners are given a riddle to think about overnight and bring their answers to the next gathering. Riddles usually begin with a phrasing about a mystery gift left by one's parents—"Agya rekɔ, ogyaw me ade bi" (My father left me a gift when leaving the house). The listeners then respond, "Ogyae wo dien?" (What did he leave you?). The conveyer of the riddle will then state the riddle. The goal of these openings is to draw listeners' attention as well as awakening their curiosity about what they are about to hear. The following are examples of some popular riddles that educators may use to encourage critical thinking in the classroom.

> *Proverb 1: Agya rekɔ, ogyaw me ade bi wo fie. Menne dan mu, na, menne abonten nnso mewo fie bia mu. Me ne hena?*
> Translation: As my parents were traveling, they left me with something, "I am neither inside nor outside, but I am in every house. Who am I?" The answer to this riddle is the door. The door is found in every home, but it is neither inside nor outside.
>
> *Proverb 2: Agya rekɔ, ogyaw me ade bi. Wɔwo me tenten nanso bre a mewu no na maye tiatia. Mene hena?*
> Translation: As my parents were leaving, they left me with an object. "I am born tall, but I die very short. I am useful inside the house. Who am I?" The answer to this riddle is the candle. The length of a candle always reduces as heat melts down the wax.
>
> *Proverb 3: Agya rekɔ no ogyaw me apono abien a debiara wo bue na wɔ tomu. Enye apon a ewɔ fie mu. Me ne hena?*
> Translation: As father/mother was leaving, they left me with two doors opening and closing at the same time. However, they are not the doors of my house. What are they? The doors are our eye.

Not only are riddles used to motivate listeners to think and rethink but are also used together with proverbs and folk stories to reiterate important lessons. Teachers can use riddles to teach parts of the human body and a lesson on virtues and responsibility, as well as creating a sense of community.

Conclusion

Within the Indigenous African context, traditional education instills values and virtues in youth to ensure discipline, respect of self, peers, and authority, responsibility, honesty, and critical engagement. Sadly, the pedagogic, instructional, and communicative significance of Indigenous African education and its ability to enhance learning outcomes for learners has received little critical exploration within the schooling and education system. However, as we have shown through several proverbs and stories we have told in this chapter, wisdom and knowledge can be acquired if they are searched from multiple centers. However, in thinking about ways to use Indigenous philosophies to teach critical thinking, the question of how best to convey spoken words as narrated in stories, fables, myths, and oral accounts of life histories requires deep analysis. There are those who argue that Indigenous oral forms capture a broader meaning in terms of their impact on the listener. For instance, to make storytelling complete and capture the attention of listeners, it has to include singing and dancing. This implies, unlike written text, where the individual reader makes mental performance without an audience, that storytelling requires whole-group participation. Such activity poses a challenge to the conventional classroom to create this needed setting for storytelling.

Again, the question of how to keep oral forms of knowledge as a pedagogical tool in the formal classroom without archiving them remains a challenging issue to educators. Even if Indigenous philosophies could be archived, how could it be done without losing its original meaning? Cruickshank (1992) argues that spoken words such as stories, fables proverbs, myths, folklore, and folk songs have long been treated as "objects" to be collected, coded, stored, and disseminated. However, it remains a challenge in how this cultural knowledge considered linguistic expression and material manifestation of ideas could be collected, represented, and stored without losing its meaning. Dei (2002), citing the works of Cruikshank (1992) and Trigger (1988), raised salient questions on how to handle oral traditions:

> What happens to the spoken words when they appear on paper or are recorded in magnetic or digital codes on tapes, disks or in film or videotape. What are the uses of material artifacts and exhibitions, stories and oral accounts as written texts in Western[-influenced] academies? Oral traditions, stories, fables, and proverbs collected from indigenous communities and written as texts in

> Western academies can become a material manifestation of the colonial encounter. (p. 15)

Dei contends further that orality raises debates about cultural/intellectual property rights and representations of culture. Within the context, oral traditions should be seen as texts to be heard but not as documents to be stored. Therefore, in reviewing the educational curriculum to make room for Indigenous philosophies, the emphasis should not be on only the written text but also on oral forms.

Again, there is also a legitimate concern about how the issue of appropriation could be addressed as one rethinks Indigenous philosophies in the academy. Indigenous knowledges belong to the community and therefore cannot be owned by individuals. Unfortunately, conventional approaches to knowledge production, validation, and dissemination demand that sources of information be cited. Similarly, the commodification and patent of knowledges as noted in Western traditions raises concerns about the inclusion of Indigenous philosophies in formal schooling. When we look at the field of medicine and how Indigenous healing practices have been corporatized and patented, this question cannot be ignored. These concerns raised should not be the basis of abandoning the whole exercise of including Indigenous philosophies in contemporary schooling but rather to search for viable ways this body of knowledge has been used in the classroom while Indigenous people's concerns are addressed.

References

Abdi, A. A. (2008). Europe and African thought systems and philosophies of education: 'Reculturing' the trans-temporal discourses. *Cultural Studies, 22*(2), 309–327.

Achebe, C. (1966). The black writer's burden. *Présence Africaine, 31*(50), 135–140.

Adjei, P. B. (2018). Adinkra symbolism of Ghana: Pedagogical implications for schooling and education. In L. Asimeng-Boahene & M. Baffoe (Eds.), *African traditional oral literature and visual cultures as pedagogical tools in diverse classroom contexts* (pp. 151–172). Information Age Publishing.

Adjei, P. B., & Gill, J. K. (2013). What has Barack Obama's election victory got to do with race? A closer look at post-racial rhetoric and its implication for antiracism education. *Race Ethnicity and Education, 16*(1), 134–153.

Agrawal, A. (1995). Dismantling the divide between indigenous and scientific knowledge. *Development and Change, 26*(3), 413–439.

Armah, A. K. (1969). *The beautiful ones are not yet born.* Collier Books.

Asimeng-Boahene, L., & Baffoe, M. (Eds.). (2018). *African traditional oral literature and visual cultures as pedagogical tools in diverse classroom contexts.* Information Age Publishing.

Bascom, W. (1965). The forms of folklore: Prose narratives. *The Journal of American Folklore, 78*(307), 3–20.

Battiste, M. (2002). *Indigenous knowledge and pedagogy in First Nations education: A literature review with recommendations.* National Working Group on Education Ottawa.

Battiste M., & Henderson, J. (2000). *Protecting Indigenous knowledge and heritage: A global challenge*. Purich Publishing.

Boadu, O. S. (1985). African oral artistry and the new social order. In M. K. Asante & K. W. Asante (Eds.), *African culture* (pp. xx). Greenwood Press.

Castellano, M. B. (2000). Updating Aboriginal traditions of knowledge. In G. Dei, B. L. Hall, & D. G. Rosenberg (Eds.), *Indigenous knowledges in global contexts: Multiple readings of our world* (pp. 21–36). University of Toronto Press.

Chance, P. (1986). *Thinking in the classroom: A survey of programs*. Teachers College Press.

Chesler, M. A., Peet, M., & Sevig, T. (2003). Blinded by Whiteness: The development of White college students' racial awareness. In A. Doane & E. Bonilla-Silva (Eds.), *White out: The continuing significance of racism* (pp. 215–230). Routledge.

Cruikshank, J. (1992). *Life lived like a story*. UBC Press.

Dei, G. J. S. (2002). Spirituality in African education: Issues, contentions, and contestations from a Ghanaian case study. *International Journal of Children Spirituality, 7*(1), 37–56.

Dei, G. J. S. (2010). *Indigenous philosophies and critical education: A reader*. Peter Lang.

Dei, G. J. S. & Asgharzadeh, A. (2001). The power of social theory: The anti-colonial discursive framework. *Journal of Educational Thought, 35*(3), 297–323.

Dei, G. J. S., Darko, I. N., McDonnell, J., Demi, S. M., & Akanmori, H. (2018). *African proverbs as epistemologies of decolonization*. Peter Lang International Academic Publishers.

Dei, G. J. S., James, I. M., Karumanchery L., James-Wilson S., & Zine, J. (2000). *Removing the margins: The challenges and possibilities of inclusive schooling*. Canadian Scholars Press.

Dei, G. J. S., Karumanchery, L., & Karumanchery-Luke, N. (2004). *Playing the race card: Exposing White power and privilege*. Peter Lang.

Dei, G. J. S., & Kempf, A. (2006). *Anti-colonialism and education: The politics of resistance*. Sense Publishers.

Dei, G. J. S., Mazzuca, J., McIsaac, E., & Zine, J. (1997). *Reconstructing 'drop-out': A critical ethnography of the dynamics of Black students' disengagement from schools*. University of Toronto Press.

Deloria, V. (1997). *Red earth, White lies: Native Americans and the myth of scientific fact*. Fulcrum Publishing.

Dzobo, N. K. (1992). African symbols and proverbs as source of knowledge and truth. In K. Wiredu & K. Gyekye (Eds.), *Person and community: Ghanaian philosophy studies* (pp. 1–16). Council for Research in Values and Philosophy.

Elder, L. (2007). *Our concept of critical thinking* [Side bar]. Foundation for Critical Thinking. http://www.criticalthinking.org/aboutCT/ourConceptCT.cfm

Eze, E. (Ed.). (1998). *African philosophy: An anthology*. Blackwell Publishers.

Fearon, J. D. (1999). *What is the identity (as we now use the word)?* [Unpublished manuscript]. Stanford University.

Fellows, M. L., & Razack, S. (1998). The race to innocence: Confronting hierarchical relations among women. *The Journal of Gender, Race & Justice, 1*(2), 335–352.

Freire, P. (2007). *Pedagogy of the oppressed*. Continuum.

Gibbons, J., & Gray, M. (2004). Critical thinking as integral to social work practice. *Journal of Teaching in Social Work, 24*(1–2), 19–38.

Graveline, F. J. (1998). *Circle works: Transforming Eurocentric consciousness*. Fernwood Publishing.

Grosfoguel, R. (2007). The epistemic decolonial turn: Beyond political-economy paradigms. *Cultural Studies, 21*(2–3), 211–223.

Gyekye, K. (1995). *An essay on African philosophical thought: The Akan conceptual scheme*. Temple University Press.

Gunn, A. P. (1986). *The sacred hoop: Recovering the feminine in American Indian traditions*. Beacon.

Huitt, W. (1998). Critical thinking: An overview. *Educational Psychology Interactive, 3*(6), 24–50.

Kuokkanen, R. (2008). What is hospitality in the academy? Epistemic ignorance and the (im) possible gift. *The Review of Education, Pedagogy, and Cultural Studies, 30*(1), 60–82.

Kurfiss, J. G. (1989). Helping faculty foster students' critical thinking in the disciplines. In A. F. Lucas (Ed.), *New directions for teaching and learning* (pp. 41–50). Jossey-Bass.

Johnson, B. (1993). *Ojibway tales*. University of Nebraska Press.

Johnson, B. (2003). *Ojibway heritage*. McClelland and Stewart.

Mayer, R., & Goodchild, F. (1990). *The critical thinker*. Wm. C. Brown.

Mulnix, J. W. (2012). Thinking critically about critical thinking. *Educational Philosophy and Theory, 44*(5), 464–479.

Mudimbe, V. Y. (1998). *The invention of Africa: Gnosis, philosophy and the order of knowledge*. Indiana University Press.

Okrah, K. A. (2003). *Nyansapo (the wisdom knot): Towards an African philosophy of education*. Routledge.

Osei, G. (1971). *The African philosophy of life*. The African Publication Society.

Paul, R., & Elder, L. (2008). *The miniature guide to critical thinking* (5th ed.). Foundation for Critical Thinking Press.

Prah, K. (1997). Accusing the victims - Review of *In My Father's House* by Kwame Anthony Appiah. *Codesria Bulletin, 1*, 14–22.

Semali, L., & Kincheloe, J. L. (1999). *What is Indigenous knowledge? Voices from the academy*. Falmer Press.

Sinclair, R. (2002). Aboriginal social work education in Canada: Decolonizing pedagogy for the seventh generation. *First People Child & Family Review, 1*(1), 49–61.

Sinclair, R. (2004). Aboriginal social work education in Canada: Decolonizing pedagogy for the seventh generation. *First Peoples Child & Family Review, 14*(1), 9–21.

Smith, L. T. (1999). *Decolonizing methodologies: Research and Indigenous peoples*. Zed Books.

Thomas, Q. R. A. (2005). Honouring the oral traditions of my ancestors through storytelling. In L. Brown & S. Strega (Eds.), *Research as resistance: Critical, Indigenous and anti-oppressive approaches* (pp. 237–254). Canadian Scholars' Press.

Trigger, B. G. (1988). *Children of Aataentsic: A history of the Huron people to 1660* (Vol. 195). McGill-Queen's Press.

wa Thiong'o, N. (1965). *The river between*. Heinemann.

wa Thiong'o, N. (1986). *Decolonising the mind: The politics of language in African literature*. East African Educational Publishers.

Wiredu, K. (1996). *Cultural universals and particulars: An African perspective*. Indiana University Press.

Yankah, K (2004). Language, the mass media and democracy in Ghana. *Annual lecture in the Humanities*. Ghana Academy of Arts and Sciences, Accra.

CHAPTER 6

Spirituality and Self-Care Among Ghanaian Social Workers: Lessons for Africanizing Social Work Education

Paul Banahene Adjei, Isaac Nortey Darko, Sulemana Fuseini, and Abigail Adubea Mills

IN THIS CHAPTER, we examine ways in which Ghanaian social workers in Ghana and the Greater Toronto Area (GTA), Canada, draw on their spirituality as a coping mechanism to deal with workplace stresses. This chapter is organized into four major sections. The first discusses how the data of the study were collected, organized, and analyzed; the second and third sections discuss some of the key findings in the study; and the fourth section focuses on some conclusions drawn from the study and their relevance for social work education. The data for the chapter were taken from a study funded by Social Science and Humanities Research Council and the Office of Vice President of the Memorial University of Newfoundland (SSHRC-VP), in which we qualitatively examined spirituality as self-care strategies among Ghanaian social workers working in Ghana and in the GTA, Canada. We hope to use the findings of the study to make a case about the importance of incorporating spirituality into social work education in Africa.

We define spirituality as

> the building and rebuilding of human spirit to embrace gentleness, humility, and compassion in learning about others and ourselves. It is about a powerful force

> beyond the immediate and more physically observable culture, one that directs social action beyond the perspective of human control in terms of that, which can be counted, measured, evaluated and physically grasped. (Dei, 2002, p. 38)

Spirituality is an important dimension of human existence and in many ways informs how some people come to know and make sense of their worlds. For many Ghanaian social workers in Ghana and the GTA, spirituality is an important self-care tool to help them deal with workplace stresses. Whether providing services for individuals, families, and communities or working to shape public policies, social workers across the globe are fully engaged and committed to helping people who are affected by social problems such as domestic violence, child abuse, poverty, homelessness, sexual abuse, and others (Bell et al., 2003). However, the cost of unconditional caregiving and emotional investment poses risks for a social worker's own physical, mental, emotional, and spiritual wellness. Despite the resistance within the social work profession to fully embrace spirituality, Tyler (2002), Coholic (2005), Graham et al. (2006), and Matthew (2009) argue that spirituality can promote health and well-being among social workers. These authors argue that spirituality is relevant to social work practice because it helps practitioners to incorporate what science, logic, and rational reasoning cannot fully explain.

Other authors have noted that the subjective side of faith and religious experience may be a vital component of self-care for practitioners experiencing stress and bereavement (Hill & Pargament, 2008; Puterbaugh, 2008). As revealed in the work of Holland and Neimeyer (2005), mental health practitioners' engagement in daily spiritual exercises helps mitigate physical, cognitive, and emotional manifestations of burnout in the workplace. Dombo and Gray (2013) further support the utility of the self-care model in clinical social work, suggesting that spiritual self-care in vicarious trauma practice facilitates compassion and improves client outcomes through continued engagement and spiritual self-care mediation practices. These findings among others reinforce a growing literature based on the value and beneficial impacts of spirituality in the psychological and physiological well-being of practitioners and clients (Williams et al., 2010). In the study, Ghanaian social workers in Ghana and in the GTA demonstrate how their spiritual knowledge and practices serve as useful coping tools to deal with workplace stresses.

Methodology

As already indicated, the data for this chapter were taken from an SSHRC/VP-funded research in which we examined how Ghanaian social workers in Ghana and the GTA understood and relied on spirituality as a self-care tool in professional practice. The data were collected qualitatively using a multifaceted research design that employed two types of methods: first, a comprehensive review of all related literature on spirituality in the social work context and, second, semistructured interviews with

Ghanaian social workers in the GTA and in Ghana. Four major questions guided the study, including the individual interviews:

a. How do Ghanaian social workers conceptualize spirituality, and if any, how do their understandings of spirituality translate into practice?
b. What are the spiritual tools and resources available to Ghanaian social workers in Ghana and in the GTA, Canada in the field of practice?
c. What are the potentials and risks/difficulties of practitioners' spirituality in the field of practice?
d. What is the relevance of spirituality in preparing students for the social work profession?

We conducted the study in Accra, in Koforidua, Ghana, and in the GTA. These selected areas serve two purposes for the study: First, the GTA has the largest concentration of Ghanaian Canadians, and the majority of Ghanaian social workers live and work within this area. Second, the majority of us (authors) are Ghanaian Canadians and have lived in Canada for many years. We have many contacts among the Ghanaian community, and these contacts were useful in identifying the potential participants for recruitment. Furthermore, some of us have worked in Ghana as social workers for some years before we relocated to Canada and still have contacts among social workers in Ghana. These contacts were also helpful in identifying potential participants for recruitment.

Recruitment

We used our established contacts in the GTA and in Ghana to identify potential participants for recruitment for the study. We used both purposive sampling and a short screening instrument to ensure an appropriate mix of Ghanaian social workers of diverse backgrounds taking into consideration participants' socioeconomic status, religion, age, gender, and ethnicity, as well as Canadian-born and immigrants from Ghana. In all, 40 individuals—20 Ghanaian social workers from the GTA and 20 from Accra and Koforidua, Ghana—were recruited for the individual interviews.

Data Collection

An in-depth interview method was employed for the data collection. The individual interviews were semistructured, and each interview lasted between 45 and 60 minutes. The interview guide included questions on demographic/socioeconomic and ethnic backgrounds of participants. Specifically, these are some of the questions posed to participants:

a. How will you conceptualize spirituality? Do you see any difference between spirituality and religion?
b. Has there been any moment in your work where issues relating to a client have affected you emotionally so that even after you left work you were still dealing with those emotional issues? How have you addressed these stresses?
c. Beside these coping mechanisms, is there anything that you do to take away some of the work-related stresses? How do you connect these coping mechanisms with your spirituality?
d. To what extent do you rely a lot on spirituality to deal with work-related stresses? Do you recall moment(s) where your spirituality has posed a challenge to your practice effectiveness as a social worker? Do you see any tension and dilemma that your spirituality poses to your work?
e. Do you consider any benefit your spirituality brings or may bring to your professional competence? If we are to rewrite the social work curricula, what would be your advice for social work education about spirituality?

In line with semistructured, in-depth interviews, several probing questions were asked to gain clarification on some of the responses of participants (Chu & Ke, 2017; Boyce & Neale, 2006). All interviews were conducted at places of the participants' choosing. With the consent of participants, all interviews with the exception of four were digitally recorded, and notes were taken to assist data analysis and interpretation.

Data Analysis

Interviews were transcribed by two research assistants—one in Ghana and the other in St. John's, Newfoundland. We used the techniques of Warren and Karner (2015) and Denzin and Lincoln (1994, 2011) for data organization and reduction. We took particular notice of the suggestion by Warren and Karner (2015) that researchers working on lengthy interview transcripts and detailed field notes in qualitative analysis must first "have an idea of where you want to end" (p. 210). In our case, the existing literature on spirituality, as well as our familiarity with interview data, was helpful in developing ideas of where the research "should end" as we openly coded and recoded themes from the data according to the interview structure and emergent themes. The use of NVivo 11, a software program designed to sort qualitative data, helped in the coding and recoding process. Participants' responses were cross-referenced with interview notes and existing literature to tease out points of convergence and divergence as well as sources of tension and pedagogic relevance. We used existing literature on spirituality as comparative bases for interrogating and interpreting local cultural knowledge and experiences on Ghanaian spiritual practices. To protect the confidentiality and anonymity of participants, we gave each participant a pseudonym as well as removed or modified any information that might compromise the identity of participants when reporting the findings. In addition, we edited each quote and statement of the participants to remove pause words (such as *like*, *uh*, and *um*), and where necessary, we corrected grammatical errors to make reading fluent. In editing the quotes, however, we were careful not to tamper with the substance of the conversation. The following section discusses the interview findings.

Findings: Conceptualizing Spirituality

In the study, we asked participants to express their understanding of spirituality. For many of the participants, spirituality is about the relationship that exists between them and a higher order. Elai, a social work supervisor who practiced in the GTA, understands spirituality as "a connection to whatever entity that is outside a person" (Interview, July 6, 2014). Siah, a clinical social worker in the GTA, also defines spirituality as "a relationship one establishes with a higher order" (Interview, December 19, 2014). Abah, a child protection worker in the GTA, similarly defines spirituality "as a relationship to a force that has answers to a lot of things" (Interview, December 12, 2014).

Similar to the views of Ghanaian social workers in the GTA, social workers in Ghana also understood spirituality as the ways in which humans deal with invisible supernatural forces beyond human grasp and comprehension. Ofado, a social worker in the Department of Social Welfare in Ghana, sees spirituality as human dependency on an omnipotent force for protection: "When you talk about spirituality, the way I understand it is that there is some omnipotent who looks down on us and protect us" (Interview, August 11, 2014). Sawa, an employee with the Child Rights Promotion and Protection in Ghana, echoes the sentiment of Ofado. She, too, believes that spirituality is about one's dealings with a supreme being from whom humans draw inspiration. Teshie, a social worker with the Department of Social Welfare in Ghana, shares the thought that spirituality is humans dealing with invisible forces: "I believe [human] is made up of the body and soul, so what I cannot see with my eye, I refer to it as spirituality. What I cannot see with my naked eye" (Interview, August 15, 2014). Datey, a hospital social worker in Ghana, adds that humans can experience the presence of those invisible forces: "It's [spirituality is] something that cannot be seen. . . . It's something that is felt" (Interview, August 19, 2014). Building on this thought, Kwoah, another hospital social worker, offered a detailed explanation about the nature of spirituality. For Kwoah, although things spiritual cannot be seen, they can be experienced. He used himself as an example to explain spirituality. Although as a human, Kwoah believes he has a spirit, like air, that he cannot see his spirit but can feel its presence. He knows when his spirit is down or excited based on things that happen to him. Similarly, spirituality operates in the same way. It is something that exists but cannot be seen:

> It's like if I have a body, do I have a soul? Do I have a spirit? I think it's spirituality. Because if I have a spirit, then where is my spirit? I cannot see my spirit, like as I cannot see air, but I can feel air. That is the same way I know I cannot see my spirit, but I can feel it, because there are times that your spirit may be down, being things that you've seen, or heard or done, yea, your spirit may be down. And there are times that your spirit may also be excited, based on maybe certain things that you've seen, heard or done; or expecting to even get. Yea, so I think spirituality entails a lot, things that we don't see with our physical eyes. (Interview, August 19, 2014)

The Ghanaian social workers in the GTA and in Ghana's understanding of spirituality—humans' relationship with a powerful force outside one's control—is consistent with African ontology. Within Indigenous African belief systems, there is an active ontological view that the physical and metaphysical worlds are connected and that there are powerful forces that keep watchful eyes over the behaviors of the living. Within Ghanaian traditional beliefs, there is a belief in the existence of four entities:

1. The Supreme God, who is the personified creator of life force. Different cultural groups in Ghana have different names for the Supreme God. The Akans call him Onyame, the Ewes call him Mawu, and the Gas call him Ataa Naa Nyongmo.
2. The deities are the smaller gods that link humanity to the Supreme God. The traditional beliefs among some Ghanaians is that the Supreme God is too big and important to be directly accessible to humanity and therefore can be accessed only through intermediaries, God's children, which are the deities. Deities exist in many forms. As spirit beings, deities live in rivers, mountains, stones, trees, forests, and other animate and inanimate objects. Hence, we have river gods, mountain gods, forest gods, tree gods, stone gods, thunder gods, and others.
3. The ancestors (the dead) are believed to watch over the living with keener interest, always willing and ready to punish evil deeds and to reward good behaviors.
4. The living, who represent living human beings, are the weakest link among these powerful entities (see Danquah, 1968; Opoku, 1978).

In a general sense, Ghanaian social workers in the GTA and in Ghana believe that humans are just a weak link in the vast chain of nature, which encompasses the living, the dead, and even the sacred (see Wangoola, 2000). Spirituality is therefore humans' relationship and dealings with these powerful entities.

Spirituality as Self-Care

Professional self-care is relevant and essential to all social work practitioners. In this study, participants shared stories about how they have relied on their spiritual knowledge, values, worldview, and practice to deal with workplace stresses. Peom, a social work in the GTA, uses prayers, the reading of scriptures, and active duties in her local church in the GTA to help deal with workplace stresses. She believes that such spiritual coping mechanisms have shielded her from traumatic experiences such as vicarious trauma and secondary trauma:

> I think that my involvement with church and my relationship with God also help. Because I have that kind of religious insight to combine all those other stuffs. I try as much as possible to read my bible, I try to pray every night when I put my kids to bed, I try to read by Bible. . . . I understand that some people go through the vicarious trauma and secondary trauma, but I have never had that experience, because for me . . . I think that my involvement with church and my relationship with God also help. (Interview, May 4, 2014)

Similarly, Awah, another social worker from the GTA, uses her dependency on God, prayers, and the reading of scriptures as spiritual self-care strategies:

> I have been so dependent on finding my sanity and peace in the word of God that if I did not have it, I don't know where I would have been able to gain the strength from to be able to go to work tomorrow morning after a terrible apprehension like what I did. This evening my husband and I will do bible studies, we will pray and that is basically how we normally end our day. Early in morning it is very busy so normally, we pray quickly, and we leave and when we leave, we always ask that the blood of God is upon us and may his grace be upon us throughout the day. If I didn't feel that shield and that protection of His grace being upon me, I don't believe it would be possible to do the work I do, I really don't. I don't think I would have the inner strength, even the ability, to deal with the emotional and psychological effects. (Interview, December 9, 2014)

Like their counterparts in the GTA, Ghanaian social workers in Ghana also spoke about the importance of prayers and faith in God as spiritual self-care practices. Soah, a male social worker in one of the hospitals in Ghana, talked about the importance of prayers, the reading of scriptures, and listening to gospel songs as spiritual self-care practices:

> Dwelling on the Word of God, because there are times that I, I normally don't sleep early. Yea, sometimes I pray, I listen to songs, gospel songs; so, I have apps

> on my phone that I can read my Bible, commentary, make notes, yea. So, I will say those are my rituals. (Interview, August 8, 2014)

Two other female Ghanaian social workers in Ghana, Abompo and Shale, also spoke about the importance of prayers and faith in God as spiritual self-care practices:

> For me when I wake up in the morning, I pray for every case that will be coming, my clients, colleague social workers, et cetera, so that God will take control. (Interview, August 11, 2014)

> I believe that whatever that I do, without God, I can't do it because in this world, I don't know where I came from and I'm here, in the first place, and once you believe and trust Him [God], whatever you ask from God, you're able to get it and aside from that too, by our own strength we are not able to do anything.... Whatever is happening, I pray to my God for my safety. (Interview, August 11, 2014)

The Ghanaian social workers' use of prayers, the reading of scriptures, and faith in God as spiritual coping mechanisms are consistent with other studies. In their study of spirituality among men with prostate cancer, Walton and Sullivan (2004) note that daily prayers to God are an important coping mechanism for people that seek assurances, comforts, and inner strengths. Similarly, Backus, Backus, & Page (1995) note in their study of emergency medical services (EMS) workers that 87% of EMS workers use prayers as a self-care tool. However, prayers, the reading of the scriptures, and faith in God are not the only spiritual self-care strategies of Ghanaian social workers. Some of them, specifically those from the GTA, listed the listening and dancing to African music as spiritual self-care strategies. Laman, a male social worker in the GTA, spoke about the importance of African music as a spiritual self-care tool. According to him, the lyrics and the drumbeat give him inner strength and sensations that help him to deal with any workplace stresses:

> I listen to mostly local Ghanaian music. I also listen to some African artists within the genre of Afrobeat; we talk about Sala, Uchindo and just the drums they give you some strength. Some of the lyrics I don't even understand but the beats make you feel some sensations, there is a visceral feeling that you get from music. (Interview, May 22, 2013)

Siah, a male social worker in the GTA, echoes Laman's sentiments about Ghanaian music. He, too, argues that whenever he listens to Ghanaian music, he feels he has momentarily left his Canadian environment and its attendant problems and is actually in Ghana:

> I will just listen to some of the Ghanaian music on the radio and it also helps me a lot. To me this may not probably apply to every Ghanaian; it just takes my mind back to the things that we used to do in Ghana, and anytime that I am listen[ing] to Ghanaian music it does not matter whether it is highlife or gospel, I just reflect on the culture or the atmosphere in Ghana. That alone helps me because I forget about everything that is happening in Canada. I don't care about the bills, work or anything. I take my mind back to Ghana and then just seeing the environment in Ghana, and it helps me a lot while enjoying the music at the same time. (Interview, December 19, 2014)

Laih, a female social worker in the GTA, also spoke about the importance of listening and dancing to Ghanaian music as self-care strategies:

> There is a lot of dancing, we love music, so this is how we escape some of these things and then I go back on Monday and deal with those issues, and on the weekends, we always have things planned. We play a lot of gospel, what we call Ghanaian music highlife gospel. Most of them are optimistic music meaning that everything will be fine, there is always light at [the] end of the tunnel. (Interview, June 7, 2013)

Although the importance of music as a spiritual self-care tool is well noted in participants' narration, it is also instructive to note that unlike Ghanaian social workers in the GTA, not many Ghanaian social workers in Ghana spoke about Ghanaian music as an important spiritual self-care tool for their well-being. In fact, in all the transcripts of the interviews conducted in Ghana, music was mentioned as an important spiritual self-care tool two times. Even with those two, only one participant, Soah, mentioned that he uses music as a spiritual self-care tool. The other participant, Abompo, who spoke about music only mentioned it as a self-care tool she recommended for a traumatized client living in an abusive home:

> I told her to read good books, listen to good music. The next time she came to see me, she was looking much better, and she thanked me for teaching her something better. She no longer dwelt on the man, but on herself. (Interview, August 11, 2014)

The question remains: Why is it that Ghanaian social workers in the GTA tend to rely more on Ghanaian music as a spiritual self-care tool than their counterparts in Ghana? The answer probably lies in the works of Adinkrah (2008), Agovi (1989), and Nketia (1957). These authors argued that the lyrics in Ghanaian music are themselves rich in Ghanaian cultural metaphors. This makes them signposts that help listeners living outside the borders of Ghana remember the forgotten Ghanaian traditional values, worldviews, and spiritual knowledge. This may explain why more Ghanaian social workers in the GTA than their counterparts in Ghana mentioned Ghanaian music as one of their spiritual self-care tools. Having lived several years outside the border of Ghana, there is a possibility that Ghanaian social workers in the GTA may have nostalgic feelings about their homeland. Thus, Ghanaian music in many ways reminds them of "home." Despite the differences between how Ghanaian social workers in the GTA and in Ghana respond to Ghanaian music, studies show that music, in general, is an important spiritual tool that connects people to nature and a higher power (Batt-Rawden et al., 2005; Bunt & Stige, 2014; Siedliecki & Good, 2006; Williams et al., 2010). Other studies even suggest that music is a useful coping tool to counter anxiety, depression, and loneliness that human services professionals experience because of their work (Bunt & Stige, 2014; Carrette & King, 2005; Dubé, 2008; Keister, 2004; Kravits et al., 2010; Showalter, 2010).

Ghanaian social workers in the GTA and in Ghana in their responses show how they are employing their Ghanaian cultural knowledge, sense of community, and spirituality to fashion genuine self-care strategies. Significantly, their responses also signal how participants learn about and negotiate between their Ghanaian spirituality grounded to Indigenous Ghanaian spiritual ontology—beliefs in the existence of the Supreme God, the lesser deities, and ancestors—and their various affiliations to formal religious institutional faiths such as Christianity and Islam. In fact, in recognizing that Christian missionaries historically established the school system in Ghana, perhaps it is not surprising that many Ghanaian social workers drew their spirituality from Christianity. The narrations of Ghanaian social workers in Ghana and in the GTA point to an inherent belief that the human search to understand their worlds should not shy away from the recognition of the existence of powerful forces—material or nonmaterial, physical or metaphysical, knowable or unknowable—beyond human grasp that manage human lives. As Dove (1998) pointed out, Africans on the continent and in the diaspora are linked to African cultural memory and spirituality and may at any time become conscious of its significance to their Africanness (p. 516). Not surprisingly, in their difficult and stressful situation, Ghanaian social workers in Ghana and in the GTA have drawn on their spirituality and religion for guidance and supports.

Spirituality in Professional Practice: Issues of Tensions, Ambiguity, Contradiction, and Possibility

Given that all Ghanaian social workers in Ghana and in the GTA expressed their spirituality through the lens of religion, questions arose as to how Ghanaian social workers' sense of spirituality can be embraced and encouraged in the workplace. Although participants spoke highly about the importance of their spiritual practices to their professional self-care, they also acknowledge moments of tension, ambiguity, dilemma, and contradiction whenever they attempt to bring their spirituality into professional practices. Although each participant expressed concerns, reservations, and hopes about integrating spirituality into social work practices, the reason differs, especially for those operating in Ghana and those operating in the GTA. For those in the GTA, their narrations point to a number of concerns, including those Sheridan (2009) has listed as rigidity, biases, judgemental, potential for proselytization and infringement of client's self-determination, blurring of professional boundaries, and impediments to social justice (p. 100). Prul, a female social worker in the GTA, spoke of her discomfort in recognizing and accepting same-sex relationship in practice as a Christian. However, she recognizes that this is something she cannot verbalize openly or even resist at work knowing that such a position will cost her job:

> Based on how I was socialized as a person and coming from Ghana and also my own religious faith, what a typical marriage looks like is more traditional for me and that is what I totally believe in and so now, I'm coming to a culture where I am sort of forced to accept what marriage should really look like that it should be an agreement between two people regardless of their sexes. It is an affront to my belief and my belief includes my religious faith. This is not something I can actually say anywhere. I will not only lose my job; I may be even sued. When I am forced to say things that I don't believe in, honestly that causes me greatest stress. (Interview, December 18, 2014)

Although Prul claimed that she keeps her homophobic sentiments to herself, one wonders if such hidden sentiments affect Prul's ability to be nonjudgmental when working with clients in same-sex relationships. Abah echoes similar sentiments, but she also acknowledges that in a liberal democratic society such as Canada, she must hold off her personal beliefs and ensure that they do not interfere with her work:

> We live in Canada and spirituality that exists here is completely different; the definition is completely mind blowing. This is a world that is very liberal; it has tolerance for certain things that one does not agree with. For example, a social worker working in an environment where I am working with homosexual individuals, I have to make sure that my thoughts, ideologies, my brain stops before I even enter my workplace just so I don't get fired, sued, or lose my license because the world that exist[s] is just different. (Interview, December 9, 2014)

Here is the paradox and the open contradiction of the responses from Prul and Abah: If spirituality is part of their well-being, then how are they able to separate or/and suppress their spirituality at their workplace? To claim to be spiritual at home and non-spiritual at work is to fail to acknowledge the mind, body, soul, and spirit interactions. Santiago Castro-Gomez (2003), the Colombian philosopher, refers to such an attitude as "point zero," a point of view that represents itself as being without a singular perspective.

It is a "God-eyed view" that always hides its local and particular perspectives under an abstract universalism (Grosfoguel, 2001, p. 214). Unlike Prul and Abah, some Ghanaian social workers in the GTA did not see any conflict, ambiguity, or tension between their spirituality and professional practices. Although these participants' spirituality is rooted in their Christian faith, they have a progressive interpretation of Christian doctrine. Laih, for example, argues that her Christian spirituality has made her a better practitioner because she draws inspiration from Jesus Christ, who never discriminated against anybody. This is why she is inspired to practice antidiscrimination at work:

> Looking at the way that I practice if you know about the Bible and you look at Jesus' life, I think that I practice in that way that Jesus never discriminated against anybody so we deal with a lot of ageism, diversity, and anti-oppression. Diversity and anti-oppression is being aware of the difference in people whether is intersection, sexism, race, or culture you have to be respectful to everybody and show fairness and equity and so I think that is the core message of Jesus Christ. That is the connection between my faith and this work, so I am not conflicted. (Interview, June 7, 2013)

The Ghanaian social workers in Ghana also expressed some concerns about integrating spirituality into professional practice for different reasons. As we mentioned earlier, the Ghanaian spiritual ontology espouses beliefs in powerful forces that watch over the living who often reward good deeds and punish bad deeds. Within this context, some Ghanaians perform charities with the sole goal of averting misfortunes or/and attracting blessings for themselves or family members. Usually, they carried out such charity work after consulting a diviner—a prophet, a *mallam*, or a traditionalist who provides specific instructions on how the acts of charity should be carried out. The instructions can include cooking for orphanage children and watching them eat everything or feeding candies to children at the orphanage. Usually, these types of donors will say, "*Eye akwankyere*"—Twi language—that translates as "it is a diviner's instruction." By that, they meant the donations must be taken with a specific instruction, even if the instructions violate the Criminal Code of Ghana, the rights of the children, or/and the Code of Ethics of Ghanaian social workers. Jasu, who works with one of the children's homes in Ghana, has many examples to share on this subject. In one such example, a donor insisted that her pastor had instructed her to only take a blank receipt for her cash donation, an action that, if complied with, constitutes a crime for the social worker:

> Somebody too will come and tell you that my pastor told me not to give me a receipt don't write it, give me a blank receipt. Then I will also let her know that your pastor has his rights and it ends somewhere, I'm doing government work. (Interview, August 11, 2014)

Shale, another female social worker in a children's home, also shared a similar experience. In her case, a donor with three dresses insisted she should be allowed to hand over the dresses directly to three children because that is the instruction she received from a diviner:

> Those who donate, some of them will tell you that "*eye akwankyere*" and tell you that "I have three dresses, the spiritual direction, I was asked to give it to three children, so give me three children to give it to them." (Interview, August 11, 2014)

The social workers working in this environment are cautious about the idea of openly integrating spirituality into social work practices for fear that such a decision will create problems for practitioners. Of course, the call to accept the relevance of spirituality as a tool of self-care is not to suggest that social workers must accept everything that is done in the name of "spirituality" or even impose their spirituality on others. In many ways, having spiritual knowledge and values is no different from those who have cultural values and worldviews. Although social workers know they cannot impose their values, worldviews, and cultures on others, they acknowledge that they cannot leave their cultural values and worldviews at home because they are what made them who they are. In the same way, the tensions, contradictions, and ambiguities that spirituality brings to individual practitioners cannot be the reason to reject spirituality in social work practice. If anything, we have learned from these responses that spirituality and spiritual practices are themselves not the problem, but how they are evoked and used in practice can make them a problem. In view of that, social workers need special training on how they can fully integrate their spirituality into practice in more inclusive and less harmful ways. We expand the last point in the discussion that follows.

Spirituality and Social Work Education

Contrary to the roots of social work originating from philanthropic motivations and faith-based moral motivations of social service and charity, social work education has undermined religious insights at the preferential acceptance of separating the sacred and the secular (Hugen & Scales, 2008). The movement toward securing professional credibility among social workers across the globe has acted to dissolve spiritual education, further bolstering narrowed conceptualizations of the value of spirituality in social service (Hugen & Scales, 2008; Moss, 2005). The effect is that social work education is currently failing to meet the spiritual needs of learners.

In an earlier study done among social work practitioners in the United States, 79% indicated that they never received or rarely received any content on religion and spirituality in their social work graduate training (Sheridan et al., 1992). Russel (1998), following the study by Sheridan et al. (1992), conducted a survey among 114 Master of Social Work programs in the United States. He noted that only 14.9% of the programs offered a course on spirituality (Russel, 1998). Russel et al. (2005) conducted a follow-up study in 2005 among 171 accredited Master of Social Work programs in the United States. They noted that only 33.3% offered a course on spirituality or religion. In the United Kingdom, a national survey among social workers indicated that they received little to nothing on spirituality in their social work education (Furman et al., 2004). In Canada, the 2018 survey among social work educators in 38 social work schools indicated that only 31.7% in the Bachelor of Social Work programs and 29.2% of the Master of Social Work programs include some content on spirituality and religion in the social work education (Kvarfordt et al., 2018). In South Africa, a survey conducted among final-year social work students (714) in 21 social work schools indicated that 53% of respondents did not hear anything about spirituality or religion in their social work education (Bhagwan, 2010). Yet a follow-up study among social work educators in 2013 indicated that 84.5% favored the inclusion of spirituality in social work education in South Africa (Bhagwan, 2013). Similar studies among social work educators in Australia and South Asian countries (India, Sri Lanka, Nepal, Bangladesh, Burma, and Bhutan) received overwhelming approval—89% in Australia and 100% in South Asian countries—about the inclusion of spirituality and religion in social work education (Lindsay, 2002; Pandya, 2015).

Considering the importance of spiritual self-care among Ghanaian social workers in the GTA and in Ghana, we asked participants to share their thoughts about incorporating spirituality and religion in social work education. Cyie, a social work educator in Ghana, explained that spirituality already plays a major role in African society. Thus, educating social workers on how to manage spirituality can only help them to offer effective and competent services to clients:

> In Africa for instance, very often, when you're dealing with clients, you realize that the spiritual aspect comes into play. You have people . . . and sometimes also it comes into play negatively. . . . You know, you have people who are sick, you know they have to go to the hospital, and they tell you it's that old woman in the village . . . let me use the Ghanaian English, who is "doing them" [*Laughs*], are you getting me? And so how do we teach our students, you know, to take that aspect into consideration? Because it does actually help! And so, if you are able to encourage the person, if it is the person's religion or whatever, that would encourage the person to think positively, why not use it? (Interview, August 26, 2014)

Another social work educator in Ghana, Kofah, echoes Cyie's sentiment. He also believes that spirituality and religion in social work education will serve as a good foundation for practice:

> Expose people [social work students] to various religious practices that are around, so that if you encounter any client, who comes from any particular background, then you will appreciate, you know . . . things about their religious beliefs. . . . All religious beliefs, Hindu, Buddhist, Christian, Muslim . . . you know, you have to learn about these religions, so that when you encounter a client . . . , and you get to know this is the religious faith they have, because you are conversant with it, you know you can deal with the person. (Interview, August 21, 2014)

Like their counterparts in Ghana, Ghanaian social workers in the GTA strongly favored the inclusion of spirituality in social work education. Abif, a social worker in the GTA, argues that the nature of social work practice and the inherent difficulties suggest that the social workers need to draw on their faith and spirituality to survive. His concern, however, is that without adequate training on how social workers employ spirituality at work, more harm than good is likely to be the results:

> Your physical being alone would not pull you through the work because day in and day out there are many challenging issues of injustices, issues of abuse, issues of people acting inappropriately, people choking on their own because of power and people doing things that are not humanly nice to others. So just to rely on your physical strength would not be enough. You have to dwell on your faith, prayer, and all those things to be able to pull you through . . . and if you don't have an instinct of what spirituality is and people are dealing with their own spiritual matrix, you are deficient. You can't help. (Interview, May 22, 2014)

Priful, a Ghanaian social worker in the GTA, shared Abif's thought. She reminds readers that social work practice is not like the banking industry, where clients come to transact on financial issues. Social work is about building relationships with people who themselves embody some form of spirituality. It is therefore fulfilling to have a framework that can teach social workers on how to draw on spiritual knowledge and practices to help clients:

> This is not a corporate world. This is not a bank, where somebody comes to redraw and go. This is different. You are building [a] relationship with the common person on the street . . . [who] embod[ies] some forms of spirituality or whatever it is for everybody. I think there is a sense of fulfillment for you as a worker that my spirituality is not being thrown out, it is being respected, acknowledged, and I can actually use it positively in my work environment. (Interview, December 18, 2014)

The African healer and diviner, Malidoma Some (1994), observed a long time ago that "you cannot be who you truly are until you can put what you remember into action in your life" (p. 309). The narrations of Ghanaian social workers in the GTA and in Ghana indicate that their spiritual knowledge, beliefs, and practices are part of who they are. Therefore, to ask them to deny those spiritual beliefs and practices before they can practice as professionals is like asking fish to give up water or fire to give up oxygen. As the French philosopher and Jesuit priest Pierre Teilhard de Chardin once said, "We are not human beings having a spiritual experience. We are spiritual beings having a human experience" (n.p., as cited in McElrath, 2008). Thus, social work education cannot be complete if curricula excludes spirituality and religion. Furthermore, the anecdotes within this study show that without adequate training on how social workers apply their religion and spirituality in practice, potential harm could be done to colleagues as well as to clients.

Conclusion

In 1972, at a meeting of the Association of African Universities in Accra, a decision was made to promote a university education that seeks to improve the social and economic development of African minds (Yesufu, 1973). Despite this vision, the search for viable educational options for Africans is still dominated by Western cultures, values, knowledge, and worldviews (Dei, 2004). Indeed, in the *Song of Lawino*, Okot p'Bitek (1986) describes typical African educators as intelligentsia with little or no stamina about how to contextualize standards and excellence to the needs and condition of their people. Siobhan Laird (2006) shared her experience as a coordinator and instructor at the Social Work Department at the University of Ghana between 1997 and 2001:

> Once I attended a lecture at the University of Ghana given by a former student of social work. Though Ghanaian, he is a professor in America now. He told us how information technology could transform our teaching. He told us of teleconferencing, of distance learning through remote computer terminals, of essential Internet access for research. But he did not seem to notice the week-long power outages we were then suffering; he did not seem to recognize our lack of resources and he seemed to have forgotten that at times it is difficult to telephone from one house to another even in the same town. In fact, he did not see us at all. He was speaking to some imaginary American audience. Certainly, he was a professor now, but somewhere on his ascendancy to professorhood he had lost Africa and Africa had lost him. He had no feel for our reality in Ghana and so he had nothing to convey to us. Franz Fanon spoke of the colonized personality, of an individual who sets aside their own cultural experience and instead puts on a borrowed mentality an Anglo-American worldview. A terribly

> high price is paid for that kind of barter and our Ghanaian professor turned American has paid it. (p. 383)

Siobhan Laird's story raises an interesting issue for discussion. Our goal here is not to blame the Ghanaian scholar who shortly lost sight of his audience and therefore suggested ideas that were at odds to the reality of frontline workers. His story, however, speaks volumes about the nature of social work education in Africa, the processes whereby African cultures, values, worldviews, and knowledge systems are overlooked while imparting Westernized methodologies of services. Not surprisingly, social work students leave classrooms sometimes with a feeling that they have received limited knowledge to address local issues. Indeed, Frantz Fanon (1963) spoke about this kind of education long ago:

> While the masses of the people maintain intact traditions, which are completely different from those of the colonial situation, the intellectuals throw themselves in frenzied fashion into frantic acquisition of the culture of the occupying power and take every opportunity of unfavorably criticizing their own culture. (p. 237)

Social work is a profession that concerns itself with helping individuals, families, groups, and communities to maximize their full potentials in society as well as fulfill their life aspirations. Working in a people-centered profession, social workers desire to help people develop their abilities and skills, as well as resources within their domain to solve their problems. This means that social work education cannot be developed outside the cultural resources, values, and worldview of the people.

As we have learned from Ghanaian social workers in our study, spirituality is the vehicle that carries African ethos, values, worldviews, and knowledge systems. In similar research among African Nova Scotian communities in Canada, David Este and Wanda Thomas Bernard (2006) noted that African spirituality is a source of strength as well as a coping mechanism in how those of African descent respond to everyday challenges and discrimination. Ani (1980) and Paris (1995) have equally noted that spiritual strivings appear to be the common denominator that unites Africans around the globe. Therefore, we are not asking spirituality to be included in Africanizing social work education in Africa because spirituality is already in the classroom through the embodied knowledge of African social work students. We are ultimately asking for Africanizing social work education to recognize spirituality, nurture it, and enhance it to be more productive to practitioners, clients, colleagues, organizations, and society.

References

Adinkrah, M. (2008). Witchcraft themes in popular Ghanaian music. *Popular Music and Society, 31*(3), 299–311.

Agovi, K. E. (1989). The political relevance of Ghanaian highlife songs since 1957. *Research in African Literatures, 20*(2), 194–201.

Ani, M. (1980). *Let the circle be unbroken: The implications of African spirituality in the diaspora.* Greenwood Press.

Backus, C. J., Backus, W., & Page, D. I. (1995). Spirituality of EMTs: A study of the spiritual nature of EMS workers and its effects on perceived happiness and prayers for patients. *Prehospital and Disaster Medicine, 10*(3), 168–173.

Batt-Rawden, K. B., DeNora, T., & Ruud, E. (2005). Music listening and empowerment in health promotion: A study of the role and significance of music in everyday life of the long-term ill. *Nordic Journal of Music Therapy, 14*(2), 120–136.

Bell, H., Kulkarni, S., & Dalton, L. (2003). Organizational prevention of vicarious trauma. *Families in Society: The Journal of Contemporary Social Services, 84*(4), 463–470.

Bhagwan, R. (2010). Spirituality in social work: A survey of students at South African universities. *Social Work Education, 29*(2), 188–204.

Bhagwan, R. (2013). Spirituality in social work in South Africa: Insights from a survey with academics. *International Social Work, 56*(3), 276–289.

Boyce, C., & Neale, P. (2006). *Conducting in-depth interviews: A guide for designing and conducting in-depth interviews for evaluation input.* Pathfinder International.

Bunt, L., & Stige, B. (2014). *Music therapy: An art beyond words.* Routledge.

Carrette, J. R., & King, R. (2005). *Selling spirituality: The silent takeover of religion.* Routledge.

Castro-Gomez, S. (2003). *La hybris del punto cero: Biopolíticas imperiales y colonialidad del poder en la Nueva Granada/ The zero point hubris: Imperial biopolitics and coloniality of power in New Granada (1750–1810).* Universidad Javeriana, Bogota, Colombia.

Chu, H., & Ke, Q. (2017). Research methods: What's in the name? *Library & Information Science Research, 39*(4), 284–294.

Coholic, D. (2005). The helpfulness of spiritually influenced group work in developing self-awareness and self-esteem: A preliminary investigation. *The Scientific World Journal, 5*(1), 789–802.

Danquah, J. B. (1968). *The Akan doctrine of God.* Frank Cass & Co.

Dei, G. J. S. (2002). Spirituality in African education: Issues, contentions and contestations from a Ghanaian case study. *International Journal of Children Spirituality, 7*(1), 37–56.

Dei, G. J. S. (2004). *Schooling and education in Africa: The case of Ghana.* Africa World Press.

Denzin, N. K., & Lincoln, Y. S. (1994). *Handbook of qualitative research.* Sage Publications.

Denzin, N. K., & Lincoln, Y. S. (2011). *The SAGE handbook of qualitative research.* Sage Publications.

Dombo, E. A., & Gray, C. (2013). Engaging spirituality in addressing vicarious trauma in clinical social workers: A self-care model. *Social Work & Christianity, 40*(1), 89–104.

Dove, N. (1998). African womanism: An Afrocentric theory. *Journal of Black Studies, 28*(5), 515–539.

Dubé, R. A. (2008). *Songs of the spirit: Attending to Aboriginal students' emotional and spiritual needs through a Native American flute curriculum.* VDM Verlag.

Este, D., & Bernard, W. T. (2006). Spirituality among African Nova Scotians: A key to survival in Canadian society. *Critical Social Work, 7*(1), 1–22.

Fanon, F. (1963). *The wretched of the earth.* Grove Press.

Furman, L. D., Benson, P. W., Grimwood, C., & Canda, E. (2004). Religion and spirituality in social work education and direct practice at the millennium: A survey of UK social workers. *British Journal of Social Work, 34*(6), 767–792.

Graham, J. R., Coholic D., & Coates, J. (2006). Spirituality as a guiding construct in the development of Canadian social work: Past and present considerations. *Critical Social Work, 7*(1), 1–17.

Grosfoguel, R. (2001). Colonial difference, geopolitics of knowledge and global coloniality in the modern/colonial capitalist world-system. *Review, 25*(3), 203–224.

Hill, P. C., & Pargament, K. I. (2008). Advances in the conceptualization and measurement of religion and spirituality: Implications for physical and mental health research. *Psychology of Religion and Spirituality, 5*(1), 3–17.

Holland, J. M., & Neimeyer, R. A. (2005). Reducing the risk of burnout in end-of-life care settings: The role of daily spiritual experiences and training. *Palliative and Supportive Care, 3*(3), 173–181.

Hugen, B., & Scales, T. L. (2008). *Christianity and social work: Readings on the integration of Christian faith and social work practice* (3rd ed.). North American Christians in Social Work.

Keister, J. (2004). The shakuhachi as spiritual tool: A Japanese Buddhist instrument in the West. *Asian Music, 35*(2), 99–131.

Kravits, K., McAllister-Black, R., Grant, M., & Kirk, C. (2010). Self-care strategies for nurses: A psycho-educational intervention for stress reduction and the prevention of burnout. *Applied Nursing Research, 23*(3), 130–138.

Kvarfordt, C. L., Sheridan, M. J., & Taylor, O. (2018). Religion and spirituality in social work curriculum: A survey of Canadian educators. *British Journal of Social Work, 48*(5), 1469–1487.

Laird, S. E. (2006). Teaching social work as a foreign language: A White European at an African university. *Teaching in Higher Education, 11*(3), 381–386.

Lindsay, R. (Ed.). (2002). *Recognizing spirituality: The interface between faith and social work*. University of Western Australia Press.

Mathews, I. (2009). *Social work and spirituality*. Learning Matters. New York: Sage.

McElrath, D. (2008). *The essence of twelve step recovery: Take it to heart*. Hazelden Publishing.

Moss, B. (2005). Thinking outside the box: Religion and spirituality in social work education and practice. *Implicit Religion, 8*(1), 40–52.

Nketia, J. (1957). Modern trends in Ghana music. *African Music, 1*(4), 13–17.

Opoku, K. A. (1978). *West African traditional religion*. FEP International Private Ltd.

Pandya, S. P. (2015). Including spirituality in the social work curriculum: Perspectives from South Asia. *Social Work Education, 34*(6), 729–746.

Paris, P. J. (1995). *The spirituality of African peoples: The search for a common moral discourse*. Fortress Press.

p'Bitek, O. (1986). *Song of Lawino*. East African Educational Publishers.

Puterbaugh, D. (2008). Spiritual evolution of bereavement counselors: An exploratory qualitative study. *Counseling and Values, 52*(3), 198–210.

Russel, R. (1998). Spirituality and religion in graduate social work education. *Social Thought, 18*(2), 15–29.

Russel, R., Ferraro, G., & Russo, A. (2005, February). *The development of MSW courses with a spiritual or religious focus* [Paper presentation]. The Council of Social Work Education, New York, NY, United States.

Sheridan, M. (2009). Ethical issues in the use of spiritually based interventions in social work practice: What are we doing and why. *Journal of Religion & Spirituality in Social Work: Social Thought, 28*(1–2), 99–126.

Sheridan, M. J., Bullis, R. K., Adcock, C. R., Berlin, S. D., & Miller, P. C. (1992). Practitioners' personal and professional attitudes and behaviors toward religion and spirituality: Issues for education and practice. *Journal of Social Work Education, 28*(2), 190–203.

Showalter, S. E. (2010). Compassion fatigue: What is it? Why does it matter? Recognizing the symptoms, acknowledging the impact, developing the tools to prevent compassion fatigue, and strengthen the professional already suffering from the effects. *American Journal of Hospice and Palliative Medicine, 27*(4), 239–242.

Siedliecki, S. L., & Good, M. (2006). Effect of music on power, pain, depression and disability. *Journal of Advanced Nursing, 54*(5), 553–562.

Some, M. P. (1994). *Of water and the spirit: Ritual magic and imitation in the life of an African shaman.* Tarcher/Putnam Books.

Tyler, W. (2002). Teaching social work values within their historical context. *The Journal of Baccalaureate Social Work, 7*(2), 33–47.

Walton, J., & Sullivan, N. (2004). Men of prayer: Spirituality of men with prostate cancer, a grounded theory study. *Journal of Holistic Nursing, 22*(2), 133–151.

Wangoola, P. (2000). Mpambo, the African multiversity: A philosophy to rekindle the African spirit. In G. D. B. Hall & D. Rosenberg (Eds.), *Indigenous knowledges in the global contexts: Multiple readings of the world* (pp. 265–277). University of Toronto Press.

Warren, C. A., & Karner, T. X. (2015). *Discovering qualitative methods: Ethnography, interviews, documents, and images.* Oxford University Press.

Williams, I. D., Richardson, T. A., Moore, D. D., Gambrel, L. E., & Keeling, M. L. (2010). Perspectives on self-care. *Journal of Creativity in Mental Health, 5*(3), 320–338.

Yesufu, T. M. (Ed.). (1973). *Creating the African university: Emerging issues in the 1970s.* Oxford University Press.

CHAPTER 7

Contextualized Role-Play, Inquiry, and Eco-Management in Teaching Environmental Education in Junior High Schools in Ghana

Louis Atsiatorme and Kolawole Raheem

GHANA IS ENDOWED with rich natural resources, which form the basis of her development. As in many developing countries, Ghana's developmental efforts have resulted in environmental degradation, particularly in some parts of the country with fragile ecosystems. For this reason, coupled with the severe droughts in Ghana as well as the extensive bushfires in 1983 and 1984, public awareness of environmental issues became heightened. The government's response to this public concern was the establishment of a National Environmental Policy aimed at ensuring that economic development took place without destroying the natural resource base of the country.

Compiled by the Environmental Policy Commission (EPC), a National Environmental Action Plan was designed to implement educational practices (EPC, 1988). Environmental education (EE) in the basic and second-cycle schools formed a major part of this National Environmental Action Plan. This was premised on the fact that EE is important and essential in the protection and conservation of the environment as observed in international conferences on the human environment. The seeming ineffectiveness of these interventions may be due to the fact that pedagogical skills adopted in teaching children in schools are not related to the philosophical thoughts of the people but instead are related to European culture with its concomitant philosophical systems. Accumulated evidence supports the thinking as proposed in this study that the effectiveness of EE will depend on the right contextualized pedagogical skills for the teaching of EE.

Literature Overview

In 1992 during the Stockholm Conference on Human Environment, it was recognized that the environment was undergoing serious degradation, and it was recommended that a common strategy and/or policy be identified to guide the people of the world to repair the damages being done to the environment due mainly to human activities. The Stockholm Conference therefore emphasized the need for an education that is environmentally oriented to help people to develop a positive attitude toward the environment and work toward its conservation (United Nations Educational Scientific and Cultural Organisation [UNESCO], 1985). Perhaps what the conference did not emphasize at that time was that education should be placed in the learners' cultural context.

EE was therefore conceived as a learning process aimed at increasing people's knowledge and awareness about the environment and its associated challenges; developing the necessary skills and expertise to address the challenges; fostering attitudes, motivations, and commitment to make informed decisions; and taking responsible action (UNESCO, 1978). People were therefore to be given opportunities through EE to acquire the knowledge and skills and to develop values and positive attitudes toward the environment. This will involve the development in students and, indeed, individuals' certain desirable skills and qualities to thoroughly and objectively analyze environmental issues and identify the linkages and synergies in the protection and improvement of the environment (Short, 2010). Key among these skills and qualities are a basic knowledge and understanding of the environment and its interrelationship with man, social values, and attitudes that are in harmony with the environmental quality; skills to solve environmental problems; and a sense of responsibility, ownership, and urgency toward the environment (Short, 2010). Acquisition of these values, skills, and attitudes suitable for environmental conservation and protection is closely related to the methods used by the teacher and the learner (Goralnik, Millenbah, & Thorp, 2012; Short, 2010).

There have been diverse studies to determine the best approach or approaches to impart these qualities to school children through EE. Yavuz et al. (as cited in Aslan Efe et al., 2012) observed that a project-based learning approach had positive effects on the development of desirable attitudes toward the environment. Britzman and Gilbert (as cited in Preston, 2011) saw the role of a teacher in that method as not to provide solutions to environmental problems, which they referred to as environmental template, but rather to provide students with opportunities to be attentive to new thoughts and the cultivation of new relations. Other researchers have found eco-school programs in which learning and action are combined to be more effective than traditional methods of teaching in which knowledge of the environment is presented to students (Bajd and Lescanec, cited in Ozsoy et al., 2012; Krnel & Naglic, cited in Ozsoy et al., 2012; Ozsoy et al., 2012). Stern et al. (2011) evaluated a constructivist and culturally responsive approach to EE for diverse audiences and established its effectiveness. In using Indigenous knowledge and theater, Lane (2012) established that a technique of personalizing the elements in the environment that the author referred to as the embodiment has the potential to enrich environmental education by promoting connections with and responsibility for the environment.

In general, three approaches in EE could be delineated. The first, the positivist approach, makes the teachers the keepers of knowledge and students passive recipients. The second is based on the activities in the environment, in which a teacher is an organizer of experiences and students active learners, and the third, the critical approach, is aimed at providing students with opportunities for action for the environment, in which teachers are collaborative participants with students who are actively generating their own knowledge (Robottom & Hart, 1993). These approaches give opportunities to pupils to gain information that is effective in bringing about a change in their undesirable behavior and that of their peers. Through their direct involvement or participation in their own learning, they gain information and skills at their respective developmental levels.

However, these approaches failed to recognize the cultural environment of the people and assumed that all cultures are the same. The collective survival of Africans depends on their philosophical thoughts. Asabere-Ameyaw et al. (2014) therefore rightly observed that every teaching and learning must stress the interdependence of society, culture, and nature and must be within the philosophical thought of Africans. In Africa, Indigenous knowledge should therefore be developed into the EE curriculum. Africans have seen their lives inextricably linked with the natural environment. Any EE that underestimates the environment of the local people and the product of their interaction with their own environment is bound to fail (Atsiatorme, 2011). Simataa (2015) observed that cultural resources are very vital to every society and should form the basis of any development and by extension education. EE for Africans and developing countries should reflect their values and lifestyle.

In Ghana, however, it does seem that despite government's efforts to make EE effective, viz, the integration of EE themes and topics in the curriculum of schools, the development of a national Environmental Education Strategy for Ghana, the introduction of EE in the curriculum of teacher training institutions, and so on, there is little impact of EE on the attitude and behavior of pupils in basic schools in the country. One key area, which the government has not tackled, is the approach of EE as the educational authorities continue to prescribe methods of teaching that do not reflect the culture of the people. There must be a paradigm shift in African EE.

Research Questions

Based on the issues raised in the literature overview, this study set out to assess the effectiveness of role-play, inquiry, and eco-management approaches in teaching EE in junior high schools in Ghana with a view to ascertaining their instructional advantages in relation to Africanizing its pedagogical strategy. More specifically, the study was set out to address the following questions:

1. What is the level of environmental literacy profiles of junior high school pupils in Ghana?
2. What differences exist in the performance of pupils on Environmental Literacy Test (ELT) between first-year junior high school pupils who are taught environmental issues using role-playing, inquiry, and eco-management approaches and those taught using traditional approaches?

Methodology

The study employed descriptive and experimental designs. The descriptive component of the study was used to ascertain the existing conditions in terms of students' literacy profile, the way EE is integrated into the school's curriculum, and teachers' pedagogical practices in teaching EE. The experimental component was implemented as an intervention to determine the effectiveness of three pedagogical approaches (role-play, inquiry, and eco-management) in EE. The study was carried out in three major phases: (1) baseline study of existing conditions in the schools in relation to EE; (2) the development of teaching materials and training of teachers, development, and pilot testing of instruments; and (3) the evaluation of the three pedagogical approaches. The framework, shown in Figure 7.1, was used to describe the approach to the study.

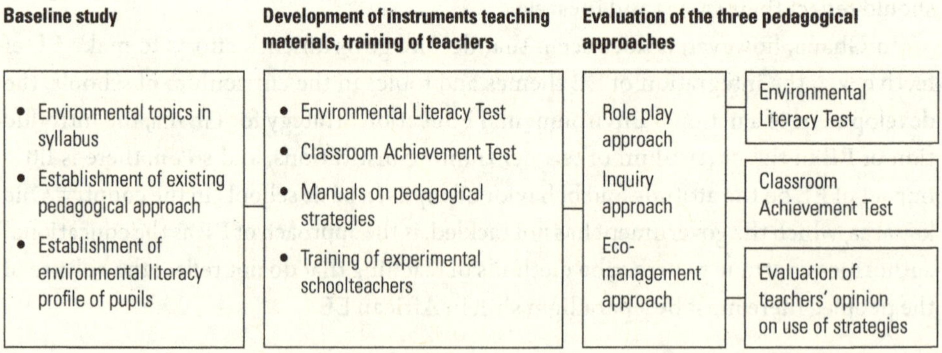

Figure 7.1. Design Approaches

The baseline data collection involved a curriculum audit to identify EE issues and topics, the nature of the integration of the topics, and the adequacy of the number of topics integrated into the syllabus of the schools. This phase also involved the establishment of the pedagogical approaches being used to teach the environmental topics/themes in the school and the existing environmental literacy profiles of pupils.

The second phase involved the development of teaching materials and training of teachers and the development and pilot testing of instruments. The instruments developed were the ELT, used to establish the general level of environmental literacy of the pupils, and the Classroom Achievement Test (CAT), used to measure the knowledge and awareness of environmental issues taught in the classroom. The ELT was pilot tested to establish its validity and reliability, and the difficulty index and the discriminatory power of the CAT were calculated. This phase also involved the development of three different manuals on how to teach the identified topics using each of the three pedagogical approaches. The manuals contained materials in the form of lesson plans and directions on how to use the pedagogical approaches to teach the topics. A 1-day training was organized for the teachers on the use of the manuals.

In connection with role-play, the workshop involved the following: teachers' own preparation, an explanation of the activity to pupils and how to help the pupils to prepare for the role-play activities, and the identification of the major issues during a discussion after the role-play. With the inquiry approach, teachers were trained to identify relevant issues for investigation and to involve pupils to conduct investigations into such issues. The teachers were also taught to help pupils to organize learning activities and analyze data resulting from those activities. Concerning eco-management, the teachers were trained to involve pupils to identify projects related to environmental issues in the syllabus and that will be relevant to the school or the community. For example, in checking erosion on the school compound on the topic "Protecting the Environment," teachers had 35 minutes of peer-teaching practice on each of the approaches.

The last phase was the evaluation of the three pedagogical approaches included the introduction of an intervention in the experimental schools in the form of the use of role-play, inquiry, and eco-management to teach identified environmental topics for 11 weeks. The outcome of the use of the approaches, which measured their effectiveness, was then determined by the performance of pupils on the ELT and the CAT and the evaluation of teachers' opinions on the use of the approaches.

Instrumentation

Two major instruments were used in this study. These were

1. the ELT and
2. the CAT.

ELT

This instrument was developed to establish the general level of environmental literacy of the pupils. The ELT was developed based on the Student Environmental Literacy Assessment, adapted from a profile of EE in Wisconsin K–12 schools (1997) through the support of the Wisconsin Center for Environmental Education (WCEE). The ELT consisted of 34 items grouped under three main sections. Section A consisted of five items to obtain the background data of pupils. Section B consisted of 12 items that were used to measure pupils' ideas about the environment. Section C consisted of 17 items. These were used to measure what pupils did to manage the environment. The validity and reliability of the Environmental Literacy Test were determined through pilot test and internal consistency (WCEE, 1997). The result of the environmental audit was carried out on the syllabus in junior high schools in Ghana. To establish the validity and reliability of the ELT, a draft test was given to experts in curriculum development, EE, and social science for comments. The comments were used to finalize the instrument, which was pilot tested in selected schools in Accra. The Cronbach's alpha of the final instrument was 0.86.

CAT

A CAT was developed based on topics taught with the instructional techniques. A table of specification to ensure content validity was developed and the number of items covering the topics was identified. The difficulty index of all the items was calculated. All the items fell within 0.30 and 0.70, the recommended desirable difficulty index level for test items.

Data Collection

The focus of this study was to determine the effectiveness of contextualized pedagogical approaches in the teaching of environmental topics/themes in the syllabus of first-year junior high school students. Data were collected on the following issues: baseline conditions, intervention to determine the effectiveness of pedagogical approaches, and opinions of teachers on the use of pedagogical approaches. Three sets of baseline data were collected to determine the prevailing situation of EE in the junior high schools. These were a curriculum audit of first-year junior high school syllabus for environmental topics/themes, the establishment of the pedagogical approaches used, and the establishment of the environmental literacy profile of pupils. The baseline conditions established the EE already taking place across the curriculum in terms of the integration of environmental topics/themes into the syllabuses and how they must be taught.

To assess the effectiveness of the three pedagogical approaches, an intervention was introduced in the experimental schools in the form of teaching the same topics with the three pedagogical strategies using the relevant manuals as a guide. Teachers from the experimental schools were giving a 1-day training in the use of the guide and the assigned pedagogical approach. Data were collected from 12 schools: six experimental and six control schools. A pretest was administered to both control and experimental schools at the beginning of the term before they were taught the environmental topics/themes. Pupils from the experimental schools were taught the same environmental topics/themes for 11 weeks using the different pedagogical approaches. Two experimental schools were assigned to each pedagogical strategy while the control schools had no exposure to any of the approaches but continued using the existing traditional or conventional method of teaching in the schools. The lessons were taught as part of the teachers' regular lessons. A posttest was administered to both groups at the end of 11 weeks after all the environmental topics/themes had been taught. During the term, researchers monitored the two sets of schools to ensure that teaching of the topics was effectively done and monitored the instructional techniques in the control schools. The third stage involved an assessment of the opinions of teachers on the use of pedagogical approaches.

Results

Comparativeness of Experimental and the Control Groups

The comparativeness of both the experimental and the control groups was established by finding out the conditions in the schools. This involves an assessment of the curriculum and the teaching methodology. The comparativeness of their attitude and actions in relation to the environment was established by comparing their performance on ELT using an independent-sample *t* test before the intervention. Table 7.1 shows the environmental literacy profiles of experimental and control groups.

Table 7.1. Environmental Literacy Profiles of Experimental and Control Groups

	Pre-test						Post-test					
	Mean	*SD*	*N*	*F*	*t(df)*	*p*	*M*	*SD*	*N*	*F*	*t(df)*	*p*
Experimental	38.40	6.79	274	.029	-.444 (552)	.657	40.22	7.44	273	.009	3.126 (549)	.002
Control	38.66	6.96	280				38.24	7.40	278			
Total			554*						551*			

*: At pre-test 554 pupils participated in the study while at post-test three mortalities were recorded from the experimental group and two from the control group.

Curriculum Audit of the First-Year Junior High School Syllabus

The curriculum audit revealed that EE topics/themes were mainly integrated into social studies and integrated science. For social studies, 21 topics are presented, and 8 topics (accounting for 38%) have direct relevance to environmental issues. In integrated science, 24 topics are mapped out; three of them (accounting for 12.5%) are directly related to the environment. The teaching methodology in the schools was based on knowledge–attitude–behavior tradition.

Effects of Pedagogical Approaches on Pupils' Attitudes and Behaviors Toward the Environment

A paired-sample *t* test was conducted in both the experimental and the control groups to find out the impact of the intervention on pupils' ELT scores. The results indicated that the intervention produced a significant change in the attitudes and behaviors of pupils toward the environment. The results are summarized in Table 7.2. A second paired-sample *t* test was conducted to find the contribution of each pedagogical approach. Table 7.3 gives a summary of the results. With role-playing, there was no statistically significant increase in the scores of pupils on ELT from pretest to posttest. Concerning the inquiry approach, there was a statistically significant increase in pupils' scores on ELT from pretest to posttest on the environmental profile of pupils. The use of the eco-management approach produced a statistically significant increase in the pretest to posttest on the environmental profile of pupils.

Table 7.2. Impact of Intervention on Pupils' Environmental Literacy Profiles

	Pre-test			Post-test				
	M	*SD*	*N*	*M*	*SD*	*N*	*t(df)*	*p*
Experimental	38.41	6.794	274	40.22	7.437	273	2.898 (272)	.004
Control	38.63	6.975	280	38.24	7.396	281	.671 (277)	.503

Table 7.3. Contribution of Each Pedagogical Approach on the Pupils' Environmental Profiles

	Pre-test			Post-test				
Dependent Variable	*M*	*SD*	*N*	*M*	*SD*	*N*	*t(df)*	*p*
Role play	38.97	7.00	119	39.61	7.474	119	.655 (118)	.514
Inquiry	38.69	6.78	61	42.41	7.68	61	2.67 (60)	.01
Eco-management	37.52	6.65	93	39.56	7.02	93	2.11 (92)	.037

Effects of the Pedagogical Approaches on the Cognitive Knowledge of Some Environmental Issues

A two-way analysis of variance (ANOVA) was conducted to explore the effect of role-playing, inquiry, eco-management, traditional approaches, and gender on pupils' cognitive knowledge of the topics they were taught as measured by CAT. Table 7.4 shows the results of the ANOVA tests of the between-subjects effects of pedagogical approach and gender on the CAT. There was a statistically significant main effect on pupils' cognitive knowledge on the topics for the approaches, $F(3, 571) = 10.589$, $p = .00$; however, the effect size was small ($\eta^2 = .05$). Post hoc comparison was made using the Tukey Honestly Significant Difference (HSD) test. The comparison indicated that the mean score for the role play ($M = 9.61$, $SD = 2.69$) was significantly different from inquiry ($M = 8.31$, $SD = 2.29$, $p = .006$), eco-management ($M = 8.04$, $SD = 2.72$, $p = .00$), and traditional ($M = 8.12$, $SD = 2.50$, $p = .00$) approaches. The main effect for gender, $F(1, 571) = .003$, $p = .953$, did not reach statistical significance.

Table 7.4. ANOVA Tests of Between-Subjects Effects of Pedagogical Approach to Gender on the CAT

Dependent Variable: Scores on CAT

Source	Sum of Squares	df	Mean Square	F	Sig.
Approach	209.309	3	69.770	10.589	.000
Sex	.023	1	.023	.003	.953
Approach * Sex	7.043	3	2.348	.356	.785
Total	45267.000	579			

Computed using alpha = .05

Effects of Role-Play, Inquiry, Eco-Management, Traditional Approaches, and Gender on Pupils' Attitudes and Behaviors Toward the Environment

A two-way between-group of ANOVA was conducted to explore the effect of the role-play, inquiry, eco-management, traditional approaches, and gender on pupils' attitudes and behaviors toward the environment as measured by the ELT. The results are shown in Table 7.5. There was a statistically main significant effect for pedagogical approach, $F(3, 543) = 3.78$, $p = .01$. There was also a statistically significant main effect for gender, $F(1, 543) = 5.224$, $p = .02$. The effect size was however small ($\eta^2 = .01$). Post hoc comparison using the Tukey HSD test indicated that the mean scores for role-play ($M = 39.61$, $SD = 7.47$), inquiry ($M = 42.41$, $SD = 7.68$), and eco-management ($M = 39.56$, $SD = 7.02$) did not differ significantly from each other, but the inquiry approach differed significantly from the traditional approach ($M = 38.24$, $SD = 7.40$, $p = .00$).

Table 7.5. ANOVA Tests of Between-Subjects Effects of Pedagogical Approach and Gender on the ELT

Source	Sum of Squares	df	Mean Square	F	Sig.
Sex	283.116	1	283.116	5.224	.023
Approach	615.317	3	205.106	3.784	.010
Sex * Approach	194.520	3	64.840	1.196	.310
Total	878426.000	571			
Corrected Total	30733.543	550			

Computed using alpha = .05

Discussion

The results of the study are discussed under the following categories: effects of the contextualized pedagogical approaches on the cognitive knowledge of some environmental issues, effects of the pedagogical approaches on pupils' feelings/attitudes and behaviors/actions toward the environment, gender differences in feelings/attitudes, behaviors/actions toward the environment, and cognitive knowledge of environmental issues and teachers' opinion on the suitability of the approaches.

Effects of the Contextualized Pedagogical Approaches on the Cognitive Knowledge of Some Environmental Issues

The higher performance of the experimental group on the CAT was expected because the experimental group was taught with a set of pedagogical approaches that made the pupils the center of the learning processes. Children like to be involved in activities and are always happy and motivated if they discover something by themselves or learn from their peers instead of a threatening adult. In the approaches, teachers in the experimental schools were facilitators. In the control schools, on the contrary, the teachers assumed the central role and just presented information to pupils. Role-play contributed significantly to the difference that was observed in the scores of the experimental and the control groups. This was followed by the inquiry approach. However, contrary to what was expected, the traditional approach, which was used in the control group, was more effective than the eco-management. The observed difference may be because it was difficult for the teachers to use the eco-management approach because it involved acting to resolve some environmental issues.

Effects of the Pedagogical Approaches on Pupils' Feelings/Attitudes and Behaviors/Actions Toward the Environment

The environmental literacy profiles of pupils from the experimental group increased more than did the control group's after the implementation of the intervention strategy. This increase, however, was observed in the behavior/action environmental profile of pupils. The absence of change in the feeling/attitude environmental profile of pupils was expected because the period of intervention was short to notice any substantial change. Moral life, including environmental attitudes, either positive or negative, are formed in our communities through life (Noddings, cited in Goralnik et al., 2012). Values ingrained in children over the years will not take one term to change substantially. Perhaps the effect of the change could be exhibited in a much more profound way sometime after the intervention strategy. The scope of this study did not permit a follow-up test to ascertain this assertion. However, the significant main effect resulting from the pedagogical approaches indicated the effectiveness of the approaches in changing behaviors. Feelings/attitudes might take a longer time to change than behaviors/actions. As have been observed by the constructivists, the individual's personal belief systems, which lead to feelings and concerns (Ajzen, 1988), consist of their conception and intuitive understanding of the issue, which are not easily broken (Pines & West as cited in Ballantyne & Parker, 1996).

The inquiry approach contributed greatly to the significant change in the environmental profiles of pupils. This was followed by role-play and eco-management, respectively. The inquiry approach was the most effective of the pedagogical strategies because it involved taking pupils out for data collection. Children by nature like going out to collect things, and they like playing with them (Lim as cited in Apedoe & Reeves, 2006). They might have therefore been more interested in EE using this approach. They encounter real problems, and they become curious and start asking questions. The inquiry approach gives pupils the opportunity to provide answers to their queries to satisfy their curiosity. They gather data, observe, verify, and draw conclusions. They are motivated if their queries are answered from their own observations and conclusions.

Things are better learned by doing them than by listening. In doing, learners gain experience subjecting their own analyses to critical thinking, organizing, and making inferences and decisions. This approach helps children to make things they have learned real because the approach involves saying, writing, observing, hearing, and doing. Getting pupils to conduct inquiry is a way of showing them respect and therefore making them feel trusted and worthwhile. Bas et al. (2011) suggested that if EE is taught with the inquiry approach, students will understand scientific and environmental concepts easily and think clearly about the connection between environmental and economic issues in more detail. The use of role-play as a pedagogical approach in the teaching of environmental education was effective because it enabled the pupils to perceive practically the various components of the environment and the roles they play. Pupils also became involved in the lesson. Role-play helps to increase the level of basic school children's skills for clarifying environmental values, which is basic to the development of positive feelings/attitudes toward the environment (Bonnet, 2000). Role-plays also can develop pupils' skills to debate environmental values. In the role-play approach, pupils' involvement, practical perceptions of the components of the environment, and acting out roles are important factors in the EE teaching and learning process.

Eco-management involves more preparation than the other approaches, including the identification of relevant projects and how pupils can learn from the projects. A lot of cooperation is needed from the school administration and other teachers in the identification of projects. Teachers therefore have to put in extra time and effort to get projects for pupils. The manual given to teachers identified some of these projects, which helped teachers prepare for the lessons.

Gender Difference in Feelings/Attitudes, Behaviors/Actions Toward the Environment, and Cognitive Knowledge of Environmental Issues

The gender difference in pupils' feelings/attitudes, behaviors/actions toward the environment, and cognitive knowledge of environmental issues is expected. Hausbeck et al. (1992), Tikka et al. (cited in Lee, 2008) and Zelenzy et al. (cited in Lee, 2008) observed that females express more positive environmental attitudes than males do. Zelenzy et al. (cited in Bas et al., 2011) observed that females tend to be more caring, selfless, and concerned about many things around them while their male counterparts are more independent and cooperative. Women are considered to be better environmental managers and are generally more concerned than men are (Alp et al., cited in Bas et al., 2011; Eisler et al., cited in Bas et al., 2011; Ozden, cited in Bas et al., 2011; Taskin, cited in Bas et al., 2011; Tuncer et al., cited in Bas et al., 2011; Yilmaz et al., cited in Bas et al., 2011).

In rural areas in Ghana, women are involved in collecting water for household use, fuelwood extraction, weeding, agriculture work, and sanitation in the home and community. This may be due to the fact that women have been found across cultures to be more caring, cooperative, nurturing, and expressive (Williams & Best, cited in Lee, 2008) and therefore might have transferred these attributes to the environment. Again, children in Ghana are always trained by their mothers to maintain cleanliness in the home and communities by sweeping; women teach their children how to maintain the home by ensuring that there is potable water and fuelwood for cooking. Ghanaian women also see to it that their children keep themselves neat. They are also engaged in farming with their husbands and children. The schoolgirls, probably due to cultural practices, might have been more exposed to environmental issues than their male counterparts.

Equipping women with environmental management skills is very necessary for sustainable environmental management. In line with the higher scores of females on ELT, it is necessary to ensure that environmental education is integrated into a variety of subjects to ensure that no matter what subjects one is reading, environmental issues would be studied because in most African countries, boys and girls are tracked into different kinds of courses and careers that have built-in gender attitudes and distinctions. Furthermore, there is a need to encourage efforts to balance attention on EE for boys and girls to ensure that boys and girls pay equal attention to environmental conservation and preservation.

Teachers' Opinions About the Pedagogical Approaches

The teachers who used role-play commented that the method was very good because it enabled the pupils to practically perceive the various components of the environment and the roles they play. Pupils also became involved in the lesson. The teachers agreed that the role-play manual given to them was helpful because it provided them with materials that gave them resources to help pupils to prepare their various roles and it gave them clear directions. The problems teachers faced were inadequate teaching periods, pupils' inability to express themselves in English when playing roles, the large number of pupils in the class, and the level of teachers' preparation required for teaching the topic. The teachers who used the inquiry approach expressed the view that it could stimulate the interest of pupils and enhance learning. However, it was time-consuming, and it needed a lot of teaching and learning materials. The problems teachers faced were lack of teaching/learning materials, insufficient time for teaching, and an inability to make field visits. Mr. K. A. of St. Barnabas Anglican School, Osu, Ghana, expressed the view that the method, although useful, required a lot of preparation on the part of the teacher and required pupils to express themselves in the English language, which was difficult for them to do. However, he argued that the approach would be relevant for students in senior high schools (personal communication, April 21, 2018).

The teachers' observations seemed to suggest that the pupils were not mature enough to draw out inferences and conclusions from the data they gather, observe, and verify. Consequently, they believed that the approach was more suitable for senior high school. Observations by teachers were, however, not consistent with the result of the study. Again, the opinions of the teachers seemed to suggest that they were not predisposed to the use of the inquiry approach in the teaching/learning of EE in the basic schools. The approach proved effective in teaching environmental topics/themes probably because of the manual that gave teachers guidance and direction to play their facilitating roles more systematically and effectively.

Teachers who used eco-management expressed the view that it was effective in teaching the topics, although it was time-consuming and required a lot of teaching/learning materials and field trips. The problems encountered by the teachers were large classes of pupils, too much time needed by the teacher to prepare and present lessons, and difficulty in involving pupils. They felt the project work component of the methodology could help students to imbibe positive attitudes toward the environment if it is well understood and the students are given sufficient opportunities.

Conclusion

On the effectiveness of the three contextualized pedagogical strategies in the teaching of environmental topics/themes in junior high schools, the conclusion from the study is that role-play, inquiry, and eco-management as approaches to teaching environmental topics/themes are effective. From the opinions expressed by teachers, it seemed that they are not predisposed to the use of these pedagogical strategies in the teaching of environmental education. Teachers would therefore benefit from any program that will afford them the opportunity to acquire skills in the use of these strategies in teaching environmental topics/themes. Concerning gender difference as related to the teaching of environmental topics/themes integrated into the syllabus of schools, the conclusion of the study is that girls express more concern and feelings toward the environment than boys and can benefit from role-play, inquiry, and eco-management as pedagogies of EE that have the propensity of developing responsible environmental behavior in pupils. This conclusion is based on the result of the study that females expressed more positive environmental attitudes than males.

References

Ajzen, I. (1988). *Attitudes, personality and behaviour.* Open University Press.

Apedoe, X. S., & Reeves, T. (2006). Inquiry-based learning and digital libraries in undergraduate science education. *Journal of Science Education and Technology, 15*(5), 321–326.

Asabere-Ameyaw, A., Sefa, G. J., & Raheem, K. (2014). *Contemporary issues in African sciences and science education.* Sense Publishers.

Aslan Efe, H., Yucel, S., Baran, M., & Oner Sunkur, M. (2012). Influence of animation supported project-based instruction method on environmental literacy and self-efficacy in environmental education. *Asia-Pacific Forum on Science Learning and Teaching, 13*(2). Retrieved from https://pdfs.semanticscholar.org/1ed0/0bcabc67b731ae0a96af13e442be7a997b6c.pdf

Atsiatorme, L. D. (2011). *Effectiveness of three pedagogical approaches in the teaching of environmental education topics in junior high schools in Ghana* [Unpublished PhD thesis]. University of Education, Winneba, Ghana.

Ballantyne, R. R., & Packer, J. M. (1996). Teaching and learning in environmental education: Developing environmental conceptions. *Journal of Environmental Education, 27*(2), 25–32.

Bas, M., Teksoz, G., & Ertepinar, H. (2011). Emphasizing local features for effective environmental education: Environmental attitudes of elementary school students living in ancient Halicarnassus (Turkey). *Science Education International, 22*(2), 119–132.

Bonnet, C. (2000). *The relevance of role-playing in environmental education.* In Proceedings of the International Union of Biological Sciences Commission for Biological Education: International Symposium on Biological Education IUFM Versailles, Centre de Cergy, France. Retrieved from http://citeseerx.ist.psu.edu/viewdoc/download?doi=10.1.1.496.7916&rep=rep1&type=pdf

Environmental Protection Council (EPC). (1988). *Ghana Environmental Action Plan Vol 1.* Accra, Ghana.

Goralnik, K., Millenbah, N., & Thorp, L. (2012). An environmental pedagogy of care: Emotion, relationships, and experience in higher education ethics learning. *Journal of Experiential Education, 35*(3), 412–428.

Hausbeck, K., Milbrath, L., & Enright, S. (1992). Environmental knowledge, awareness and concern among 11th-grade students: New York State. *Journal of Environmental Education, 24*(1), 27–34.

Lane, J. (2012). Toward a model of embodied environmental education: Perspectives from theatre and Indigenous knowledges. *Journal of Experiential Education, 35*(3), 395–411.

Lee, K. (2008). Making communications meaningful to female adolescents. *Science Communication, 30*(2), 147–176.

Ozsoy, S., Ertepinar, H., & Saglam, N. (2012). Can eco-schools improve elementary school students' environmental literacy levels? *Asia-Pacific Forum on Science Learning and Teaching, 13*(2), 1–25.

Preston, L. (2011). Green pedagogy – guidance and doubt in teaching outdoor and environmental education. *Asia-Pacific Journal of Teacher Education, 39*(4), 367–380.

Robottom, I., & Hart, P. (1993). *Research in environmental education: Engaging the debate.* Deakin University.

Short, P. (2010). Responsible environmental action: Its role and status in environmental education and environmental quality. *The Journal of Environmental Education, 41*(1), 7–21.

Simataa, S. (2015, 10-12 December). *The role of culture in the implementation of the 2030 Agenda for Sustainable Development* [Hangzhou, People's Republic of China]. The International Conference on Culture for Sustainable Cities, Hangzhou, China.

Stern, M., Powell, R., & Ardoin, N. (2011). Evaluating a constructivist and culturally responsive approach to environmental education for diverse audiences. *The Journal of Environmental Education, 42*(2), 109–122.

United Nations Educational Scientific and Cultural Organisation (UNESCO). (1978). The Tbilisi Declaration. *Connect, 3*(1), 1–8.

United Nations Educational Scientific and Cultural Organisation (UNESCO). (1985). *Environmental education: Module for pre-service training of social science teachers and supervisors for secondary schools.*

Wisconsin Center for Environental Education (WCEE). (1997). *A profile of environmental education in Wisconsin K-12 Schools based on statewide surveys and assesments of students, teachers, curriculum, coordinators, and principals.* Stevens Point: Wisconsin Center for Environmental Education.

CHAPTER 8

Global Anti-Blackness and Resistance: Implications for Educating African Learners

Rowena Linton

In 1959, at the age of 9, Ken Morgan arrived in the United Kingdom from Jamaica as a British subject. Jamaica gained independence 3 years later. Morgan grew up and established life in the United Kingdom. Years later, Morgan returned to Jamaica to attend a family member's funeral, however, upon returning to the United Kingdom, Morgan's British passport was confiscated without explanation. Unable to persuade the British High Commission that he was British, he was denied entry. After years of financial struggles, Morgan reestablished life in Jamaica as a local store owner. In 2018, the British High Commission offered Morgan a visa to visit Britain. Although Morgan was happy to return to his childhood neighborhood in Britain, he suspected that this offer was Britain's attempt to conceal damaging Windrush revelations ("Windrush Scandal," 2018; "Windrush Victim Back Home," 2018). Similarly, Hubert Howard was born in Jamaica and died 3 weeks after finally being granted British citizenship. Howard arrived in London in 1960 at the age of 3 and lived there for 59 years. Howard, who had not left the United Kingdom since his arrival, only realized that there were issues with his residency status when his employer requested that he show that he was living in the United Kingdom legally. Shortly after, he tried to acquire a passport in order to visit his sick mother in Jamaica, but immigration officials indicated that there was no record of him and warned that if he left the United Kingdom, he would not be allowed back into the country. His mother died before he was able to see her again. In 2012, Howard was dismissed from his job because he was unable to prove his legal status in the United Kingdom and consequently died in debt (Loop News, 2019).

Morgan and Howard were among the many Black children who arrived in the United Kingdom with their parents from the Caribbean in the 1950s as colonial subjects. The United Kingdom was commonly referred to as the "mother country" by Caribbean colonial subjects (see Ramrayka, 2020). Those migrating included individuals whose parents fought in the two World Wars for Britain and others who were invited to rebuild the country in different industries. Upon settling in the United Kingdom, most of these individuals faced a significant number of challenges, racism, discrimination, and later deportation. They worked and built lives in the United Kingdom, but years later, having only known Britain as "home," they were publicly humiliated upon learning that they were illegal immigrants. This open humiliation, famously known as the Windrush scandal, broke in April 2018 (The Joint Council for the Welfare of Immigrant, n.d.). This scandal is of particular interest to me as it finally explains why so many Jamaicans ended up in the United Kingdom. Strangely, when I first read about the Windrush scandal, it took me back to my primary school education received in Jamaica that had a heavy British influence and that I now view as a colonial product.

As I recall, the education system in Jamaica modeled British standards. In many instances, Britain was depicted as the hub of education, economic, and social opportunities, and very often individuals who excelled academically hopped on the opportunity to migrate to Britain. However, the same education failed to reveal the harsh reality that some migrants faced on settling in Britain. The case of the Windrush scandal makes one question the role education plays in (re)producing systems and structures that devalue Blackness within society. For me, as an anticolonial, antiracist scholar, history plays an important role in helping me understand the impacts of colonialism, ongoing colonization, or the changing face of racism. This chapter focuses mainly on Blackness, anti-Blackness, and education, particularly how Black and African students, especially in the diaspora, experienced and continue to experience schooling through a colonial education system and curriculum. Nevertheless, there remains a deafening silence and denial of anti-Blackness and its damaging effects on Black students' experience. In discussing the urgent need for decolonial education, I draw on reggae music, which embodies as a legitimate form of decolonization against colonial structures.

Global Anti-Blackness

The Windrush scandal captures the systematic control of Black bodies and represents anti-Black racism that is present in the United Kingdom and varyingly around the globe. Anti-Black racism speaks to practices that reinforce beliefs, attitudes, and prejudice toward people of African descent. It refers to a negative reading of the Black/African body, particularly a reading that is framed by racist thoughts such as Blacks as laborers and subalterns (see Dei, 1996; Dei & Linton 2019; Dei & Vasquez, 2017). In the case of the Windrush scandal, Black bodies are read as valuable to work and build the economy but not valuable enough to obtain citizenship and legal protection from the state. Put another way, Black bodies are permitted insofar as they serve the economic interests of the state or the ruling elites. Such a reading robs Black people of humanity and dignity, reducing them to subhumans or commodities. Notably, a similar logic was used to enslave people of African descent. Although slavery has been a part of different civilizations throughout history, the transatlantic slave trade was unparalleled in vehemently disrupting and damaging the humanhood of people of African descent. For some three centuries, millions of innocent people from the continent of Africa were kidnapped, forced out of their homes, and transported across the Atlantic Ocean to the Americas by European slave traders. Many of their children were born into slavery and spent their whole lives as subhuman or property working to build Britain and the Americas (Davis, 2010). Ranked as one of history's greatest crimes against humanity, slavery robbed these people of their mortality, identity, pride, and right to their own way of life.

Although our Black communities are still dealing with the stifling impacts of transatlantic slavery, some of its tenets are still governing contemporary society. For instance, slavery turned African captives into transatlantic commodities in the same way entertainment and sports industries today commodify Blackness and the Black body. Saidiya Hartman (Hartman & Wilderson, 2003) discusses the Black body as the property of enjoyment. Entertainment industries bloom significantly off Black bodies' athleticism and Black culture but still deny them of the mental intellectual capacity of the Black personhood. Furthermore, these industries provide no insurance or genuine protection for these Black bodies once they are no longer of service. They are tossed like the slaves were in the Zong Massacre (see Dei & Vasquez, 2017; Hartman & Wilderson, 2003; Smallwood, 2007). Modern variations of slavery are still a part of society but packaged and labeled differently. One of the long-term effects of slavery is the widespread contempt and even racist hatred for people of African descent (Davis, 2010). This hatred also reproduces the belief that Black people are less than White and any other people; it has made segregated schools acceptable, mass incarceration possible, and the rapidly increasing police violence permissible. Anti-Black racism is so enmeshed in the fabric of society, yet it is still being ignored by the masses and almost completely erased from discussions on racism (Dei, 1996; Ladson-Billing, 1998).

Anti-Blackness is a global phenomenon. First, all forms of racism are rooted in anti-Blackness. Take, for instance, colorism—which is a type of discrimination among people of the same ethnicity in which lighter skin is privileged over darker skin—so a regular adage in contemporary society such as "Filipinos are the Blacks of Asia" is derived from anti-Blackness. Ironically, some of these non-Black communities subscribe to the negatives stereotypes about Black people and will distance themselves to maintain some degree of power (see Newton, 2017). In some instances, many non-Black communities around the world still settle with the Europeans narratives of Africa and its people as supposedly dark, uncivilized, deviant, and criminal world (Dei, 2017). Consequently, this provides the prescription for the treatment of African people despite their geographical location.

Many other groups and communities have experienced varying forms of oppression, cruelty, and inhumane treatment throughout civilized society; however, the experiences of Black people across the globe have been unmatched. Irrespective of social status or social context, displacement, excluded, and inferiorized are common experiences of Black people around the world. In some instances, anti-Blackness is the mass killing of Black bodies. For example, every 23 minutes a Black youth is murdered in Brazil (Vinícius, 2017). In India, there have been many reported instances of students of African descent being persecuted. Ezeugo Nnamdi, secretary general at Africa-Asia Youth Foundation in Central Delhi, shared that Africans in India believe that history in South Asia is rife with anti-Blackness, and just having Black skin is a badge of guilt to many Indians (Balram, 2019). Anti-Blackness is even perpetuated in popular culture and entertainment in India. For example, in the Indian film, *Fashion* (Bhandarkar et al., 2008), an ambitious small-town girl, played by actress Priyanka Chopra, wants to make it big in the fashion industry as a supermodel. After turning to different vices, that is, drugs and alcohol, as she struggled to reach the top, the worst of her situation was sleeping with the Black man. Although often hypersexualized, the Black man here symbolizes the worst of all evils (Balram, 2019; "Esha Gupta: Has Instagram", 2019). In South Africa, Black communities still experience racial discrimination, which is remnant of the apartheid era of racial hierarchy and tensions. Regardless of the region, race disparity widens for especially the Black population (Cupido, 2019). Statistics across countries with a small Black population often indicate that Black people are more likely to be stopped and searched by police than their White other counterparts, to be held in custody, or to be unemployed. Similarly, Black students often experience racial discrimination on school grounds and college and university campuses around the world.

The United States has a long history of overt, institutional, and systemic discrimination against not just Blacks communities but other ethnic groups as well. Racism against Black communities in the United States began with a structured institution of slavery. America's economy thrived off slavery; subsequently, slavery helped to build the world's economy. After slavery was abolished (1865), new forms of legal structures ensured that Blacks were legally marginalized and separated from the general populace through segregated institutions, services, and opportunities, including military, employment, housing, medical care, and education (Constitutional Rights Foundation, n.d.). Although labeled as the postracial era, today, there are still extreme manifestations of discrimination against Black people in the United States. In the United States, Black women, men, and youth make up a disproportionate amount of the prison population, with police brutality continuing to plague Black communities (Morris, 2014). Because of the severity of racism in America, most people fail to recognize racism within their local context or rationalize that their racism is not as bad as their American counterparts.

In Canada, racism surfaces as more sophisticated and covert. Although a multicultural state, Black people continue to experience exclusion and discrimination in Canada, yet in many cases, it is denied (Howard, 2018; Patel, 2018; Phillips & Pon, 2018). Diversity, inclusion, and cultural tolerance are among Canada's cultural strengths; however, this approach also certifies the myth that racism does not exist in Canada. In some Canadian history textbooks, it is evident that people of African descent have been historically excluded from Canada's grand narrative. For example, although initially rejected from fighting in the two World Wars, Black men were only "allowed" to fight at the shortage of soldiers. Upon return, these veterans were relegated to "less than human" and subjected to discrimination and violence in Canada (N. Henry, 2019; Winks, 1997). Furthermore, research on Canada's Black population confirms the long-standing institutional and systemic disadvantages that Black communities continue to endure, although multicultural rhetoric, inclusion, and diversity strategies often make it more difficult to be detected and subsequently be addressed (Ahmed, 2012; Clément 2018; Dei, 2017; F. Henry et al., 2017).

Theorizing Anti-Blackness

> *Human life is dependent on Black death for its existence and for its conceptual coherence. There is no world without Blacks, yet there are no Blacks who are in the world.*
>
> —FRANK WILDERSON III (2016, PARA. 10)

Blackness is an identity and experience with shared, contested, and contingent histories and specific geographies. It is an identification that comes with a political consciousness, Black agency, and resistance. Although weaponized, Blackness is knowledge about politics, culture, history, and present understandings of the experiences of Black and African people. Simone Browne (2015) locates conditions of Blackness as a key site through which surveillance is practiced, narrated, and resisted (see Browne, 2015; Dei, 2017, 2018; Sexton 2011, 2015; Sharpe 2016; Walcott, 2003). Any effort to depreciate or inferiorize Blackness is anti-Blackness. Anti-Black racism and anti-Blackness are interconnected, but anti-Blackness is the denial of the unique challenges Black people face in society and failure to acknowledge the various interconnected ways in which people of African descent are contextually, systematically, and institutionally marginalized. It is tiptoeing around matters relating to Blackness; it is addressing racism but ignoring the Black experience; it is positioning Blacks as deficient and in need of being saved. Anti-Blackness reveals the specific kind of racial prejudice and hatred directed toward only Black people, even though it is manifested differently in the diverse contexts. Michael Dumas and Kihana Ross (2016) argue that anti-Blackness is not simply racism against Black people; rather, anti-Blackness refers to a broader antagonistic relationship between Blackness and (the possibility) of humanity. Anti-Blackness is an embodied lived experience of social suffering and resistance, in which the Black is a despised thing in itself (but not the person for him- or herself) in opposition to all that is pure, human(e), and White (Dumas, 2014; Dumas & Ross, 2016).

Frank B. Wilderson III (2016), in his essay "Afro-Pessimism and the End of Redemption," discusses the tenets of Afro-pessimism in relation to the condition of slavery, Blackness, and Black nonexistence. He defines Afro-pessimism as an ontological account of White supremacy and the tenacity, perdurance, and radicality of anti-Blackness. He also states that it clarifies the irreconcilable difference among the violence of capitalism, gender oppression, and White supremacy in contrast to the violence of anti-Blackness. Although believed to be cynical, especially based on the premise that Afro-pessimism positions that Black people today are not viewed differently than slaves and that is it critical in how we understand and talk about Black people, Afro-pessimism is rather a useful lens to help understand the global anti-Blackness present in current society. For some people, the reference point for Black people is slavery. The history of slavery is true to the Black experience irrespective of regions, country, social status, and political affiliation; however, it is dangerous to use this as a prescription for the treatment of all Black people or as the marker of the beginning Black people's existence. Moreover, it is unfitting to interpret this as anything more than an interruption to Black history. Dumas (2016) asserts that Afro-pessimism theorizes that Black people exist in a structurally antagonistic relationship with humanity. That is, the very technologies and imaginations that allow a social recognition of the humanness of others systematically exclude this possibility for Blacks.

Seemingly contrasting to Afro-pessimism is Black optimism. Black optimism rejects the notion that Black people, as the historical subjects of slavery and colonialism, are pure absence; the artifact of imposition and negation; a socially dead, nonhuman, pathological entity without remainder (Hart, 2018; Moten, 2008; Sexton, 2012, 2015). Rather than pathologizing Blackness, Black optimism speaks to the inclination to hope. Psychological definitions of both optimism and pessimism tend to deal with confidence and motivation in dealing with life and possibilities, present or lack thereof. Whereas pessimism expresses doubt, hesitancy, or a general disposition that focuses on the dark side, optimism symbolizes confidence, hope, and persistence, especially in the face of adversaries. Scholars indicate that both Afro-pessimism and Black optimism offer juxtaposing responses to anti-Blackness, even though they both seem to share similar understandings and views of how capitalism, racism, and White supremacy function in society (Sexton, 2011). Anti-Blackness theory emerged from Afro-pessimism and Black optimism, which both, complementarily, help to explain the social reality of Black people around the globe. Black optimism takes into consideration that while slavery and capitalism continue to plague the Black experiences, it is not enough to focus solely on the deficiencies; rather, it prioritizes Blackness and resistance and the hope and optimism often displayed by Black people in the face of despair. Wilderson (2016) argues that Blackness is essential to human existence. Whether as colonial subject, Black death, or the absented-presence Blackness has in society, he states that there is no world without Blacks, yet there are no Blacks who are in the world. Black optimism spotlights this vitality of Blackness in ways that will affect positive changes and garner different outcomes. Although a deeper examination of the influence and contribution of both frameworks is beyond the scope of this chapter, both are important considerations for understanding anti-Blackness globally.

Global Anti-Blackness in Education and School

The work of many critical race and anticolonial scholars affirms that the crisis of anti-Black racism in schools persists across generations (see Dei 1996; Dumas, 2014, 2016; James & Turner, 2017; Ladson-Billing, 1998; Maynard, 2017; Walcott, 2003). Education, whether formal or informal, has always been a part of civilization; it ensures learning and the acquisition of knowledge, skills, values, beliefs, and habits considered essential in society. Education is important for nation building. Especially through formal education, individuals learn the skills deemed necessary for survival in society. As a vital element in society, it is important to question how education constructs and preserves some of the issues present in society and globally. Based on the premise of Afro-pessimism (discussed earlier) and colonialism, which gave birth to global prejudice toward people of African descent, education about colonialism and its relatives should then be analyzed to investigate how education shapes and preserves anti-Blackness globally.

For many, colonialism is characterized as a good thing, justified in the name of modernization and advancement. Rules, regulations, policies, and practices of the colonizers were imposed on colonies. As mentioned earlier, in Jamaica and other former colonies of Britain, the education system and its administration are fashioned after the British system. As a result, curriculum resources in the Caribbean still inform students that Christopher Columbus "discovered" Jamaica and highlight all the benefits the country reaped under British rule. With this colonial education still entrenched in the fabric of Jamaican society, a recent survey revealed that approximately 60% of Jamaicans believe that the country would be in a better state, especially economically, if still under Britain rule (Wallace, 2011). Colonial education in the Jamaican context blindfolds the Jamaican people, preserving a culture and mindset of dependency.

Growing up in Jamaica, this message was commonly reflected in reggae music. This genre of music originated in the late 1960s in Jamaica and is closely tied to Rastafarianism, which is an Africentric faith system developed in Jamaica in the 1930s. A common theme in reggae music is criticizing colonialism. Reggae music and Rastafarian subculture for the mass were, and possibly still are, deemed as controversial, oppositional, and marginalized by society. However, reggae artists continue to challenge government systems and institutions. In fact, the colonial education system was regarded as untrue and a tool for brainwashing and distracting people from the truth. For example, Burning Spear ("This Man—Burning Spear," n.d., para. 8) sings about the systems failing to tell the people about their roots:

It's the system, the system, the system
Any nation without their roots
Is like the trees without their root
Any nation without their roots
Is like the trees without their root

Reggae artists would conclude that colonial education systems obscure the well-being of Jamaicans and continue to diminish our ancestral heritage.

In the North American context, colonial education has spared children from the terrible reality about slavery in U.S. history whereas in Canada, the existence of a slave or its colonial past is completely erased from the Canadian grand narrative. In place of historical precision, curricula and textbooks tend to highlight the victor's triumphs and tactics in a way that legitimizes the violence inflicted on people of African descent during slavery. In some American textbooks, slavery is lightly described as another "pattern of immigration" and slaves are referred to as "workers" from Africa to the southern United States to work on agricultural plantations (Helm, 2019). Amid public outcry, one textbook publisher later apologized for what was deemed an editorial error (Helm, 2019). However, this "mistake" aligns suspiciously with the global anti-Blackness within the social structure. Curriculum planning and development have clear ideas of the nation's developmental goals and social and political realities that are subsequently reflected in curricula. In the same way, education policies, processes, and implementation are also intentional. Therefore, anti-Blackness, which is deeply rooted in education, is not merely by chance but perhaps is structured.

In the literature on Black student experience in the Canadian public education system, Black students are labeled as "at risk" or as unintelligent, treated as inferior, or make up the vast majority of students in special education or gifted programs, suspended or expelled at disproportionately higher rates than their counterparts, have access to inadequate resources, and lower graduation rates (see Dei et al., 1997; James & Turner, 2017; Maynard, 2017). However, anti-Blackness in education is more than the symptoms that Black students experience in schools. Rather, it speaks to the structural and systemic efforts to blindfold Black students and to conceal the truth about their history, identity, and ancestors. Dumas (2016) states that education policy, as a site of anti-Blackness, speaks fundamentally to acknowledging the long history of the Black struggle for educational opportunity, which is to say a struggle against what has always been (and continues to be) a struggle against specific anti-Black ideologies, discourses, representations, (mal)distribution of material resources, and physical and psychic assaults on Black bodies in schools.

Implications for Educating African Learners

Experiences of racism combined with other social and economic factors have been proved to negatively impact the physical, emotional, and psychological health and well-being of African people. Anti-Black racism is the invisible institutional hand that Dei (1996) mentions as pushing out Black African youth from schools at alarming rates, thus destroying their dreams. I hereby outline the following implications for educating African learners: (a) continue efforts to reclaim a diverse Africa, (b) encourage African learners to be more critical of international influence and to analyze the ways in which they may continue colonial projects or obstruct decolonial politics, and (c) ensure young people to embrace their African roots and defy other narratives that portray Africa and Blackness as limited, catastrophic, and destitute.

Colonial education tends to separate the diaspora, for example, Jamaica, from the continent of Africa. The practice of prioritizing Western knowledge while silencing or erasing African influence and knowledge has led to some Black people in the diaspora disassociating themselves from Africa and condemning African knowledge. Dei (2017) states that there is an urgency of reinventing an Africanness in diasporic contexts; therefore, Black and African bodies should continue to challenge the constructed tension between continental Africa and diasporic Black communities and quickly dismantle any urge to divide our community based on identity or differences. Second, the transatlantic slave trade radically impaired Africa's potential to develop economically and shattered African communities while Britain, on the other hand, greatly benefited (M'baye, 2007). Similarly, the Windrush migration, which in some ways was disguised as providing economic opportunities to Caribbean people, instead supplied Britain with "laborers" to help rebuild the economy, but Britain later mistreated them. It is therefore important to examine the opportunities offered to Black/African communities as to ensure that they are not masked to reproduce or maintain anti-Blackness and further destruction of the continent and diaspora. Finally, as African learners and scholars, we have a responsibility to tell the stories of precolonial Africa, Blackness as powerful, Black resistance, resilience, and hope. This kind of education can also embrace alternative forms of knowledge sharing and allows Black students to engage with critical scholarship on Black power and pride and Black economics, which are typically divorced from the stifling slave narratives commonly found in colonial education. This will help demolish the sense of hopelessness buried in most conventional teaching and learning practice; it is also a part of decolonization.

Anti-Blackness, Decolonization, and Resistance

Anti-Blackness and decolonization are not just temporary or trendy rhetoric but, rather, are critical ongoing processes. For many, decolonization is imagining a different possibility; it is a way of being that interrogates colonial structures and power, it is uncomfortable, but it is also necessary. Decolonization can be framed and led by these three Rs: remedial, resistance, and restorative, taking into consideration the history of violence, dispossession, and oppression. In no particular order, remedial involves acknowledging the historical violence inflicted on Black bodies, educating, and making efforts to reclamation and restructuring. As decolonization is taking place within the current colonial systems, resistance is crucial to the process. Indeed, resistance and decolonial work can be emotionally exhausting; therefore, as a community, restorative practices should always be a part of what we do. Even amid violence, it is necessary to hope to be present and for healing to take place (hooks, 2003).

What does remedial look like in the decolonization process? In accordance with transformative ideologies, colonial structures must be deconstructed and reconstructed. This can be represented through new laws and policies recognizing colonial logic and offering restitution. In 2003, Brazilian federal education legislation passed Law 10,639/03 as an acknowledgment and proposed remedy to the Eurocentric Brazilian educational system. This law represents a significant moment in the institutionalization of ethno-racial policies in Brazil over the past 15 years. It makes obligatory the teaching of African and Black Brazilian history and culture in all school subjects and requires in-depth study of Black contributions in the social, economic, and political spheres. The law also requires that school curricula develop in-depth engagements with Black participation in national society so as to make visible their contributions in social, economic, and political spheres (Da Costa, 2016). In the same way, there needs to be more laws and policies, perhaps international laws, which at most acknowledge how the enslavement of African people was the economic engine of the world and the role colonialism plays in the current social order of global society. Furthermore, new policies will sanction education and critical integrated learning and, moreover, dismantle false narratives about Blackness that are embedded in a colonial curriculum, textbooks, and language.

Reggae music captures resistance and it is restorative. By its very nature, reggae music embodies decolonization and resistance. Generally, reggae music refuses to condone the degradation of Africa. As discussed earlier, reggae as an art form has been challenging colonialism and imperialism from its inception in the 1960s. Because of its resistance basis, reggae music has been condemned by many mainstream institutions, religions, schools, and so on. Nevertheless, the genre remains committed to unconventional storytelling and has always promoted knowledge and critical learning for the youth. Reggae music combines both Afro-pessimism and Black optimism to deal with the colonial structures in Jamaica. On one hand, Afro-pessimism is present in the sense that the genre frequently references slavery while speaking out against government and systematic corruptions, hardships, and barriers recurring in Jamaica society. At the same time, reggae artists sing about hope, unity, Black pride, and truth. Essentially, reggae artists refuse to promote the colonial narrative of African and Black communities as deficient or deficit (Dei, 2017). An example is depicted in contemporary reggae artist Chronixx's "Black is Beautiful" (2017, para. 2):

> We love the children of Africa
> Teaching the children
> Black eye, Black hair, Black skin
> Black queen stands majestic with the Black king
> Today I'll sing you a Black song, you need to hear about beautiful Black things
> 'cause most time we hear about Black, we hear about Black magic and Black
> witches, Blacklist, Black book, Black market
> Black Friday, ya spend off your Black riches
> I've never seen a doctor in Black nor seen a Black pill fi cure no Black people . . .
> So, when the little offspring asking, tell them . . .

Although rebellious and celebratory, reggae is also lively and uplifting, which captures the final "R" of the decolonization process, that is, restorative. Whether for natural therapy or its positive energy, reggae is also about love and healing, which are often cited in the lyrics; for example, reggae artist Sizzla states in his song "Bless Up" ("Sizzla—Bless Up," n.d., para. 7), "Only love is di answer, and [Rastafari] always conquer."

Conclusion

I started this chapter with the case of the Windrush scandal. Growing up in Jamaica, colonial education regarded the United Kingdom as the "motherland"; however, decolonial education will teach the reverse. Whenever I am asked if there will ever be an antiracist curriculum or a decolonized education system, without hesitation, I share my confidence in a Black future which is different from the now. I demonstrated earlier that anti-Black racism and violence against Black bodies have been a part of Black history, but it is not the only history. Therefore, I based this critical optimism on history. Ending chattel slavery may have seemed impossible for some enslaved, but it was eventually abolished. Although slavery was eventually abolished, mostly on economic grounds, we cannot discredit the strategies employed by the enslaved to rebel against the institution. Throughout history, Black communities have and continue to resist against structural oppression using creative forms. I believe a critical step to moving forward is through education. Education should create opportunities to engage in honest and very specific conversations about Black bodies, Blackness, Black historical memories, and Black resistance. Black and African scholars have a responsibility to create legitimate spaces of power for Black people to develop and maintain liberatory practices.

References

Ahmed, S. (2012). *On being included: Racism and diversity in institutional life.* Duke University Press.

Bhandarkar, M. (Director), Monga, A., Iyengar, N, Tiwari, A., Nath, S., Siddiqui, I., & Ghorpade, A. (Writers). (2008). *Fashion* [Film]. Bhandarkar Entertainment.

Balram, D. (2019, April 9). *Violence towards Africans in India has roots in Anti-Blackness that has existed for centuries.* Media Diversified. https://mediadiversified.org/2019/04/09/violence-towards-africans-in-india-has-roots-in-anti-blackness-that-has-existed-for-centuries/

Browne, S. (2015). *Dark matters: On the surveillance of Blackness.* Duke Review University Press.

This Man—Burning Spear. (n.d.). *Genius.* https://genius.com/Burning-spear-this-man-lyrics

Chronixx—Black is Beautiful. (2017). *Genius.* https://genius.com/Chronixx-black-is-beautiful-lyrics

Clément, D. (2018). Review of the book *The Equity Myth: Racialization and Indigeneity at Canadian Universities,* by Frances Henry et al. Labour / Le Travail, *81,* 285–287.

Constitutional Rights Foundation. (n.d.). *Southern Black codes.* https://www.crf-usa.org/brown-v-board-50th-anniversary/southern-black-codes.html

Cupido, C. (2019, September 24). *In her own words: Confronting anti-Blackness in South Africa.* Global Citizen. https://www.globalcitizen.org/en/content/cape-town-flats-coloured-identity-south-africa/

Da Costa, A. (2016). Training educators in anti-racism and pluriculturalismo: Recent experiences from Brazil. *Race Ethnicity and Education, 19*(1), 23–45.

Davis, D. (2010). Foreword. In D. Eltis, D. Richardson, D. Davis, & D. Blight, *Atlas of the transatlantic slave trade* (pp. xvii–xxii). Yale University Press. www.jstor.org/stable/j.ctt5vm1s4.4

Dei, G. J. S. (1996). *Anti-racism education in theory and practice.* Fernwood Publishing.

Dei, G. J. S. (2017). *Reframing Blackness and Black solidarities through anti-colonial and decolonial prisms.* Springer.

Dei, G. J. S. (2018). "Black like me": Reframing Blackness for decolonial politics. *Educational Studies, 54*(2), 117–142, doi:10.1080/00131946.2018.1427586

Dei, G. J. S., & Linton, R. (2019). Racism in schools and classrooms: Towards an anti-racist pedagogy of power and systemic privilege. In A. Julé (Ed.), *The compassionate educator: Understanding social issues and the ethics of care in Canadian schools* (pp. 271–293). Canadian Scholars Press.

Dei, G. J. S., Mazzuca, J., McIsaac, E., & Zine, J. (1997). *Reconstructing 'dropout': A critical ethnography of the dynamics of Black students' disengagement from school.* University of Toronto Press.

Dei, G. J. S., & Vasquez, A. (2017). The foundation of transformative anti-racism: A conversation. *Canada Education, 57*(3), 50–52.

Dumas, M. J. (2014). "Losing an arm": Schooling as a site of Black suffering. *Race Ethnicity and Education, 17*(1), 1–29. doi:10.1080/13613324.2013.850412

Dumas, M. J. (2016). Against the dark: Anti-Blackness in education policy and discourse. *Theory Into Practice, 55*(1), 11–19. doi:10.1080/00405841.2016.1116852

Dumas, M. J., & Ross, K. M. (2016). Be real Black for me: Imagining BlackCrit in education. *Urban Education, 51*(4), 415–442.

Esha Gupta: Has Instagram exposed everyday racism in India? (2019, February 1), BBC News. Retrieved from https://www.bbc.com/news/world-asia-india-47042681

Fanon, F. (1968). *The wretched of the earth.* Grove Press.

Hart, W. D. (2018). Constellations: Capitalism, antiblackness, Afro-pessimism, and Black optimism. *American Journal of Theology & Philosophy, 39*(1), 5–33.

Hartman, S., & Wilderson, F. B., III. (2003). The position of the unthought. *Qui Parle, 13*(2), 183–201.

Helm, J. (2019). Teaching America's truth. *Washington Post.* https://www.washingtonpost.com/education/2019/08/28/teaching-slavery-schools/?arc404=true

Henry, F., James, C., Li, P. S., Kobayashi, A. L., Smith, M., Ramos, H., & Enakshi, D. (2017). *The equity myth: Racialization and indigeneity at Canadian universities.* UBC Press.

Henry, N. L. (2019, May 28). Racial segregation of Black people in Canada. In *The Canadian Encyclopedia, Historica Canada.* https://www.thecanadianencyclopedia.ca/en/article/racial-segregation-of-Black-people-in-canada

hooks, bell. (2003). *Teaching community: A pedagogy of hope.* Routledge.

Howard, P. S. (2018). On the back of Blackness: contemporary Canadian blackface and the consumptive production of post-racialist, White Canadian subjects. *Social Identities, 24*(1), 87–103.

James, C. E., & Turner, T. (2017). *Towards race equity in education: The schooling of Black students in the Greater Toronto Area.* York University.

The Joint Council for the Welfare of Immigrant. (n.d.). *Windrush scandal explained.* https://www.jcwi.org.uk/windrush-scandal-explained

Ladson-Billings, G. (1998). Just what is critical race theory and what's it doing in a nice field like education? *International Journal of Qualitative Studies in Education, 11*(1), 7–24, doi:10.1080/095183998236863

Loop News. (2019, November 25). *Anger after Jamaican Windrush victim dies without compensation.* http://www.looptt.com/content/anger-after-jcan-windrush-victim-dies-without-receiving-compensation-3

M'baye, B. (2006). The economic, political, and social impact of the Atlantic slave trade on Africa. *The European Legacy, 11*(6), 607–622.

Maynard, R. (2017). *Policing Black lives: State violence in Canada from slavery to the present.* Fernwood Publishing.

Moten, F. (2008). The case of Blackness. *Criticism, 50*(2), 177–218.

Morris, M. (2014). *Black stats: African Americans by the numbers in the twenty-first century.* The New Press.

Newton, J. (2017) Anti-Black racism, resistance, and the health and well-being of Black bodies in public education. In J. Newton & A. Soltani (Eds.), *New Framings on Anti-Racism and Resistance: Volume 2—Resistance and the new futurity* (pp. 45–64). Sense Publishers.

Patel, A. (2018). 3 reasons why anti-Blackness still exists in multicultural cities like Toronto. *Global News.* https://globalnews.ca/news/4178811/anti-Blackness-toronto/

Phillips, D., & Pon, G. (2018). Anti-Black racism, bio-power, and governmentality: Deconstructing the suffering of Black families involved with child welfare. *Journal of Law and Social Policy, 28* (1–2), 81–100.

Ramrayka, P. (2020). Journeying through the 'motherland'. In J. Webb, R. Westmaas, M. Del Pilar Kaladeen, & W. Tantam (Eds.), *Memory, migration and (de)colonisation in the Caribbean and beyond* (pp. 79–84). University of London Press.

Sexton, J. (2011). The social life of social death: On Afro-pessimism and Black optimism. *Tensions Journal, 5*, 1–47.

Sexton, J. (2012). Ante-anti-Blackness: Afterthoughts. *Lateral, 1*. Retrieved from https://csalateral.org/issue/1/ante-anti-blackness-afterthoughts-sexton/

Sexton, J. (2015). Unbearable Blackness. *Cultural Critique, 90*(1), 159–178.

Sharpe, C. (2016). *In the wake: On Blackness and being.* Duke University Press.

Sizzla—Bless Up. (n.d.). *Jah Lyrics.* https://www.jah-lyrics.com/song/sizzla-bless-up

Smallwood, S. (2007). *Saltwater slavery: A middle passage from Africa to American diaspora.* Harvard University Press.

Vinícius, L. (2017). *Reports from Agência Brasil.* https://agenciabrasil.ebc.com.br/en/direitos-humanos/noticia/2017-12/forum-reports-black-genocide-brazil-un

Walcott, R. (2003). *Black like who? Writing Black Canada* (2nd rev. ed.). Insomniac Press.

Wallace, K. (2011). Most residents think Jamaica 'better off as a British colony,' poll suggests. *The Star.* https://www.thestar.com/news/world/2011/06/29/most_residents_think_jamaica_better_off_as_a_british_colony_poll_suggests.html

Wilderson, F. (2016, March 30). Afro-pessimism & the End of Redemption. *The Occupied Times.* https://theoccupiedtimes.org/?p=14236

Winks, R. (1997). *Blacks in Canada: A history.* McGill-Queen's University Press. www.jstor.org/stable/j.ctt7zq6b

Windrush scandal: 'I had no roof over my head, no money.' (2018, May 25). *The Guardian: International Edition.* https://www.theguardian.com/uk-news/2018/may/25/windrush-scandal-i-had-no-roof-over-my-head-no-money

Windrush victim back home after 25 years in Jamaica. (2018, October 15). *The Gleaner.* http://jamaica-gleaner.com/article/news/20181015/windrush-victim-back-home-after-25-years-jamaica

CHAPTER 9

How the Mainstream Media Signified Ben Johnson: A Tale of a Black Canadian Sports Hero Turned Jamaican Villain and the Implications for Black Students

Patrick Radebe

In Canada, discussions centered on race are conspicuous by their absence. Moreover, there has never been an open and honest public debate on race. Those who would dare to initiate one are immediately shouted down as racist. Most Canadians, and Whites in particular, prefer to avoid the subject for fear of resurrecting the specter of racism, long thought laid to rest as evinced by nearly half a century of official multiculturalism and the highest third-world immigration rate among developed countries. Indeed, over the course of this period, one is hard-pressed to find any evidence of overt and/or concerted acts of racism on the part of the White majority. So why is it so many Black Canadians view race as a serious issue? Some argue that this preoccupation with race and racism represents a kind of catharsis from historic wrongs, and as such a precondition for healing. For some White Canadians, on the other hand, it speaks to a Black belligerence, stemming from hypersensitivity and an unforgiving spirit. For them and their allies within the Black community, multiculturalism is sufficient recompense, and it is incumbent on Blacks to bear their pain, cut their losses, and bank on a better Canada moving forward.

I believe the answer to this question lies largely with mainstream media representations of Black Canadians. More often than not, the latter are signified as incorrigibly irresponsible, prone to criminality, a burden on the country's social services, and a threat to public safety. Put into context, Black crime is often signified as a pathology whose roots lie deep within the Black family, community, and, ultimately, the culture. This is in sharp contrast to the ways in which mainstream media tend to frame White crime in either medical terms, such as the story of Eric Harris, one of the Columbine High School shooters, who was reported to be "under a doctor's care and had been prescribed an anti-depressant medication" (Salvatore, 1999, para. 1), or as a sociological category. Regarding the latter, *The Washington Post* reported,

> The [Columbine] shooters . . . were members of a small clique of outcasts who always wore black trench coats and spent their entire adolescence deep inside the morose subculture of Gothic fantasy . . . the group [was] also interested in the occult, mutilation, shock-rocker Marilyn Manson and Adolf Hitler. (Brockell, 2019, para. 9)

In either case, professional intervention is recommended as an appropriate remedy. Thus, while Black crime is demonized and the Black criminal is viewed as beyond rehabilitation and therefore a permanent threat to Canadian society, the White criminal is medicalized (Wortley, & Owusu-Bempah, 2016). Moreover, for a Black man or woman, merely to be accused of committing a crime or engaging in some lesser form of unethical behavior is to be presumed guilty. In 1988, one such man was tried and condemned by the media for allegedly using a performance-enhancing substance to win the 100-meter dash at the 1988 Seoul Olympic Games. His name was Ben Johnson.

I wrote this chapter not because of any interest in sports or in Ben Johnson, per se, but because I am acutely aware of the power of media representations to inform public attitudes and assumptions, often to the disadvantage of minorities. As an educator, I have firsthand experience of how stereotypical depictions of Black people and Black life can demoralize students to the point where their academic performance suffers or they drop out of school. This chapter in no way excuses Black crime or misconduct of any kind; rather, it foregrounds the impact on Black Canadians, and especially Black students, of media representations that demean their race and cultural heritage. In internalizing such representations Blacks come to think and behave in ways that are consistent with societal expectations.

Using media coverage of the Ben Johnson doping scandal as a case study, this chapter examines how Black students are impacted by negative media depictions of their race and culture. It also elucidates how deeply entrenched racism is within the mainstream media. This chapter has four objectives, the first of which is to provide an overview and analysis of the media coverage of the scandal that would end Olympic athlete Ben Johnson's brilliant career. Next, I reveal how media representations work to perpetuate racial stereotypes. I then discuss the "new racism," a subtler variant of earlier forms, that seeks to avoid offending the racial sensibilities of a multicultural Canada. Finally, drawing on cultural deficiency theory (CDT) and the theory of biological determinism, I examine the impact of negative media representations on Black students and on the public education system as a whole. Regarding terminology, the term *Black* is used here to refer to Canadians who self-identify as Africans on the basis of parentage, ancestry, or country of birth. The terms *cultural deficit theory* and *CDT* are used interchangeably.

A Canadian Sports Hero Turned Jamaican Villain

How often does one hear the cliché that race doesn't matter? Advocates of multiculturalism don't think so, or at least pretend they don't, for their object is to urge all Canadians to accept and even celebrate differences across the full spectrum of humanity—and this despite the fact that poll after poll indicates race does matter (Harriot, 2019; Javed, 2017). Indeed, among other things, it remains a principal determinant of who is singled out for praise and who is punished.

While competing in the 1988 Seoul Olympic Games, Ben Johnson would discover this for himself after being disqualified for testing positive for a performance-enhancing substance. Previously hailed by the media as Canada's greatest athlete, he would soon discover that his status had changed dramatically overnight: No longer a "Canadian" sports hero, he had reverted to being another Jamaican Canadian, warranting the kind of hyphenated citizenship conferred on Black Canadians who fall afoul of the law (Bissoondath, 1994). Once a "Canadian" hero, that is, "one of us," the beleaguered athlete was reduced to "one of them," that is, "a Jamaican-Canadian" (Bissoondath, 1994, p. 116) and thus fair game for a national media intent on prying into every nook and cranny of his life in the hope of discovering other newsworthy failings. Interrogating his true Canadian identity in the wake of the scandal, the media had this, among much else, to say about the dethroned sports hero:

> The transition to Canada's schools proved difficult for Johnson. His Jamaican accent and stutter [a childhood-onset fluency disorder] led to placement in remedial classes. . . . He did manage to graduate from Yorkdale High, though his reading and mathematics skills were judged to be very basic. (Kram, 2020, "Academic Trouble")

The media was also quick to report that the "federal sports minister Pierre Cadieux [had] called Johnson a national disgrace, and suggested he consider moving back to Jamaica" (Ansah, 2016, "Major Accomplishments").

The country's reputation had been tarnished, and so it was imperative that Johnson be shorn of his Canadian identity and signified instead as the product of the Black community and Jamaican culture from which he hailed. The ensuing media narrative would absolve Canada, to which he had immigrated at the age of 14; the school system;

the country's Olympic team; and immigration policy of all responsibility in this matter. Instead, the media blamed him, and by implication the Black community, for the scandal (Denton, 1987; James, 2003). They also downplayed his Canadian citizenship while foregrounding his Jamaican nationality, relegating the former sports hero to the status of what Walcott (1997) calls an "absented presence" (p. 37), meaning a person who, although residing in Canada and identifying themselves as Canadian, is never recognized as such and invariably treated as an outsider—a not-uncommon fate for those accused of violating laws or norms. In the aftermath of the scandal, *Macleans* reported that "Johnson's commercial contracts for everything from shoes to milk began to dry up, and the golden promise of millions more in endorsement dollars disappeared overnight—*leaving the Jamaican immigrant* [my emphasis] with an uncertain future at best" (Levin, 1988, para. 9; also see Denton, 1987).

Wielding "value-free" language, Johnson's media critics set about dethroning him from the pantheon of Canadian sports heroes. The racist undertone and stereotypes they used worked to represent him, and by implication all Black Canadians, as coarse and ignorant. Emphasizing his accent, which prior the scandal had never been deemed newsworthy, served to signify him as foreign, as outside White Canada. Moreover, even Johnson's speech impediment now loomed large as a personal failing. Paradoxically, in disposing of him, the mainstream media would tap into the very racist stereotypes and fear of the "other" that they had worked so assiduously to exorcize from Canadian society with a view to advancing a multicultural agenda.

According to Hall & Hall (1990), textualizing and mediatizing race works to reproduce White supremacy. The media framed the doping scandal to reinforce the dominant expectations of Black Canadians, who must learn to obey the law or be punished. In the dominant–subordinate relationship, Jiwani (2016) argues that

> "(a) [the racialized group] assumes the position of subordination; (b) [its] behaviours . . . [are] naturalized ... [and] are regarded as . . . inherent [among] the individuals within that group; [and] (c) the behaviours ... of the subordinated group are [stripped] of all historical traces . . . (p. 44)

In naturalizing, essentializing, and decontextualizing Black "criminality," media narratives not only reveal where the locus of power lies; they also underscore the dominant order's ability to thwart any critical discussion of discourses that continue to portray Blacks accused of illegalities as deviants requiring stringent laws to regulate or modify their behavior.

How Media Representations Worked to Reproduce Racial Stereotypes

Media representations of Ben Johnson can hardly be viewed as race-neutral. Rather, their aim is to perpetuate racial stereotypes with a view to reproducing the dominant order and thus maintaining the status quo, including Black subordination. Two theoretical perspectives are used here to elucidate this project: biological determinism and CDT. The former has been used by scholars to question the intellectual capacity of persons of African heritage; the latter, to interrogate the commitment on the part of Black parents to educating their children (Herrnstein & Murray, 1994; Rushton, 1994; Rushton & Jensen, 2003, 2005). Viewed from these twin perspectives, Ben Johnson's story is that of a man doubly damned by genetic inheritance and family upbringing.

Biological determinism was long used to attribute low levels of academic performance and high suspension and dropout rates among Black and other minority students to genetic inheritance (Dei et al., 1997; Valencia, 2010). Even though generally discredited, the theory remains popular among some influential scholars and policy makers as well as those opposed to education reform, specifically in the form of targeted programs to enhance learning among racialized students (Valencia, 2010). This theoretical model works to absolve the public education system and multiple levels of government of any blame for the perennial underperformance of Black students (Valencia, 2010). In highlighting Johnson's speech impediment and struggles in school, the media inadvertently gave credence to a theoretical perspective long abandoned by all but a few recalcitrants (Valencia, 2010).

In referencing Johnson's Jamaican heritage, the media, consistent with CDT, signified the Black family and community as a principal source of academic underperformance and unethical behavior on the part of all those of Caribbean stock. Regardless of birthplace, the latter are assumed to be part of a dysfunctional family and community wherein good moral values and a strong work ethic are seldom fostered, thus limiting the academic potential and career prospects of Black students (Valencia, 2010). This same model also frames the Black family as large, disorganized, and, for the most part, headed by an uneducated matriarch (Walker, 2008), the stereotypical "welfare mother" (Henry, 1993, p. 209), whose views on education are at odds with standard school curricula. However, while the media were quick to point to Johnson's heritage as the source of his failings, regarding his family it was strangely silent, perhaps with a view to conveying a subliminal message, namely, that Black families play little or no meaningful role in their children's education—an assumption discredited by numerous studies (Dei et al., 1997; Valencia, 2010), albeit used repeatedly to stave off calls for education reform. So, what was it that motivated the media to represent Johnson in so negative a fashion? And why did they link the doping scandal to his heritage, his struggles in school, his accent, and even his speech impediment, a medical condition that ought to have been ignored given the sensitivity with which physical disabilities were signified then as today? The answer, I contend, lies with racism.

The New Racism

Racism is entrenched across a broad swath of Canadian discourse. Unlike the standard variant that is direct and confrontational, however, the so-called new racism is cordial in the sense that it conceals its true intent so as to avoid offending marginalized groups and raising accusations of racism. Cordial racism is difficult to identify, given that under the guise of friendship, it perpetuates stereotypes that can be "easily seen . . . [while hiding] strong feelings [that] flow underneath the surface" (Boechat, 2015, p. 12). According to Goldberg, moreover, "[in neoliberal Canada] contemporary discourse on race and racism [has become a] privatized affair" (Goldberg as cited in Jiwani, 2016, p. 44). Although most Canadians view racist stereotypes or even the most subtle hint of bigotry as un-Canadian and worthy of condemnation, a subset of the population continues to practice "inferential racism." Hall defines the latter as

> naturalized representations . . . relating to race, whether 'factual' or 'fictional' . . . [or] hav[ing] racist premises and propositions inscribed in them. . . . These enable statements to be formulated without ever bringing into awareness the racist predicates on which these statements are grounded. (Hall as cited in Jiwani, 2016, p. 44)

Bonilla-Silva's analysis of racism is instructive in this regard. In his view, efforts by liberal democracies to build inclusive societies have not eliminated racism (Bonilla-Silva, 2015). If anything, the "new racism" has supplanted overt racism. He characterizes the "new racism" as a friendlier variant of its predecessor that is "(i) covert, (ii) avoid[s] . . . direct racial terminology, (iii) elaborate[s] . . . racial political agenda[s] that eschew direct racial references, (iv) [presents a] subtle character . . . [and] reproduce[s] racial privilege, and (v) rearticulate[s] . . . racial practices of the past" (Bonilla-Silva, 2015, p. 1362). Although many White Canadians claim color-blindness with the popular refrain "I don't see color," they are also largely disinterested in race or racism or any other issue that does not weigh heavily on their pocketbooks. How they perceive the racialized "other" is informed by their Whiteness and their White privilege (McIntosh, 1986; Wihak, 2004). Although most are quick to deny the latter, whether earned or unearned, and invoke the liberal truism that all are equal, being White comes with an "invisible package of [privileges, earned or otherwise]" (McIntosh, 1986, p. 1). Always able to cash in on one's Whiteness, one need never worry about being measured against racialized and/or minoritized groups.

Whiteness constitutes, by default, a yardstick against which non-Whites are measured—in other words, a universal standard. Writing on the subject of racial identity, Rinaldo Walcott (1997) argues that "Blackness in Canada is situated on a continuum that runs from the invisible to the hyper-visible" (p. 36). As I understand Walcott, where Blacks fall along this continuum is contingent not on their quality of character or personal achievements but, rather, the interests of the dominant order. Thus, Black Canadian achievements that fall within normative boundaries typically receive little or no recognition or are sanitized; those deemed to violate White Canadian values, on the other hand, receive a plethora of media attention aimed at presenting Black Canadian values as antithetical to those of their "true" Canadian counterparts.

How Media Representations Impact Black Canadian Students

Owing to their ubiquitous presence and power to shape and circulate meaning in the form of values, attitudes, assumptions, and norms, mass media can impact whole societies in ways that should not be underestimated (Jiwani, 2016). By bringing news to mass audiences that is decontextualized, framed in ways that advance the interests of the dominant order, and uninformed by a diversity of views, the media can shape public opinion by, for example, generating "schemas . . . [that] influence the interpretation of new information such that recently and/or frequently activated ideas come to mind more easily than ideas that have not been activated once perceivers encounter similar stimuli" (Dixon et al., cited in Jiwani, 2016, p. 49). One such schema, namely, media stereotypes of Black males, works to induce the public, including some Blacks, to perceive all Black people as potential thugs. Assaulted, seduced, and tranquilized by compelling narratives and powerful imagery repeated over and over again, media audiences are unable to bring to bear their critical faculties and so mistake factoids for truth.

In *Race in the Schoolyard: Negotiating the Color Line in Classrooms and Communities*, Amanda Lewis (2009) describes a heart-wrenching experience not uncommon among Black students. When a "Ms. Sullivan," a Southern California (Lewis, 2009, p. 7) elementary school teacher, asked "Rodney," a Grade 4 African American student, what he planned on doing with his life, the child replied that "he wanted to go to college, but first he had to go to prison" (p. 54). Pressed further, he explained that "all Black men go to prison [and so] it would be more efficient to get his prison term out of the way before he went to college than having to do it afterward" (Lewis, 2009, p. 54). Ms. Sullivan's efforts to disabuse this student of what she viewed to be a preposterous assumption would fall on deaf ears, however. It is more than likely that Rodney's perception of his future prospects speaks to the impact of negative media representations on impressionable Black students. In demeaning their heritage, family life, and communities and featuring Black heroes/role models often steeped in criminality and/or the culture of victimhood, such representations go a long way to ensuring that many students come to view failure and incarceration as not only unavoidable but also the norm.

Media stories filed after the Ben Johnson doping scandal surfaced were filled with such representations. For example, in reporting that the "transition to Canada's schools proved difficult for Johnson [and that] [h]is Jamaican accent and stutter led to placement in remedial classes" (Kram, 2020, "Academic Trouble"), the media were implying that Black Canadian students generally have little motivation and are poorly equipped—in Johnson's case "linguistically deficient" (Gorski, 2008, p. 32)—to learn. Indeed, it is the "mismatch between the . . . culture [within Black homes and communities] and the school culture" (Valencia, 2010, p. 3) that accounts for their poor academic performance and low teacher expectations (Dei et al., 1997; Kong, 1996; Roberts-Fiati, 1996; Solomon, 1995). It should be noted, however, that this view is at odds with findings from a number of studies that indicate disaffected Black students can perform above expectations if given the requisite opportunities and support (Lewis, 2009).

I now wish to share my understanding of the nexus between media representations and how Africa and Africans are perceived by White Canadians. On November 9, 2011, I spoke on the subject of social justice in education before a group of students enrolled in the Teacher Education program at the University of British Columbia. I began by asking my audience, which was predominantly White, to record on a slip of paper, and in as few words as possible, what they thought of Africa and Africans. The purpose of the exercise was to demonstrate that despite the best of intentions, even the educated can inadvertently perpetuate racial stereotypes. The following are listed descriptors randomly selected from the responses provided by seven students:

> Student 1: continent, poverty, safari
> Student 2: Black, desert, dependent on Christian help
> Student 3: safaris, huge continent, extreme poverty in some areas, lots of people
> Student 4: safari, animals, poverty, hunger, heat, AIDS, Black
> Student 5: small, uneducated population, comprised mainly of Black people
> Student 6: continent, underdeveloped part of the world with great poverty
> Student 7: Diversity, different cultural traditions, marginalized, sometimes discriminated against or treated differently, possessing little knowledge because not taught.

These descriptors conjure up images of a "dark continent" while working to reinforce racial stereotypes that these teacher-candidates have culled from the media and will soon bring into the classroom. The picture emerging from these responses suggests that some individuals lack the ability to succeed solely because of their cultural background. Africa is signified as a basket case, its achievements of no account, its people devoid of agency. Consistent with mainstream myths, Blacks are represented as uneducated, poverty-stricken, disease-ridden, and antipathetic to everything modern. This notion lies at the heart of CDT. CDT argues that the cultural attributes or practices often associated with historically disenfranchised racial/ethnic groups (specifically Blacks and Latinos) have prevented them from assimilating and attaining social mobility within U.S. society. Examples of cultural deficiencies include limited outlooks and attitudes toward the future, a failure to internalize the work ethic, instant gratification behavior, a lack of parent involvement in schools, low intellectual abilities, an emphasis on masculinity and honor, and an aversion to honest work. Other so-called deficiencies may include female-headed households, a fatalistic attitude toward life, and a limited interest in education (Fergus, 2008)

Although CDT was discredited for lacking "empirical verification [and relying] more on ideology than science [to promote] . . . classi[st], sexi[st], and racis[t stereotypes]" (Valencia, 2010, p. 7), it resurfaced in "the 1980s and 1990s [under the rubric of] . . . the cultural deficit model" (Solorzano, 1997, p 17). "At the highest levels of educational policy, [it has] moved from deficiency theory to theories of difference, back to deficiency theory" (Kretovics & Nussel as cited in Solarzano, 1997, p. 17), further complicating efforts to eradicate it. Moreover, some of its racist and classist assumptions still inform teacher expectations where minority or impoverished students are concerned, resulting in further disaffection and higher dropout rates (Dei et al., 1997).

For critics of the public education system, Black student alienation, as evinced by poor academic performance and high suspension and dropout rates, comes as no surprise. This phenomenon stems, in part, from a mindset entrenched within public schools that attributes poor academic performance on the part of these students to their culture, as hypothesized by cultural deficiency theory. According to the Toronto District School Board (TDSB), of those "students born in English-speaking Islands in the Caribbean who entered Grade 9 in 2000, 40 per cent had dropped out by 2005" (Brown, 2006, para. 17). The report further states that the high dropout rate "applies more to second generation male . . . students than their female peers" (James, 2011, p. 193), a trend the Royal Commission on Learning in Ontario reports (1994) signifies an "education in crisis" (Royal Commission on Learning in Ontario, cited in James, 2011, p. 199).

As educators, we cannot absolve ourselves of "cultural deficit thinking." Many of us enter the profession encumbered with values and biases that work to segregate students into categories predicated on cultural background and academic ability. From birth onward, many of us have been socialized in ways that lead, inexorably, to viewing students from disadvantaged backgrounds in highly pejorative terms: *dumb, lazy, irresponsible, undisciplined,* and *fatalistic* (Solorzano, 1997, p. 9). It is but a short step to linking such attributes to the culture of underperforming students, and particularly those belonging to visible minorities. In examining cultural deficit thinking among teachers, and especially those from the White middle class, my aim is not to tar all with the same brush, but to single out those who, as several studies have shown (Dei et al., 1997; Kong, 1996), harbor cultural stereotypes of students (Dei et al., 1997) that are shaped by cross-cultural misunderstanding and that lead to negative learning outcomes for Black students. I begin this section with Mark's story, a narrative that reflects the experiences of so many Black students who struggle daily in the public education system.

For the first month of classes, "Mark," a Grade 2 Black student, worked alone at his desk even though his teacher urged all students to work in pairs. By the second month, the teacher was growing increasingly concerned over this student's antisocial behavior, which she attributed to an "adjustment problem" (Roberts-Fiati, 1996, p. 75). The real problem, however, lay not with Mark but with his White classmates who refused to partner with him. And so it was that he continued to work alone, all the while expecting one of them to join him eventually. His is an experience all too familiar for Black students attending mainstream public schools (Roberts-Fiati, 1996). The events described highlight how, in the mainstream public school system, race and culture come to mediate the Black experience. Both student and teacher were in various ways complicit in perpetuating a standard racial representation; in the latter's eyes Mark, like all Black children, was somehow tainted and thus undesirable. Raby (2004) asserts that "[White] teachers and students often downplay "the personal relevance of "race . . . through the erasure of race itself" (p. 371), even though their actions foster an atmosphere of racial intolerance. Rather than deal with the problem head-on, the teacher chose instead to ignore it, perhaps owing to a reluctance to talk about race or perhaps a conviction that it was irrelevant in the classroom and that to address it would require interrogating her own dominant attitude and that of her White students. For his part, Mark would be entirely justified were he to conclude that the school environment was hostile and the teachers uncaring. His perception of the school and teachers could translate into diminished "self-confidence" and "pride" (James & Brathwaite, 1996, p. 20), resistance to authority, and, potentially, a life of crime.

What "Mark" experienced as a Black student attending a predominantly White school speaks to the lack of empathy and even overt hostility that often characterizes relations between White teachers and their Black charges (Kong, 1996). This student's self-esteem was shattered when her Grade 3 teacher announced before a group of her peers that she "would never amount to anything" (Kong, 1996, p. 60). Perceiving the school environment to be detrimental to their sense of personhood and self-esteem, many Black students choose to drop out and others to detach themselves psychologically. Dei et al. (1997) challenge the wholesale use of the term *dropout* to describe the fate of so many Black students in the public education system. In his view "pushed out" would be more accurate (p. 36). Black students who are "pushed out" of school are not averse to education, knowing the future that awaits the uneducated. Dei et al. (1997) attribute the "pushed out" phenomenon to the lack of support provided "at risk" students by "school agents (teachers, guidance counsellors, administrators)" (p. 70), who are less responsive, indeed mostly indifferent, to their adverse experiences. For these school agents, a lack of academic success is the product of a Black identity and culture and, as such, beyond the purview of the public education system—hence the futility of providing Black students with the support required to excel academically. In the words of one student, the high dropout rate in the public education system is due, in part, to a prevailing "network of disinterest" (Dei et al., 1997, p. 72) that leaves the disadvantaged to their own devices, which invariably leads to their dropping out of school.

Critics of the public education system often target cultural stereotypes that appear both endemic and pervasive and work to blight the youngest and most innocent in particular (Roberts-Fiati, 1996). The defense put forward by the school authorities, that is, that the experiences of the Marks are anomalies and thus in no way reflect what is really going on in the classroom, serve only to reveal their discomfort with having to deal with racism and racialized students. For Mark's teacher to attribute his behavior to an "adjustment problem" (Roberts-Fiati, 1996, p. 75) stemming from some unspecified cultural deficiency is to shift the focus from race to culture, thus reproducing the illusion of a race-free classroom while reassuring Black parents who would rather believe that the teacher knows best and has the best interest of the student at heart.

Within the public education system, racial and cultural stereotypes remain key determinants of streaming Black students into vocational, technical, English development skills, or sports programs (Calliste, 1996; Dei et al., 1997; James, 2005, 2011; James & Brathwaite, 1996). With Black student underperformance foremost in mind, guardian counselors often advise Black parents to enroll their children in vocational or technical programs at a far greater rate than is the case for White students and with no thought given to the inequities pervading the school system or their impact on educational outcomes (Dei et al., 1997). While the practice of streaming has a legitimate place in the school system, one must question its disproportionate application to Black students with a view to reducing their high dropout rates and the costs incurred from the high dropout rates. Streamed away from friends and placed in nonacademic programs, students come to feel discriminated against and as a result adopt behaviors—refusing to study, acting out, truancy, and dropping out of school—that further jeopardize their limited opportunities for success (Dei et al., 1997).

As is the case with streaming, the TDSB "catchment zone" provision denies Black students from immigrant neighborhoods equal access to quality education. Stipulating the use of area codes to determine in which school(s) a student can be enrolled, this provision effectively prevents Black students from poor immigrant communities from attending schools in wealthy areas of the city. Although the "catchment zone" provision may be deemed essential to preempting logistical problems, such as over-enrollment in any given school, it could just as easily be viewed as promoting school segregation. It would appear that regardless of the lip service paid, the principle of racial equality, racist educational policies—"catchment zones," gifted student programs, and advance placement courses—however subtle, still exist. The greater educational opportunities available to students residing in middle-class neighborhoods provide them with a "better shot" in life vis-à-vis their less privileged peers.

Conclusion

It is high time the public was disabused of popular notions such as the mainstream media function as a *Fifth Estate* "speaking truth to power" or media coverage is neutral, objective, and balanced. A chief assumption informing this chapter is that the media work to advance the interests of the dominant order of which they are an integral part. It is also imperative for individual media firms to generate the broadest range or multiplicity of meanings/representations if it is to capture the largest possible market share—something for every audience member. This explains why racist narratives and their representations appear alongside those working to reproduce the dominant order. Thus, at the same time media denounce racism and promote multiculturalism and massive third-world immigration and policies aimed at securing low-wage labor and inflating assets, they also signify, albeit in subtle ways, the "racialized other" as foreign, inferior and threatening—not "one of us."

As educators, we bear witness to the harm done by media representations that exalt privileged groups while demeaning those that are marginalized and subordinated. In working to criminalize race and racialize crime, among other things, these significations are at least, in part, responsible for alienating Black students from the learning process, which explains their defiance of authority, their propensity to violence, their poor academic performance, and their high suspension and dropout rates. As educators, it is incumbent on us to provide all students, and in particular those belonging to visible minorities, with a modicum of media literacy so that racist representations might be seen for what they are, namely, part of a grand project aimed at reproducing the status quo.

References

Ansah, J. (2016, January 21). Ben Johnson. *Prezi.* https://prezi.com/7auiakoexq9d/ben-johnson/

Bissoondath, N. (1994). *Selling illusions: The cult of multiculturalism in Canada.* Penguin Books.

Boechat, W. (2015, Fall). Cordial racism: Race as a cultural complex. *Jung Society of Atlanta,* pp. 12–14.

Bonilla-Silva, E. (2015). The structure of racism in color-blind, "post-racial" America. *American Behavioral Scientist, 59*(11), 1358–1376.

Brockell, G. (2019, April 20) Bullies and black trench coats: The Columbine shooting's most dangerous myths. *The Washington Post.* https://www.washingtonpost.com/history/2019/04/19/bullies-black-trench-coats-columbine-shootings-most-dangerous-myths/

Brown, L. (2006, June 23). Dropout, failure rates linked to language: Study compares countries of origin Spanish-speaking parents worried. *The Toronto Star.* http://www.yorku.ca/goldring/clippings/dropout__rates_link_language.pdf

Calliste, A. (1996). African Canadians' organizing for educational change. In K. S. Brathwaite & C. E. James (Eds.), *Educating African Canadians* (pp. 87–106). James Lorimer & Company Ltd.

Dei, G. J. S., Holmes, L., Mazzuca, J., McIsaac, E., & Zine, J. (1997). *Reconstructing 'dropout': A critical ethnography of the dynamics of Black students' disengagement from school.* Toronto University Press.

Denton, H. H. (1987, September 6). Ben Johnson suddenly a hero in Canada: He's a native of Jamaica, but they love him north of the border. *LA Times.* https://www.latimes.com/archives/la-xpm-1987-09-06-sp-6199-story.html

Fergus, E. (2008). Cultural deficiency. In *Encyclopedia of Race and Racism, 2nd Edition.* Cengage Learning.

Gorski, P. (2008). The myth of the "culture of poverty." *Educational Leadership, 65*(7), 32–36.

Hall, E.T., & Hall, M.R. (1990) *Understanding Cultural Differences: Germans, French and Americans.* Intercultural Press, Boston.

Harriot, M. (2019, September 4). White people still tripping. *The Roots.* https://www.theroot.com/report-white-people-still-tripping-1833915981

Henry, A. (1993). Missing: Black self-representations in Canadian educational research. *Canadian Journal of Education, 18*(3), 206–222.

Herrnstein, R. J., & Murray, C. A. (1994). *The bell curve: Intelligence and class structure in American life.* Free Press.

James, C. E. (2003). Schooling, basketball and US scholarship aspirations of Canadian student athletes. *Race, Ethnicity, and Education, 6*(2), 123–144.

James, C. E. (2005). *Race and play: Understanding the socio-cultural worlds of student athletes.* Canadian Scholars' Press.

James, C. E. (2011). Multicultural education in a color-blind society. In C. A. Grant & A. Portera (Eds.), *Intercultural and multicultural education: Enhancing global interconnectedness* (pp. 191–210). Routledge.

James, C. E., & Brathwaite, K. (1996). The education of African Canadians: Issues, contexts, expectations. In K. S. Brathwaite & C. E. James (Eds.), *Educating African Canadians* (pp. 13–31). James Lorimer & Company Ltd.

Javed, N. (2017, October 27). Race matters when awaiting trial, data shows. *The Toronto Star.* https://www.thestar.com/news/queenspark/2017/10/22/race-matters-when-awaiting-trial-data-shows.html

Jiwani, Y. (2016). Mediations of race and crime: Racializing crime, criminalizing race. In B. Perry (Ed.), *Diversity, crime, and justice in Canada* (pp. 43–62). Oxford University Press.

Kong, N. A. H. (1996). Confronting a history of exclusion: A personal reflection. In K. S. Brathwaite & C. E. James (Eds.), *Educating African Canadians* (pp. 58–68). James Lorimer & Company Ltd.

Kram, M. (2020). Ben Johnson 1961—. In *Encyclopedia of Contemporary Black Biography.* https://www.encyclopedia.com/people/literature-and-arts/english-literature-1500-1799-biographies/ben-jonson

Levin, B. (1988, October 10). The steroid scandal: Was he drugged? After the games, Ben Johnson's fight to prove he was 'clean.' *Macleans.* http://archive.macleans.ca/article/1988/10/10/the-steroid-scandal

Lewis, A. E. (2009). *Race in the schoolyard: Negotiating the color line in classrooms and communities.* Rutgers University Press.

McIntosh, P. (1986, April). *White privilege and male privilege: A personal account of coming to see correspondences through work in women's studies* [Paper presentation]. The Virginia Women's Association, Richmond, VA, United States. Retrieved from https://www.collegeart.org/pdf/diversity/white-privilege-and-male-privilege.pdf

Raby, R. (2004). 'There's no racism at my school, it's just joking around': Ramifications for anti-racist education. *Race Ethnicity and Education, 7*(4), 367–383.

Roberts-Fiati, G. (1996). Effects of early marginalization on African Canadian children. In K. S. Brathwaite & C. E. James (Eds.), *Educating African Canadians* (pp. 69–80). James Lorimer & Company.

Rushton, P. J. (1994). *Race, evolution and behavior: A life history perspective.* Transaction Publishers.

Rushton, P. J., & Jensen, A. R. (2003). African-White IQ differences from Zimbabwe on the Wechsler intelligence scale for children-revised are mainly on the g factor. *Personality and Individual Differences, 34*(1), 177–183.

Rushton, P. J. & Jensen, A. R. (2005). Wanted: More race realism, less moralistic fallacy. *Psychology, Public Policy, and Law, 11*(2), 328–336.

Salvatore, S. (1999, April 29). *Columbine shooter was prescribed anti-depressant.* CNN. http://edition.cnn.com/HEALTH/9904/29/luvox.explainer/

Solomon, P. R. (1995). Beyond prescriptive pedagogy: Teacher in-service education for cultural diversity. *Journal of Teacher Education, 46*(4), 251–258.

Solorzano, D. G. (1997). Images and words that wound: Critical race theory, racial stereotyping, and teacher education. *Teacher Education Quarterly, 24*(3), 5–19.

Valencia, R. R. (2010). *Dismantling contemporary deficit thinking: Educational thought and practice.* Routledge

Walcott, R. (1997). *Black like who? Writing Black Canada.* Insomniac Press.

Walker, B. (2008, May 19). Africentric schools deserve a chance. *The Toronto Star.* https://www.thestar.com/opinion/2008/05/19/africentric_schools_deserve_a_chance.html

Wihak, C. (2004). The meaning of being White in Canada: A personal narrative. *TESL Canada Journal, 21*(2), 110–115.

Wortley, S., & Owusu-Bempah, A. (2016). Crime and justice: The experiences of Black Canadians. In B. Perry (Ed.), *Diversity, crime, and justice in Canada* (pp. 140–167). Oxford University Press.

CHAPTER 10

Rethinking Curriculum Through Critical Blackness and African Indigenous Knowledges: A Black Educator's Response

Janelle Baptiste-Brady

Black and African students, educators, and administrators have linked and shared experiences globally. As a Black educator, I think critically about my role in supporting students and dismantling systems of oppression through curriculum and anticolonial pedagogical practices. I also think critically about my positionality as a Black woman educator. I explore how can Black educators anchor their experiences in a Black political perspective rooted in African Indigeneity? How are the experiences of Black communities connected both on the continent and in the African diaspora? What is the role of community-based practices in reimagining education? What are some of the Indigenous knowledges theories that can inform decolonial and anticolonial praxis in education? And finally, what are some practices that can be rooted and grounded in Black/African educators' experiences to engage Blackness as a political tool through anticolonial and decolonial praxis?

To answer these questions, I organize the chapter into three main sections. The first section includes the theoretical framing where I engage the idea of Blackness as a political tool and the linkages to African Indigeneity globally and my positionality. The second section raises critical questions regarding Indigenous knowledges in education and its implications. The final section provides seven practical examples of rethinking curriculum anchored in my experiences as a Black educator. The key examples are community-rootedness, humility and reflexiveness, rethinking the classroom in time and space, mentorship, love and care, storytelling, and bold acts of disruption.

Blackness as a Theoretical and Political Framework

The first two questions explore how can Black educators anchor their experiences in a Black political perspective rooted in African Indigeneity and how are the experiences of Black communities connected both on the continent and in the African diaspora? Thinking about global education and the Africanization of the curriculum, it is imperative to critically engage the conceptualization of Blackness. Within my context of an African diasporic educator, I use both Blackness and Africanness interchangeably as Dei (2017) posits to "strategically evoke Blackness and Black subjectivity as part of an invention of an Africanness in a Diasporic context to gesture the particular intellectual politics I wish to pursue" (p. 2). Dei furthers this argument by stating,

> We must search for new analytical systems for understanding the Black and African experience and our human condition in the global space of transnational mobility. I am emboldened to situate African Indigeneity in these discussions. Claiming African Indigeneity is resistance to amputate: history, culture, and identity as the African body... and asserting land, cultural, spiritual and psychic memories as "living forces" we learn from. (2017, p. 3)

Dei engages the significance of employing Blackness as a political tool. Furthermore, Blackness cannot be separated from Africanness and by extension African Indigeneity. Through this extension on reframing Blackness, Dei emphasizes the importance of diasporic contexts in the pursuit of articulating African Indigeneity. Such a reframing and global perspective help to move beyond simplistic binaries that separate our communities in simply choosing African over Black or Black without linking Blackness to a larger identity grounded in African indigeneity or the fight against global anti-Black racism. By imposing purposeful and intentional politics to Blackness, it stands in opposition to ahistorical, apolitical, or even accidental articulation of Blackness. Attached to the Black body are the views that we are too "subjective," coupled with the constant surveillance and invisibility in the academy. In my work, I intentionally employ Blackness as a political tool despite my prior *multicultural* formal educational and schooling background that serves to erase, silence, neutralize, and amputate my Blackness through color-blind and sameness tropes. Hence, I am politically and actively engaged in a process of decolonization, unlearning, and learning as a Black educator and learner.

Central to the idea of Blackness and Africanness is the question of land. As a Black woman on Turtle Island whose family and ancestors engaged in acts of resistance during the transatlantic slave trade to the Caribbean and then in Canada (Turtle Island), I am in constant negotiation when it comes to land. I experience loss and grief in terms of Africa and home precontact, as well as rejuvenation and hope when it comes to the long history of precolonization. Thus, in employing Blackness, it is imperative that the idea of land is central to understanding, remembering, and disrupting. Dei (2008) sets forth that for Indigenous people, land is conceptualized beyond the physical space (as cited in Karanja, 2019). This demonstrates the centrality of land to the question of identity, self-hood, and, by extension, self-determination. Land goes beyond physicality to other aspects as highlighted in the quotation and provides a basis or form of interconnection beyond a physical space (Simpson, 2014).

I engage my own experiences and entry point to higher education and teaching to answer the question, What is the role of community-based spaces in reimagining education? My path to Black educational scholarship comes from my experiences as a Black working-class youth who was engaged in community-based projects to enhance Black and racialized students' outcomes. During my years as an undergraduate student studying sociology, I co-organized a community-based, after-school program that allowed me to see some of the systemic injustices faced by my Black peers in the Toronto context beyond my anecdotal experiences. I was mentored by Black faculty, racialized working-class graduate students, and White women faculty who encouraged me to articulate these problems through graduate research. I continued this academic journey and met Black faculty who mentor me. I stayed grounded in community organizing that informs my work and applied my lived experiences to my scholarship. I am both a mentee and a mentor; following African Indigenous knowledge principles, this is not a unidirectional relationship. I am grateful for the opportunity to teach at the postsecondary level that allows me to further my community-based and activist education. As a Black educator, I inform my practice with Africanness and Blackness as intentional, political, and on the forefront.

When I teach in the formal education system as a college faculty member, I purposefully employ "community-based" pedagogical approaches as discussed further later in this chapter. Mirza and Reay (2000) extend Collins's (1990) concept of "community connectedness" that Black females enjoy. As well, hooks (2015) states that "many people raised in black communities experienced this type of community-based childcare" (p. 145). In this way, I am connected to my childhood experiences where it truly took a community to raise me. As a Black woman, I embrace the community-connectedness based as a countering to individualistic tropes of success, and this informs my academic work and pedagogical style. This exemplifies one of the forms of resistance strategies that Black women have, and continue to, employed through this idea of community-connectedness. Furthermore, it reinforces the idea of African Indigeneity as central to Black African diasporic identities as mentioned earlier. Often, community is informed by division, as Dei et al. (2018) state:

> In Euro-American contexts claims of community are always contested with arguments of differences and divisions, however . . . the most important thing is to try and teach the value of community, and also articulate critical understandings of community that appreciate the essence of sharing, reciprocity, caring for each other and co-operation, all the while remaining mindful of divides that pit groups against each other. (p. 15)

Dei et al. (2018) go on to state that learners are not merely individuals and are part of larger collectives where schools can be part of a pursuit of what they call "schooling as community" to teach values of community and reciprocity. Hence, I use this understanding and employment of community and am critical of tropes that dismantle community through claims of essentialism while still being aware of forms of oppression and exclusion posed by community.

Returning to the project of Blackness as a political tool, we need to move away from the fragmentation that seeks to divide our communities, often along colonial national borders. Dei (2001) states that we must identify "our collective struggle" as Black people rather than becoming immersed with divisions (p. 148). I agree with the engagement of our "collective struggle" globally on the continent, on Turtle Island, in Latin America and beyond. With reference to the Toronto District School Board's (TDSB) "Don't Ask Don't Tell" (DADT) policy, Villegas (2019) states that

> when the DADT policy was introduced at the TDSB many individuals within the Board, across the media, and within the DADT Coalition treat the topic of something new. This lack of institutional history would lead to prolonged difficulties in addressing exclusion from schooling for undocumented students, particularly as it took over a year for the TDSB to pass the DADT policy and ten years later, it has yet to be fully implemented. (p. 177)

Villegas describes the loss of community history in the development of the DADT policy that dates to the 1960s and states that resistance ought to be part of the institutional history. In community-based education and forms of resistance, there is often a sense of *newness* when critical questions that are being asked. However, I would argue that as part of Black political education, the historical forms of resistance must be articulated when bringing forth new questions or acknowledging systemic barriers. This is another form of divide-and-conquer politics that treats youth as new knowledge carriers and/or community leaders, without acknowledging the work, struggle, and spirit injury that our elders have endured in White spaces. Knowing these histories would not remove from projects that youth carry out but, rather, enrich them by avoiding aspects of erasure through "institutional forgetfulness" that leaves our communities behind each time something like "racism" is treated as a new form of oppression.

Many scholars and educational researchers, such as James (2019), have acknowledged the long history of community calls for reforms to formal educational systems. James (2019) highlights the community advocacy around the urgency of collecting race-based data (p. 335) and employs "Community-Referenced Approach to Education (CRAE)," which "places students and their communities at the centre of their schooling and education" (p. 336). CRAE can only be accomplished with an acknowledgment of community, the ideals of community-connectedness, rather than fragmenting and individualizing tropes of difference (a discussion of difference is presented later). Careful considerations need to be made when engaging Blackness and indigeneity. I anchor this in Indigenous knowledges and anticolonial strategies discussed in the subsequent section where I ask, "What are some of the Indigenous knowledges theories that can inform decolonial and anticolonial praxis in education?"

Indigenous Knowledges as a Theoretical Framework for Decolonial and Anticolonial Praxis in Education

For non-White educators, particularly Indigenous, there is the constant negotiation of the formal education system in its entirety and the implications it presents. N. Nakata et al. (2012) cite Smith (1999), who highlights "at the heart of these tensions is Indigenous contestation of Western worldviews, philosophies, knowledge, theories, methods, histories, and positioning of Indigenous people, as well as the well-being of the planet" (p. 122). Fundamentally, Indigenous educators grapple with the tensions regarding their knowledge systems when employed in Western educational systems. N. Nakata et al. (2012) further explain that "education is also a site of contestation for Indigenous Studies (Nakata, 1993, 2006). And so, the content, processes, methods, and forms of education are also a contested matter, caught up as they are in the colonial and decolonial impulses" (p. 122). The mere subjugation of Black, Brown, and Indigenous bodies by disciplines within the Western academy are points of contestation, which leads to, in many accounts, communities of learners turning to "politics of resistance" (Dei, 2018). Resistance can happen within these very institutions by way of critical engagement of Indigenous knowledges as a "writing back" to the politics of erasure and subjection. Because Nakata (1993, 2006) engages the question of education being a form of contestation for Indigenous studies, important questions are raised about what do we consider education; how do we parse out the project of schooling and education and find the fluidity and connections between the two; how are politics, land, communities, ancestors, spirituality, and healing all part of the project of education; how can we posit critical engagement of racism, sexism, gender-based violence, transgender violence, ableism, anti-Black and anti-Indigenous racism, and tropes of citizenship and belonging as integral parts of the educational project; and how can we reimagine education. These questions can be answered through a critical engagement of Indigenous knowledges furthering the project of decolonization.

Decolonization can eventually lead to social and educational change. It calls for a re-visioning of the existing social order by the self and being critical of what we do in our daily lives and communities as learners. (Dei et al., 2018, p. 12). Here, the authors allow for critical thought and reflection regarding the internal manifestations of decolonization and community and broader implications for change. They go on to ask,

> How can we decolonize schooling and education using counter epistemologies and narratives? We reiterate as learners; how do we equip ourselves using multiple lenses of critical inquiry or multiple ways of knowing? And as educators and learners, how do we frame an inclusive anti-colonial global future. (p. 12)

Questions regarding epistemological transformation in schooling and education through counter-epistemologies are integral. The authors posit themselves as learners, reinforcing their humility in knowing and they transcend their local situatedness to frame antiglobal futurities. For myself, as a Black educator, I am confronted with these issues on an ongoing basis through constant reminders that the academic institution was not made for me or people like me, and the same goes for racialized, Black, and Indigenous students I teach. The gestures that I receive, whether subtle or overt, remind me that the academy needs to be reimagined, and rather than reproducing meritocracy and comfort, decolonial educators who engage critical Blackness must remain steadfast and deeply rooted in our communities and histories. This is not to be confused with the "savior" approach, where one individual—be them Indigenous or not—saves people through education. Bianchi (2018) provides a response to the savior approach by articulating that education ought to be the reciprocal transmission of knowledges. Hence, decolonizing the curriculum is not merely about the production of knowledge; rather, it engages transformation of knowledge and knowing. The savior approach is individualistic and part of a Western-colonial logic that is not embedded in communities of learners. Furthermore, Dei et al. (2018) state that decolonizing curriculum is not merely about "transplanting" African knowledges into schools (p. 13). Rather, there must be thoughtful engagement regarding which students the curriculum serves and what other systemic changes are taking place.

Many Indigenous scholars and activists grapple with the issue of transplanting Indigenous knowledges into White institutions or systems without critique, systemic change, or thought. For example, Simpson (2004) postulates that the Western academy has become increasingly occupied with the Traditional Ecological Knowledge (TEK) aspect of Indigenous knowledges as a response to modern environmental problems (p. 373).

Simpson engages critical questions about *when* the Western academy is interested in Indigenous knowledges and, in this case, TEK. Without a political stance and critical understanding of histories related to colonization, patriarchy and state violence, and the role that the academy has played in these atrocities, this becomes a fraught and, if anything, an on-the-surface exercise. Critical interventions need to be made. M. Nakata (2002) states, "To capitalist interests, Indigenous Knowledge is merely another resource for potential profit" (p. 281). This is fundamentally against the principles of Indigenous knowledges, which are holistic rather than fragmenting and compartmentalizing.. Thus, Indigenous scholars and activists have been rather critical of the profit motive embedded in the academy "Indigenizing" itself without context, history, community engagement, and accountability.

M. Nakata (2002) further engages the issues of fragmentation of Indigenous knowledges when he states, "Indigenous Knowledge has become more fragmented and specialized as scientists and humanitarians pick at the bits and pieces that fit with their interests and disciplines" (p. 282). The compartmentalization of knowledges merely seeks to fit within a Euro-colonial educational trope that is based on "disciplines" rather than the interconnectedness of knowledges, histories, people, communities, land and plants, and water and life. Furthermore, Nakata warns us about the drawbacks of simplistic binaries, particularly for Indigenous educators as "they confine Indigenous peoples to the position of 'Other' by reifying the very categories that have marginalized us historically and that still seek to remake and relegate us within the frameworks of Western epistemes" (2002, p. 285). These very categories between Western/Indigenous can serve as purposeful analytic tools and as an introduction to these arguments and discussions. However, these very binaries can reintroduce the very tropes of compartmentalization that Indigenous educators seek to deconstruct. Scholars, activists, and communities have all engaged educational change through multiple entry points. Kerr and Andreotti (2019) examine how social inequality is taken up in Initial Teacher Education within neoliberal contexts. Based on their findings, they theorize that

> rather than seek[ing] an illusive form of equity as an achievement, our work seeks to engage different possibilities for knowing, being and relating in the world. We believe that in order to understand how education might work in support of more emancipatory participation in society, we need to understand the ways that societal inequities are reproduced through education. (Kerr & Andreotti, 2019, p. 661)

Kerr and Andreotti (2019) seek possibilities for change and transformation in teacher education and call for questioning and contestation of "equity" as an achievement. This level of reflection and critical change is important from primary through to postsecondary levels of education where equity is presented as a checkbox that institutions ought to achieve. The authors offer more critical understandings of the possibilities around the ontologies, epistemologies, and ways of connecting to the world. When considering Africanizing the curriculum, we can draw on these conversations for liberatory or emancipatory participation in education and the world more broadly. Furthermore, to advance this critical engagement and thoughtfulness, it requires an engagement of how education produces and reproduces the very injustices that educators seek to entangle.

Nakata et al. (2012) state that "the decolonising rationale" in Australian universities has "secured its legitimacy as a teaching framework" (p. 123). They go on to examine how the decolonial framework aligns with the liberatory politics of social justice education, "inclusive curriculum," and "multicultural education." This alignment "all comes together to represent the institutional accommodation of diversity more generally and embed the agendas of social justice and reconciliation with Indigenous Australia, more specifically" (Nakata et al., 2012, p 123). The same can be said for the Turtle Island/Canadian context. For example, these *accommodations* can be seen by some of the uncritical take up by White neoliberal institutions of the Truth and Reconciliation Commission's 94 calls to action to address the legacy of residential schools and to ultimately lead to reconciliation with Indigenous communities in Canada (Truth and Reconciliation Commission of Canada, 2015). However, I maintain that many institutions still merely treat these calls as accommodations as posited earlier by Nakata. Several institutions simply apply a "stir-and-add" method to questions of Indigeneity, and it is done in very problematic ways, such as not taking up of anti-Indigenous racism with anti-Black racism within the larger project of colonization. Apolitical and ahistorical "application" of Indigenizing allows for the reinforcement of anti-Black racist tropes that seek to divide Turtle Island Indigenous peoples from African Indigenous peoples.

Seven Principles for Rethinking Curriculum as a Black Educator

In this section, I engage the question: what are some practices that can be rooted and grounded in Black/African educators' experiences to engage Blackness as a political tool through anticolonial and decolonial praxis? I explore seven practical examples of rethinking curriculum anchored in my experiences as a Black educator: community-rootedness, humility and reflexiveness, rethinking the classroom in time and space, mentorship, love and care, storytelling, and bold acts of disruption.

Community-Rootedness

In harmony with African Indigenous principles, I refer to a community-rootedness approach. By this, I mean that I actively and intentionally move beyond the formal classroom setting into community spaces. This is in line with Dillard's (2008) "Endarkened Feminist Epistemology," which is embedded in the African cosmology and includes spirituality, community, and praxis. Black and African political principles center community ways of knowing and being rather than treating community as separate and disconnected from academic space. This relates to King (2015), who troubles tropes of objectivity and states that fragmented and meaningless educational contexts further harm Black children in the education system. Instead, King calls for transformative public scholarship rooted in liberatory Africentric praxis that provides opportunities for expression and community building. For example, in my 4 years teaching an Introduction to Sociology course, I end the term with a site visit to Black Creek Community Farm (BCCF) in the well-known "Jane-and-Finch" neighborhood. This is the community where I spent most of my childhood years and now reside and it is no stranger to the mainstream media.

Although it is one of the most ethnically diverse neighborhoods in the province, it is painted as a Black-only community, and with that comes surveillance, antagonization, and a preoccupation with the Black body. However, almost missing entirely from mainstream media outlets are the various community-led projects focused on sustainability, social justice, food security, housing, tenant rights, senior groups, youth projects, the arts, and more. BCCF is a large farm just north of the Jane–Finch intersection where many Black, racialized, and White working-class members of the neighborhood come together to address food insecurity, mutual aid, and sustainability. When I take my students to visit the farm, they are often amazed and shocked to know that such an extravagant and vital community feature exists in the neighborhood. It helps confront some of the negative ideas that they receive about the neighborhood and provide a sense of pride to those who live in the community themselves. As the director, Leticia Deawuo, leads the tour and discussion, many students are often shocked by her very embodiment as a Black womxn in a prominent leadership role. Aware of these dynamics, Leticia and I use this as a moment of unlearning. Several students have continued to volunteer at BCCF or be part of their own local community-farm initiatives. Experiences such as these cannot fully be captured by a textbook or lecture and must be rooted in community. I employ this approach of community-rootedness by intentionally inviting students to address issues that are important to them through various volunteer opportunities. For example, I invite students who are engaged in issues of race, Indigeneity, and intersectionality to help organize the biennial Decolonizing Conference led by Dr. George J. S. Dei, the director of the Centre for Integrative Anti-Racism Studies (CIARS). As well, I have invited students to be part of the Women's March Toronto organizing committee, and they have led the charge in intersectional and transnational frameworks based on their lived experiences to reimagine gender and feminisms.

Although I am a contract lecturer, I work prior to the commencement of the term to think of various guest lecturers who represent diverse lived experiences and bring a critical lens to their work. By doing so, I facilitate the questioning and disruption the of embodiment of the mastery of knowledge as being linked to White, male, heterosexual, able-bodied, middle-class identities. Instead, by inviting in speakers who represent diverse groups and take up critical leadership roles, I invite students to rethink the confines of knowledge and to also create sustained networks and possibilities for mentorship. Akua (2020) posits that "traditional African values promote cooperation over competition, collectivism over individualism, and principles and people over corporate profits. Traditional African culture values family, character, and community over ill-gotten gain and greed" (p. 115). I use these traditional African values to reimagine educational spaces and outcomes by grounding lessons in community.

Humility and Reflectiveness

I center humility and reflectiveness, which is part of African Indigenous knowledge principles. As an educator, I need to be aware of my power and powerlessness and as such actively ensure that I extend humility. By actively engaging humility and reflectiveness, I employ decolonial principles, which is a process and not an arrival and is grounded in learning and unlearning. As Dei (2008) states, "these [Indigenous] knowledges are reflective of the humility of knowing and respecting our viewpoints and cosmologies" (p. 2). By engaging in humility, I actively disrupt tropes that emphasize mastery of knowing and the educator as being the all-knowing subject in the class. When I teach, I remind students that I do not know everything and that I am there to learn from them as much as they are to learn from me. Following a Freirean model of education, I disrupt the banking approach to education (Freire, 1968/1970), which is top down, and invite critical discussion and engagement. For example, in my first year of teaching at the postsecondary level, I would say, "Those who are shy can also engage using the online discussion board." In doing so, I thought I was being accommodating to the various learning styles. However, I was later confronted by a student who stated that not everyone who is silent is "shy" and that instead students who deal with anxiety, muteness, and other barriers will not speak aloud in class. At first, I was shocked by this oversight on my part but started to think it is not about me; rather, it is about creating a classroom of learners who truly feel a sense of community. I erased this from my language and checked my own personal privilege as not only an able-bodied but also an able-minded person and what that meant from a critical disability approach in terms of how I have been able to navigate the education system by not only being somewhat outspoken but also having the privilege to *be able* to engage in debate and conversation.

By employing principles of humility, I also reimagined the classroom and through empathy and consultation, started to think of ways to redesign my classroom and learning opportunities so that students have multiple modalities and ways of engagement. This is one example of many where I have had to employ humility and reflexiveness. As a Black educator, I can relate to my students who face oppression and violence and work to actively unsettle these tropes of "normality."

Rethinking the Classroom in Space and Time

As educators, we face a challenge with the postsecondary schedule that coincides with an academic calendar. Educators often speak about the difficulties of engaging students meaningfully within this semester-long, or sometimes a two-semester schedule, while meeting the learning requirements. This can become a balancing act. However, I try to employ what Mignolo (2007) calls "epistemological disobedience." M. Nakata et al. (2012) cite Mignolo, who "makes the argument for 'epistemic disobedience' as a way to 'delink' from the Western epistemological assumption that there is a "detached and neutral point of observation" (p. 124) through which to interpret and know the world. Epistemic disobedience is not easily achieved as it calls for delinking, and the implication is that these educational settings are inside of the White-Western academic institutions. However, it does provide opportunities for critical thought and engagement within these confines. For example, acts of epistemic disobedience can be rethinking time on a linear scale and the temporal confines set out by the project of modernity. Kerr and Andreotti (2019) draw on Mignolo and Santos in stating that we need to think about possibilities beyond "border thinking" or "abyssal lines." Take, for example, the formal education that students in the bridge program from college to university undergo. They take a variety of classes that are based on the disciplines (sociology, psychology, philosophy, biology, creative writing, among others) to gain exposure to a diverse range of knowledges. However, this can lead to border thinking, in which students see these courses as separate and apart and disconnected from their own lived experiences.

Further to that, this demonstrates the results of modernity and its deep rootedness in academic institutions where learners can engage in theories and philosophies from the "cannons." I engage in epistemic disobedience in the classroom by deconstructing the disciplines and by providing a review of modernity and categorical thinking that facilitates pedagogical opportunities for rethinking, reimagining, and questioning their formal education through critical thought and engagement in Indigenous knowledges as a way of delinking. As well, I provide opportunities beyond the class curriculum for this epistemic disobedience such as rearranging the room, arts-based pedagogies, Latinx versions of Theatre of the Oppressed (see Boal, 1979), popular education, hip-hop education, bonus opportunities, grace periods, and extensions without shame or judgment. This is all informed by my ongoing commitment to rethink the classroom's limits of spatial and temporal confines.

Mentorship

Mentorship has been a central component to my own trajectory to the academy as an early scholar. Particularly, I started a mentorship program in the Jane–Finch community with a close friend to provide students with "tools" for navigating undergraduate, entering postsecondary, and locating job opportunities. We started this program, Mentoring Arts Tutoring Athletics, because of the barriers that we experienced within our first year of university. For years, the program became a feature of C. W. Jefferys Collegiate Institute (a local high school) with an after-school program, a mentor-matching system, monthly social and community-based trips, and a sister organization operating as a student organization out of the nearby York University. As mentioned earlier, my exposure in the club highlighted some of the barriers I witnessed anecdotally such as limited educational pathways, streaming into lower levels such as "applied" and "workplace" within secondary schools, lower expectations of Black and African learners, and more severe use of disciplinary measures (suspension and expulsion). I was encouraged by Professor Joseph Mensah at York University after I met him at a community event where I gave a keynote address to continue graduate studies to further explore these issues rather than my original plan of taking a year off "to do more community work." He challenged me and said, "Why not do both?" So said, so done! I have been and continue to be mentored by many academics and community leaders, who support me to navigate the academic space. I continue to provide mentorship to undergraduate and high school students as they continue their studies. Luckily, as a postsecondary educator, I can continue this model support, keeping in mind that it is not a one-way relationship and that these relationships both challenge me and help me grow personally and professionally.

This mentorship journey falls in line with what Dei (2017) advances: "Black learners have a responsibility to mentor each other if we want to create learning communities. Mentorship is about building community and in the academic institution the whole area of building community is vital to educational and social success" (p. 209). As Black educators, we cannot engage in individualistic principles because our very existence in the academy is based on communities of Black scholars and activists who have fought for us to be in these spaces. We cannot pretend that this is based on our own personal merit. Intentionality must be central to our approaches and thus must engage active mentorship. It can be tiring as a part-time contract lecturer, graduate student, and community activist, but it is important work that must be done, and by drawing on community, it is possible.

Love and Care

Part of the work of mentorship must engage the politics of Blackness which involves a commitment to love and care. Dei (2017) forwards that "to see Blackness as community, we must acknowledge and love our Blackness" (p. 209). Dei goes on to state that the concept of "loving Blackness" comes from hooks (2001), who describes it as collective welfare, destiny, and hope and highlights the importance of community, reciprocity, sharing, and giving back (Dei, 2017, p. 209). As such, love is a rebuttal to tropes of Whiteness that makes Blackness (un)invisible (McKittrick, 2006) and erases Blackness. The erasure and invisibility–hypervisibility relation of Blackness require decolonial responses rooted in care, as such loving Blackness becomes a fundamental and integral response to imagining new futurities. It takes a community spirit and approach to reclaim Blackness and Black love. Love is part of what Dillard (2008) includes in the endarkened feminist epistemology, which involves reciprocity, gratitude, and ritual as methodology. Also, Dove (1998) draws on Karenga (1994), who postulates love as one of the principles of *Maat* (p. 162). Love is important for Black educators to survive the academy and to encourage a spirit of giving back. By approaching the classroom with love, Black educators can form communities of learners and have an openness to learn and unlearn on their own academic and personal journeys.

Storytelling

Storytelling is an important aspect of Indigenous knowledges and serves as a form of passing down intergenerational learnings. Battiste (2013) describes storytelling as part of their upbringing and introduces/reintroduces it in classroom settings as an Indigenous educator and states, "bell hooks has noted that women from oppressed groups have stories to tell, and to tell these stories is an act of resistance" (p. 17). These very stories, as highlighted, are acts of resistance, often stories are positioned as secondary, or even counter to knowledge and academic spaces. However, by telling stories we reimagine formal education and create opportunities for sharing. I remember taking a course with Professor Aparna Tarc during my Master of Education degree, and as a class we engaged in group readings of articles aloud. This profoundly influenced my pedagogical style where instead of creating an environment of shame if students have not completed readings, it encouraged students to tell their own stories and to actively engage their own lived realities in relation to course material. This follows Black feminist epistemologies that center the subjectivities, experiences, and realities of people rather than assuming "objectivity" and a disconnection from knowledge (Collins, 2000; hooks, 2015; King, 2015). Storytelling serves as a form of reimagining education.

Bold Acts of Disruption

In this section, there are several forms of disruption that I explore, including disrupting curriculum, disrupting neutrality, inclusion, and rethinking difference. Scholars, researchers, and activists have written on the various ways that educators can disrupt curriculum (Brady & Abawi, 2019; Dei, 1992, 1994, 1995, 1996, 2001; Dei & Kempf, 2006; Dei & McDermott, 2019; Gaztambide-Fernández, 2008, 2011; Lopez & Olan, 2018, 2019; Zainub, 2019). In my teaching practice, I find transformative ways to disrupt curriculum no matter the age group. For example, I work with K–6 students on a weekly basis out of a Black-focused community organization in the inner suburbs of Toronto. Our team was trying to figure out ways that we could address the spirit injury imparted on these young Black learners in some of their formal educational spaces. And so we developed numerous diverse curriculum practices, one of which involves "African Proverbs Exit Cards." We meet as a group in a circle at the end of the session to reinforce Indigenous knowledge practices, a different student recites their exit card and written on it is an African Proverb (Dei et al., 2018). As the learners engage in reading, they reflect on what the proverb means to them, their connection with their family, and the community.

Furthermore, as activist educators, many of us are engaged in political acts of disruption where we subvert "normal" educational tropes of neutrality and inclusion and rethink difference. Maldonado-Torres's 2004 paper (as cited in Andreotti, 2011) engages the idea of neutrality and universality, which reproduces "epistemic blindness" that reproduces colonial and imperial relations. Furthermore, in 2000, Quijano (as cited in Andreotti, 2011) highlights coloniality, which are the ways whereby colonial ways of knowing become deeply entrenched in daily practices. Furthermore, Andreotti (2011) goes on to cite Maldonado-Torres's critique of the "multicultural attempts to 'include' different voices in Eurocentric sites of conversation" (as cited in Andreotti, 2011, p. 388). Many scholars in Canada have also written extensively on this issue of an "add-and-stir" approach to multiculturalism, diversity, and inclusion, whereby Whiteness is still dominant and becomes normalized (Bannerji, 2000; Henry & Tator, 2006; Mackey, 2002; Razack, 1998; Thobani, 2007; Walcott, 2019). Thus, critical decolonial educators reject multicultural educational principles with their foundations of neutrality and move into a realm of antiracist, anticolonial, and culturally relevant pedagogies (CRPs).

In calling for the need for CRPs, Ladson-Billings (1994) states that Black children are not White children who are painted Black (as cited in Akua, 2020) Ladson-Billings (1995) situates CRP within a Black feminist philosophical standpoint that centers social location, self-definition, and recognition of systemic oppression. I keep this in mind with the young Black students I work with by intentionally drawing on their lived experiences rather than drawing from abstract narratives or lessons rooted in a false sense of neutrality that have nothing to do with them. This requires an active engagement of difference, McLaren (1995) states, "Difference is always a product of history, culture, power, and ideology. Differences occur between and among groups and must be understood in terms of the specificity of their production" (p. 99). Difference ought to be grounded in historical processes. Without examining the role of power, history, and culture, difference is pathologized and juxtaposed to dominant groups and peoples. As educators, we must disrupt difference along the lines of race, class, gender, religion, ethnicity, language, ability, and sexuality, among others. However, this is not to achieve sameness but to instead reclaim difference beyond deficit tropes. How can we reimagine and reclaim difference to situate bold acts of disruption in education? For me, as a Black educator, it is about using the varied lived experiences and differences among students as entry points to engage various subjects, along with drawing on my own lived experiences to engage specific topics.

Conclusion

Reimagining education can be done with careful examination of the role of the educator, their context, and social position. In this chapter, I have examined my specific entry point as a Black educator by examining the role of community and the theorization of Blackness as a diasporic African. I have also engaged the role of Indigenous knowledges and important implications for Black educators across global contexts. Finally, I engaged seven ideas for rethinking education along Black political frameworks and Indigenous knowledges through anticolonial and decolonial strategies. Black and African Indigenous education is an ongoing process that takes careful and critical consideration. As Black educators, we engage our own difference to engage the classroom and rethink education for African/Black learners for transformative pedagogical outcomes, resistance, and change.

References

Akua, C. (2020). Standards of Afrocentric education for school leaders and teachers. *Journal of Black Studies, 51*(2), 107–127.

Andreotti, V. (2011). (Towards) decoloniality and diversality in global citizenship education. *Globalisation, Societies and Education, 9*(3–4), 381–397.

Bannerji, H. (2000). *The dark side of the nation: Essays on multiculturalism, nationalism, and gender.* Canadian Scholars' Press.

Battiste, M. (2013). *Decolonizing education: Nourishing the learning spirit.* Purich Publishing Limited.

Bianchi, C. (2018). Reflections on the implications of western theories on Indigenous populations: Decolonizing and Indigenizing the classroom. In G. J. S. Dei & C. S. Jaimungal (Eds.), *Indigeneity and decolonial resistance: Alternatives to colonial thinking and practice* (pp. 51–75). Myers Education Press.

Boal, A. (1979). *Theater of the oppressed.* Pluto Press.

Brady, J., & Abawi, Z. (2019). Disrupting princesses: A pedagogical moment in dismantling colonial norms and representations of beauty through an anti-colonial framework. In F. J. Villegas & J. Brady (Eds.), *Critical schooling: Transformative theory and practice* (pp. 128–146). Palgrave Macmillan.

Collins, P. H. (1990). *Black feminist thought: Knowledge, consciousness, and the politics of empowerment.* Routledge.

Collins, P. H. (2000). *Black feminist thought: Knowledge, consciousness, and the politics of empowerment* (2nd ed.). Routledge.

Dei, G. J. S. (1992). *The challenges of anti-racist education in Canada.* Ontario Institute for Studies in Education.

Dei, G. J. S. (1994). Afrocentricity: A cornerstone of pedagogy. *Anthropology and Education Quarterly, 25*(1), 3–28.

Dei, G. J. S. (1995). Integrative anti-racism: Intersection of race, class, and gender. *Race, Gender, and Class, 2*(3), 11–30.

Dei, G. J. S. (1996). The role of Afrocentricity in the inclusive curriculum in Canadian schools. *Canadian Journal of Education, 21*(2), 170–186.

Dei, G. J. S. (2001). Rescuing theory: Anti-racism and inclusive education. *Race, Gender and Class, 8*(1), 139–161.

Dei, G. J. S. (2008). Indigenous knowledge studies and the next generation: Pedagogical possibilities for anti-colonial education. *Australian Journal of Indigenous Education, 37*(Suppl.), 5–13.

Dei, G. J. S. (2010). Theorizing Africa beyond its boundaries. In G. J. S. Dei (Ed.), *Teaching Africa: Towards a transgressive pedagogy* (pp. 47–60). Springer.

Dei, G. J. S. (2017). *Reframing Blackness and Black solidarities through anti-colonial and decolonial prisms.* Springer International.

Dei, G. J. S. (2018). "Reframing Education through Indigenous, Anti-Colonial and Decolonial Prisms". In. Peter McLaren and Suzanne Soohoo (eds.). *The Radical Imagine-Nation.* (pp. 214–235). New York: Peter Lang.

Dei, G. J. S., & Kempf, A. (2006). *Anti-colonialism and education.* University of Michigan Press.

Dei, G. J. S., & McDermott, M. (Eds.) (2019). *Centering African proverbs, Indigenous folktales, and cultural stories in curriculum: Units and lesson plans for inclusive education.* Canadian Scholars.

Dei, G. J. S., Nortey, I. N., McDonnell, J., Demi, S. M., & Akanmori, H. (2018). *African proverbs as epistemologies of decolonization.* Peter Lang.

Dillard, C. B. (2008). *On spiritual strivings: Transforming an African American woman's academic life.* State University of New York Press.

Dove, N. (1998). *Afrikan mothers: Bearers of culture, makers of social change.* State University Press.

Freire, P. (1970). *Pedagogy of the oppressed* (M. Bergman Ramos, Trans.). Seabury Press. (Original work published 1968.)

Gaztambide-Fernández, R. A. (2008). The artist in society: Understandings, expectations, and curriculum implications. *Curriculum Inquiry, 38*(3), 233–265.

Gaztambide-Fernández, R. A. (2011). Musicking in the city: Reconceptualizing urban music education as cultural practice. *Action, Criticism and Theory for Music Education, 10*(1), 15–46.

Henry, F., & Tator, C. (2006). *The colour of democracy: Racism in Canadian society.* Thomson Nelson.

hooks, b. (2001). *Salvation: Black people and love.* William Morrow.

hooks, b. (2015). *Feminist theory: From margin to center.* Routledge.

James, C. E. (2019). Community, schooling, and the education of racialized students [Postscript]. In F. J. Villegas & J. Brady (Eds.), *Critical schooling: Transformative theory and practice* (pp. 327–338). Palgrave Macmillan.

Karanja, W. (2019). Land and healing: A decolonizing inquiry for centering land as the site of Indigenous medicine and healing. In N. N. Wane, M. S. Todorova, & K. L. Todd (Eds.), *Decolonizing the spirit in education and beyond: Resistance and solidarity* (pp. 45–61). Palgrave Macmillan.

Karenga, M. (1994). *Maat, the moral ideal in ancient Egypt: A study in classical African ethics, 1.* Ann Arbor, MI: UMI Dissertation Services.

Karenga, M. (2004). *Maat, the moral ideal in ancient Egypt: A study in classical African ethics.* Routledge.

Kerr, J., & Andreotti, V. (2019). Crossing borders in initial teacher education: mapping dispositions to diversity and inequity. *Race Ethnicity and Education, 22*(5), 647–665.

King, J. E. (2015). *Dysconscious racism, Afrocentric praxis, and education for human freedom through the years I keep on toiling: The selected work of Joyce E. King.* Routledge.

Ladson-Billings, G. (1994). *The dreamkeepers: Successful teachers of African American children.* San Francisco, CA: Jossey-Bass.

Ladson-Billings, G. (1995). Toward a theory of culturally relevant pedagogy. *American Educational Research Journal, 32*(3), 465–491.

Lopez, A. E., & Olan, E. L. (Eds.) (2018). *Transformative pedagogies for teacher education: Moving towards praxis in an era of change.* Information Age Publishing.

Lopez, A. E., & Olan, E. L. (Eds.) (2019). *Critical action, agency, and dialogue in teaching and learning contexts.* Information Age Publishing.

Mackey, E. (2002). *The house of difference: Cultural politics and national identity in Canada*. University of Toronto Press.
McKittrick, K. (2006). *Demonic grounds: Black women and cartographies of struggle*. University of Minnesota Press.
McLaren, P. (1995). Chapter III: White terror and oppositional agency: Towards a critical multiculturalism. In P. McLaren, R. Hammer, D. Sholle, & S. S. Reilly (Eds.) *Counterpoints, Vol. 4. Rethinking media literacy: A critical pedagogy of representation* (pp. 87–124). Peter Lang.
Mignolo, W. D. (2007). Delinking. *Cultural Studies, 21*(2–3), 449–514.
Mirza, H.S., & Reay, D. (2000). Spaces and places of Black educational desire: Rethinking Black supplementary schools as a new social movement. *Sociology, 34*(3), 521–544.
Nakata, M. (1993). Culture in education: For us or for them? In N. Loos & T. Osanai (Eds.), *Indigenous minorities and education: Australian and Japanese perspectives of their Indigenous peoples, the Ainu, Aborigines and Torres Strait Islanders* (pp. 334–349).
Nakata, M. (2002). Indigenous knowledge and the cultural interface: underlying issues at the intersection of knowledge and information systems. *IFLA Journal, 28*(5–6), 281–291.
Nakata, M. (2006). Australian Indigenous Studies: A question of discipline. *The Australian Journal of Anthropology, 17*(3), 265–275.
Nakata, N. M., Nakata, V., Keech, S., & Bolt, R. (2012). Decolonial goals and pedagogies for Indigenous studies. *Decolonization: Indigeneity, Education and Society, 1*(1), 120–140.
Razack, S. H. (1998). *Looking White people in the eye: Gender, race and culture in courtrooms and classrooms*. University of Toronto Press.
Simpson, L. (2004). Anticolonial strategies for the recovery and maintenance of Indigenous knowledge. *The American Indian Quarterly, 28*(3–4), 373–384.
Simpson, L. (2014). Land as pedagogy: Nishnaabeg intelligence and rebellious transformation. *Decolonization: Indigeneity, Education and Society, 3*(3), 1–25.
Thobani, S. (2007). *Exalted subjects: Studies in the making of race and nation in Canada*. University of Toronto Press.
Truth and Reconciliation Commission of Canada. (2015). *Calls to action*. http:// www.trc.ca/websites/trcinstitution/File/2015/Findings/Calls_to_Action_English2.pdf
Villegas, F. (2019). Active communities and practices of resistance: Brief history of the use of schools as border zones in Toronto. In F. J. Villegas & J. Brady (Eds.), *Critical schooling: Transformative theory and practice* (pp. 128–146). Palgrave Macmillan.
Villegas, F., & Brady, J. (Eds.) (2019). *Critical schooling: Transformative theory and practice* (pp. 128–146). Palgrave Macmillan.
Walcott, R. (2019). The end of diversity. *Public Culture, 31*(2), 393–408.
Zainub, A. (Eds.). (2019). *Decolonization and anti-colonial praxis: Shared lineages*. Brill Sense.

EPILOGUE

Connecting Missing Links: A Voice From the Diaspora

Rukiya Mohamed

THROUGHOUT THIS VOLUME, key issues and challenges in decolonizing the African school curriculum were presented. Authors focused on the necessity of decolonizing the curriculum while offering their own critiques and interrogations of Black and African education and suggesting concrete ways of making the curriculum more inclusive and accessible to all learners. Chapters in this edited collection highlighted key philosophical arguments on the necessity surrounding inclusive and decolonized curriculum, pointing specifically to the challenges and possibilities in achieving these goals in a meaningful manner. In discussing the Africanization, Indigenization, and decolonization of education, the authors advanced the relationship between *restoration* (a deep reflection on past, history, culture, and psychic memories) and *liberation* (the pursuit of educational praxis informed by an interconnectedness of body, mind, soul, and spirit). From a diaspora perspective, it is useful to use the Ghanaian proverbial instruction of "Sankofa" bird—going back to fetch the forgotten—as a symbol for Africans in the diaspora to keep a knowledge of the history and rich legacies of African thought in the forefront of students' consciousness when building agency and self-determination for new anticolonial futures.

In writing this epilogue, I am reflecting critically on the ways in which decolonization is marked onto bodies and spaces and how we come to know and act in said spaces. When I decided I was going to apply to do my Bachelor of Education, I was 22 years old, and my views of the education system were changing drastically. While I was still grappling with my own experiences of schooling as a Black Somali Muslim woman, a turning point for me was the last year of my undergraduate degree while I was volunteering for Pathways to Education, a community learning program. After many instances of questioning for whom the education system was conceived and how institutions center student culture and experiences, two particular students, recent immigrants from St. Vincent, were the catalysts for my pursuit in education. Incredibly bright and articulate, the two brothers, one in Grade 8 and the other in Grade 7 were placed in an English as a Second Language (ESL) program—although English is the national language of St. Vincent. After a few weeks, I met their mother, a young woman who radiated love and compassion for her two children, was excited for the opportunities they were to have in Canada, and was grateful for the teachers and community volunteers that were supporting her family.

Midway through the term, I could not grasp how and why the boys were still in an ESL program and what it was that I saw in them that their teachers did not. I also was at odds with the work they were assigned—tasks that looked more like they was meant for a primary student than young teenagers on their way to high school. After having borrowed science and math textbooks from the public library (none were available within the school), we began doing grade-level work after completing their assigned classroom tasks. Their mother was equally confused but was unsure as to how to advocate for her children and was worried about creating tension within the school. One evening session, excited to hear about the younger brother's speech presentation, he approached me sulking and whipped his rubric at me. Shocked by his aggression, as I took the page from him, he said, "The teacher said I plagiarized it and I have to do it all over again. She thinks I'm dumb and she was correcting the way I spoke when I was presenting in front of everyone." Noticing the look of bewilderment on my face, his brother added, "They all think we're dumb, Miss; that's why they give us this baby work to do and think we can't speak English." I didn't know what to feel that night and many days afterward. I was angry with the school, hurting for the boys, frustrated that this was happening, and powerless because I did not know how to support the family in navigating the public education system.

Fast-forward to the end of that year; I had graduated from my initial degree and was 4 months into my preservice education program in Toronto, a much larger urban community. It was here where I became increasingly curious about teaching practices that focused on community engagement and highlighted multicentric cultural knowledge within an education system that I now saw as replete with anti-Blackness. What became evident within the sociopolitical context in which education took place was the systemic devaluation of Blackness within society. My two teaching placements were in a downtown community called Regent Park, which was undergoing a revitalization process. During my free time, I also had decided to continue volunteering at an evening tutoring program with predominantly African families. As these families were dealing with displacement and inequitable access to information regarding their housing and financial needs, I noticed the spatialization of racial inequities that was ultimately contributing to the limited opportunities made available within an institution not designed for Black children to succeed. At the end of that year, I was hired as a permanent teacher within the Toronto District School Board (TDSB), the largest school board in Canada (Toronto District School Board, 2014), serving the same community in which I initially began my educational journey. My first foray into African-centered education was in 2012, with a rejuvenated soul and a determination to do better for the younger version of me, the two boys from St. Vincent and their mother, the Black and African families in Regent Park, and the generations of brilliant Black and African children to come.

I'm not sharing with you my story and my experiences with racially and historically marginalized students for you to simply read but rather to position a new model of Black and African education—a model of the people, by the people, and in the service of the people. There is theory and practice in the narratives shared in this volume and parallels can be drawn to diverse membership communities. This epilogue highlights the inevitable need to decolonize education structures by means of reclaiming African voices through curriculum reform and transformative pedagogical practices. The purpose of this epilogue is twofold: to position within the diasporic context a critical regeneration of what it means to Africanize the education system as it relates to current issues within the Canadian public education system, and to challenge you, the reader, to consider your role and responsibility in ensuring that necessary opportunities to learn and thrive are provided equitably to Black and African learners. Educational and life opportunities are distributed moment to moment in society. How can educators, policy makers, and educational leaders say they are promoting excellence and achievement within public education systems if they are not both affirming and uplifting the culture and stories of Black and African learners? How can real structural transformation occur without us critically reflecting on our own teaching practice? The politics of indigenizing education requires that educators pause, step backward, and rethink new and varied ways for creating spaces that allow for multiple knowledge systems. What then are the roles of the different stakeholders within the education system to work on promoting an inclusive curriculum and expand pedagogical frameworks for teaching to the lived experiences and cultural frameworks of Black and African learners?

Educational institutions are responsible for perpetuating the inequities embedded within society. For as long as people of African descent have been in Canada, the engagement in the educational pursuits of their children have been negatively portrayed. Black families have been in regular advocacy for equitable access and opportunities in education. The following section examines the historical context and presents challenges within the Ontario education system as it relates to the experiences of Black and African learners. It will then be followed by a critical examination of what it means to Africanize the education system in Ontario connecting missing links to previous chapters. I conclude with some responses to the earlier questions and pose new questions as we engage in the process of challenging the dominance of the teacher to create space for students to share their culture and experiences, especially in ways that center embodied knowledge.

Understanding the Current Situation in Canada

For more than 40 years, the government of Ontario, Canada has recognized the inequities within academic institutions for Black and African learners and their families. This has stretched across governments, system leaders, school administrators, and classroom educators. As the history is documented in the following, it is important to note that while in Canada, there are three levels of government (municipal, provincial, and federal) and elections are held every 4 years, many steps have been taken to respond to the cultural and racial diversity of students in the public education system, but limited policies have helped to address the inequities that impact the achievement and well-being of Black and African learners.

In 1988, the Ontario Ministry of Education developed a policy titled *The Development of a Policy on Race and Ethnocultural Equity* to examine strategies that ensure school board policies reflect a commitment to antiracist and ethnocultural equity practices as the province was engaged in a journey to eliminate racism within schools and in society at large. Around this time, the city of Toronto was reeling with a string of shooting incidents involving Toronto-area police and Black civilians, with limited justice for the Black and African community. As a result, in 1992, the Black Action Defence Committee and its allies took to the streets, decrying anti-Black racism within the city in a protest called the "Yonge Street Riot." In response to conversations and analyses surrounding race relations, the government finally named anti-Black racism and acknowledged the lack of progress within the education system (Lewis, 1992). In the aftermath of this report, the New Democratic Party (NDP) made amendments to the Education Act. It was also in 1992 that the provincial government called for school boards to develop and implement antiracist and equity policies that would promote explicit strategies to identify within systems and procedures the barriers and prejudices that underpin inequitable outcomes for the achievement of Black learners (Toronto District School Board, 1988). In centering the need for professional development around equitable educational practices for staff, the NDP government put in motion an employment equity legislation in 1994 and established the Anti-Racism Secretariat.

Unfortunately, one year later, all the inroads that were made were undone by the Progressive Conservative government following the 1995 election. In sum, the changes made by this government subsequently granted educators (administrators and classroom teachers) more authority to suspend and expel students without critical reflection about educator power and privilege, recognizing bias and prejudice with the enforcement of policies and promoting positive student–parent–teacher relationships (McMurtry & Curling, 2008). It is now widely recognized that this approach to school discipline disproportionately targeted Black students, and they were being suspended at much higher rates than their counterparts in Toronto (James & Turner, 2017; Puxley, 2007).

By 2007, the Ontario Human Rights Commission (OHRC) began investigating the Ministry of Education and the TDSB due to concerns initiated by wider Black and African communities. Within the complaints lodged, issues were raised regarding the discriminatory impact of the changes on Black and African learners. By 2009, more than 20 years after the initial report *The Development of a Policy on Race and Ethnocultural Equity* (Ontario Ministry of Education, 1988), the Ontario government launched the Equity and Inclusive Education Strategy (Ontario Ministry of Education, 2009) to support educators in identifying, addressing, and eliminating discriminatory biases and systemic barriers present within institutions to promote equitable learning environments. Given that the Equity and Inclusive Education Strategy did not direct school boards to explore an antiracist, anti-oppressive approach to their structures or procedures, and did not extend to anti-racist pedagogical professional learning, in 2016, the provincial government established the Anti-Racism Directorate (ARD). The ARD had a mandate to eliminate systemic racism in government-regulated institutions, ensure inclusive and equitable working environments (from hiring policies and procedures, to practices that promote racial equity), and build relationships with community and caregivers alongside enacting the change forwarded by the OHRC (2016).

In 2017, more explicit recognition of racism, prejudice, and discrimination directed at people of African descent rooted in their unique history and experience of enslavement became necessary (Javed, 2016; Dei, 2006). Although antiracism named issues of race and social difference as issues of power and equity, anti-Black racism examined the intersections of identity markers (gender, class, ability) alongside Blackness. This is when Ontario developed its Anti-Black Racism Strategy to build awareness of the deep entrenchment of anti-Blackness in Canadian institutions and to critically challenge the policies and practices that normalize or render anti-Black racism invisible to the wider society (Government of Ontario, 2017). Anti-Black racism lies in the historical and current social, economic, cultural, and political marginalization of Black bodies. It is experienced as a lack of access and barriers to opportunity and inequitable outcomes in the social determinants of health and well-being, education, housing, and income (see Dei, 1996, 2006, 2013; Dumas, 2016). Anti-Black racism is deeply invested in upholding and sustaining power structures within the dominant society while anti-Blackness, as examined by Dei (2018), connects to conversations of "...Black disposability, particularly, the apparent state's disregard for Black Peoples' welfare and aspirations, concerns about the ways how Black lives are wasted through incarceration, a dysfunctional educational system, and additional forms of state sanctioned violence (p. 120).

By this point, race-based studies such as the *Towards Race Equity in Education* (James & Turner, 2017) were released which examined the schooling of Black students in the TDSB and supported the anecdotal experiences many Black families have been sharing for decades. Black families navigating the school system have varied concerns stemming from the academic achievement to the socio-emotional well-being of their child(ren) (TDSB, 2013a, 2013b, 2016). Coupled with disproportionate disciplinary measures, a greater likelihood to be streamed into applied and locally developed programs, and recurring racial discriminatory within the institution, many families are exploring alternate measures to provide their child(ren) the best opportunity for academic success (James & Brathwaite, 1996; Dei & Kempf, 2013; James & Turner, 2015, 2017). As clearly articulated in the report, "Many participants felt that stereotypes of Black students limited the ability of educational staff to see Black students as academically competent individuals whose abilities, talents, and strengths went beyond the artistic and athletic" (James & Turner, 2017, p. 44). This report, along with countless narratives shared by Black communities all over the country, highlighted stories of exclusion, dehumanization, and disregard for the intellect and capability of Black students.

Implications of Recognizing Historical Pitfalls to Ground Present Practices

The legacy of anti-Blackness manifests itself within Canadian society in a myriad of ways. These highlight the institutional biases in policies, practices, and procedures that continue to disadvantage Black bodies. They are not new and have not been new for centuries. Exploring Black geographies (McKittrick, 2006, 2011) draws attention to the links between Blackness and the spaces we occupy. There is significant scholarship that articulates how forms of colonialism rooted in slavery and anti-Blackness have created intersecting structures of oppression and obscure interpretations of cultural practice (Dei, 2018; McKittrick, 2006; Walcott, 2003). The signifier Black carries with it a mark of exclusion, a badge of foreignness, and of racial and social inferiority. In highlighting how a Black sense of place (Dumas, 2016; Walcott, 2018) is consistently attacked by White supremacist hegemony, it is important to recognize how education systems sustain the racial disparities that shape the experiences and outcomes for Black and African learners. Embracing the anticolonial framework offers vast possibilities for understanding and reimagining the education system. It is through awareness of the legacy of anti-Blackness in society that we might deconstruct the implications of colonial structures on knowledge production, validation, and dissemination, recognizing the significance of Indigenous knowledge systems and the agentive capacity and resistance of Black and African learners to establish an African-centred counter-vision to the education system.

As demonstrated in the previous section, many themes have emerged from over 40 years of reports, policies, and data, most predominantly being low expectations and frequent stereotyping, a lack of access to culturally responsive material, and the absence of a climate of belonging for Black and African learners in the education system (James, 2019; James & Turner, 2017). An indicator of a positive school climate reflective of the student body is the pedagogical practices of its educators and the curriculum being pedaled by the institution. Many students, families, and communities have alluded to the narratives within the chosen resources in their respective classes, the knowledge that was being shared in their classrooms, and to whom it belonged. They voiced their concerns about not seeing themselves as reflective of what was being taught, feeling that instruction was stripping them of their cultural legacies and leaving them to question their adequacy and potential for success.

Regardless of how you feel about the data and where you sit within our own positional power, what is crystal clear is that Black and African learners in the diaspora continue to experience schooling through colonial educational systems and curriculum that negates and devalues experiences, cultures, and histories. There continues to be a deafening silence about anti-Blackness with a persistent denial of its damaging effects on the Black and African student experience. Historically, Black bodies have been fragmented. However, knowledge resides in the body and cultural memories, which encourages not only troubling the imposition of colonial knowledge systems, the oppressiveness of the education system, but also the universalizing of identity markers that allow for a one-size-fits-all approach to curriculum reform. Culture is the way that our brain makes sense of the world around us. It is how we approach learning as we engage in a quest to find truth in our experiences and values. It reveals how our activities and thoughts acknowledge and appreciate the beauty within ourselves and the belief systems we have of wider societal cultures. It impacts the opportunities we have to develop habits of mind that would prepare us to take on more social roles and academic tasks. It is an all-encompassing identity that for many students is not validated or referenced in their education and often takes many more life experiences for them to unpack.

In the following section, we examine what a critical regeneration of the education system could entail and factors that contribute to establishing a community of caring, greater achievement, and an increase in a sense of belonging for Black and African students. These issues highlight the importance of ensuring curricula that enables a reconnection to and reclamation of African Indigenous ways of knowing and being as well as challenging the current education system that divorces African people from their collective histories and legacies.

Critical Regeneration

What makes an educational model one that is of the people, by the people, and in service of the people? What fosters unity among students, teachers, caregivers, and their allies in the process of committing to the reformation of education systems? Is it that the pedagogical practices are geared toward strengthening local knowledge and cultural resources and further engendering human capacity building to respond to the needs of and issues within the community? Is it the embodiment of learning as it relates to how one identifies themselves and their experiences within society? The authors of this volume recognize that education must speak to learners' lived experiences—it must be an intellectual and emotional journey, one that evokes emotion, rejuvenates the spirit, ignites a desire for civic action, and ultimately provides spaces and opportunities to locate the self and their power within. The starting point is the idea of "being" in the world, that is, being situated in a physical and social space. The significance of Africanizing education is a process that takes place in the mind and serves to begin with African value systems within the theory and practice of pedagogy. Ultimately, education must be a holistic and spiritually affirming endeavor.

An integration of African epistemology in education systems defines the dictum that Africans are agents of their own history and masters of their destiny. To bridge educational theory into practice entails that a curriculum must be designed as both an instrument of liberation and one of empowerment. To Africanize our education system, we have to take the teachings of African languages, cultures, identities, and politics as critical entry points of conversation/dialogue. The more holistic the cultural knowledges that are affirmed, the deeper the connections learners make of body, mind, soul, and spirit. This decolonization of curricula ultimately increases student and caregiver agency as they become more equipped to respond to colonialism and its narratives to better navigate the education system. In this section, I bring full circle two strategies mentioned in the introduction of the volume: Africa as our intellectual anchor and decolonizing the curricula as a means to connect the missing links and respond to the questions noted in the beginning of this chapter.

Africa as Our Intellectual Anchor

Africa must be the epicenter of learning and becoming for the Black and African learner. In doing so, they engage with the schooling process in ways that promote taking ownership of knowledge and education by framing their own lived experiences and cultural connections with the content being presented. Thus, they center an embodied approach to learning reflective of the collective nature of African culture and epistemology and in Indigenous knowledge systems. It is a pedagogical practice that emphasizes agency, resistance to cultural dominance in education, and Indigeneity.

As mentioned in the introduction, transforming schooling and education *about* and *on* African and Black peoples to schooling *by* and *for* African and Black peoples (Afful-Broni et al., 2021) necessitates that we critically examine structures that for over 40 years have been recognized as deficient and disjointed yet not dismantled. By reimagining our education system, we have the opportunity to achieve African-centeredness by identifying and teaching through facets from the culture and history of a people. This can be done while simultaneously ensuring that the experiences of Black and African learners in terms of their lived realities, community relations, and cultural legacies are supported as fundamental knowledge systems and disseminated as such. Africanizing the education system is not an exclusionary approach. It denotes a form of inclusivity and community that goes beyond the individual and centers the collective (Dei & Kempf, 2013, p. 15). It is a humanist and communal learning journey where students come to perceive Blackness as a continuum transcending all borders and to understand that we are one people with our strength lying in unity (Dei, 1996).

Decolonizing the Curricula

Schools are microcosms of society. As such, education systems take the neoliberal and capitalist goals within society and mold them into curriculum content that ultimately captures and makes provision for the passing on of aspects of culture deemed relevant and valuable. In doing so, messages of worth, importance, and validity are transmitted to students as young as 3 years of age when they begin preschool—let alone what they glean from the media! Curriculum is also about power. It is an academic blueprint that has the power to construct, validate, and legitimize knowledge. It is about values, ideas, and practices, as well as identities (class, race, ethnicity, gender, sexuality, disability, language, religion, etc.) and how they connect with knowledge production. As mentioned in the introduction, "educators must embrace a Freirean 'consciousness,' pedagogies of liberation, and Fanonian decolonization, all of which extend the discussion beyond our mental universe to what it means to engage in true practice for educational change" (Afful-Broni et al., 2021, p. 19). Education is a key instrument for transformation.

Decolonizing the curricula stresses the importance of both teachers and students in developing an understanding of the interconnectedness between an individual's thoughts, experiences, power, and identity/culture and how such aspects either support or hinder going beyond pedagogies of oppression. The integration of pedagogical approaches framed within the cultural references and identities of Black and African learners affirms the development of a strong sense of identity, self-worth, sense of connectedness, and belonging to a community of learners that supports the right of a subject in resistance to define their own reality. This falls in line with hooks' (1994) assertion that education is the "practice of freedom" complete with a holistic history of ideas and events that have, and continue to, shaped human growth, development, and the creation of alternate possibilities. This cannot be possible without educators investing in and taking personal responsibility for students' success by developing their awareness of themselves as practitioners to deliver programming "[in] a manner that respects and cares for the souls of students" (hooks, 1994, p. 13). By choosing not to decolonize the curricula (whether intentional or not), education systems continue to pedal a wounded existence for Indigenous learners while forcing them to seclude their cultural knowledge, values, and worldviews (Dei, 2010) from a learning journey that is supposed to support them in the process of becoming. This cannot continue to be an option.

African-Centered Education: Inclusionary and Emancipatory Practice

Within Ontario, Africanizing the education system manifests itself through the Africentric curriculum. A pedagogical approach centered on the continent of Africa and peoples of African descent and in the African diaspora. Using African students' cultural strengths as integral parts of instruction and socialization grounds African Canadian students in the histories, legacies, and values of African peoples. While advancing and infusing African knowledge, students are set within the context of their own frames of reference so that they become more connected to and take ownership of their learning journey in collaboration with community and family. Learning experiences highlighting Black and African individuals in positions of power within the local community, teaching through African proverbs, engaging in storytelling (folktales and counternarratives), arts-based approaches, and Black and African inventors, innovators, and contributors across various fields and examining early civilizations of Africa are all ways that affirm the cultural legacies of learners, serve as a context for learning, and provide students with a holistic understanding of the histories and cultural heritage of African peoples.

In the Africentric perspective, family and caregiver relationships along with community partnerships are central to students' success. The importance of *Ubuntu* is rooted in African philosophy, and it espouses the ideals of interconnectedness or sense of collective identity among people, such as kindness, compassion, sensitivity, and consideration. Through the development of African ways of knowing and understanding as part of a broader inclusive approach to education, Africentric education provides opportunities for students to actively act on societal injustices in ways that center African values, principles, and traditions (e.g., pride, mutual respect, social and economic responsibility, community belonging, cooperation, and academic excellence). When the communal aspects of African epistemology are infused in education, a community of learners is generated, and the histories, knowledge systems of African Canadian perspectives are fully integrated within curricula and educational policies.

Conclusion

The dire necessity to reimagine the sociocultural purpose of education is what brought me into teaching and research. Ethics resides in us as educators, not within institutions. It is important as we examine approaches to Africanize the education system that we hold accountable education policies and procedures that continue to denigrate and devalue Black and African learners. Relationships and accountability are critical. As we critically evaluate our own complicities within an oppressive system, educators and community practitioners must engage in self-reflection that troubles their discomfort. Establishing curricula centered on communal cultural knowledge and the acknowledgment of and teaching through the history and totality of the Black experience ensures that every student in the classroom has the opportunity to be their best self and have both their cultural legacies and brilliance affirmed. It is only then that we may begin to challenge the dominance of the teacher and to create space for students to share their knowledge and experiences, especially in ways that center embodied knowledge.

Throughout this volume, the authors have highlighted the violence and complexities of decolonization, but within each narrative, there have been possibilities for building new relationships and harnessing local and global community connections. It also sought to identify both the challenges of Africanizing school curriculum and critically questioned the pedagogical practices that dismiss the voices of the African students. As you engage in the process of subversion, consider the following: what might the possibilities for codeveloping with community partners conditions for holistic and authentic relationships entail for education? What action-oriented approach to education might be undertaken that ensures the centrality of Black and African learners, engaging them from their identities and lived experiences, and presenting education that is holistic in the making of a whole, embodied learner who is able to act for change?

References

Afful-Broni, A. Anamuah-Mensah, J. Raheem, K., & Dei, G. J. S. (2021). *"Africanizing the school curriculum: Promoting an inclusive, decolonial education in African contexts": An introduction* (pp. 1–31). Myers Education Press.

Dei, G. J. S. (1996). The role of Afrocentricity in the inclusive curriculum in Canadian schools. *Canadian Journal of Education, 21*(2), 170–186.

Dei, G. J. S. (2006). On race, anti-racism and education. *Journal of the Canadian Race Relations Foundation, 3*(1), 27–33.

Dei, G. J. S. (2010). Theorizing Africa beyond its boundaries. In G. J. S. Dei (Ed.), *Teaching Africa: Towards a transgressive pedagogy* (pp. 47–60). Springer.

Dei, G. J. S. (2013). Reframing critical anti-racist theory (CART) for contemporary times. In G. J. S. Dei, & M. Lordan (Eds.), *Contemporary issues in the sociology of race and ethnicity: A critical reader* (pp. 1–14). Peter Lang.

Dei, G. J. S. (2018). "Black like me": Reframing Blackness for decolonial politics. *Educational Studies, 54*(2), 117–142

Dei, G. J. S., & Kempf, A. (2013). *New perspectives on African-centred education in Canada.* Canadian Scholars' Press.

Dumas, M. J. (2016). Against the dark: Antiblackness in education policy and discourse. *Theory into Practice, 55*(1), 11–19.

Freire, P. (1970). *The pedagogy of the oppressed.* The Seabury Press.

Government of Ontario. (2017). *A better way forward: Ontario's 3-year anti-racism strategic plan.* https://www.ontario.ca/page/better-way-forward-ontarios-3-year-anti-racismstrategic-plan

hooks, b. (1994) *Teaching to transgress.* Routledge.

James, C. E. (2019). *We rise together.* York University.

James, C. E., & Brathwaite, K. S. (1996). *Assessing the educational experiences of African Canadians.* In K. S. Brathwaite & C. E. James (Eds.), *Educating African Canadians* (pp. 13–31). Our Schools/Our Selves & James Lorimer Ltd.

James, C. E., & Turner, T. (2015). *Fighting an uphill battle: Report on the consultations into the well-being of Black youth in Peel region*. F.A.C.E.S. of Peel Collaborative.

James, C. E., & Turner, T. (2017). *Towards race equity in education: The schooling of Black students in the Greater Toronto Area*. York University.

Javed, N. (2016, December 2). Parents file human rights complaint against York school board. *Toronto Star*. https://www.thestar.com/yourtoronto/education/2016/12/02/parentsfile-human-rights-complaint-against-york-school-board.html

Lewis, S. (1992). *Stephen Lewis report on race relations in Ontario*. Government of Ontario.

McKittrick, K. (2006). *Demonic grounds: Black women and the cartographies of struggle*. University of Minnesota Press.

McKittrick, K. (2011). On plantations, prisons, and a black sense of place. *Social and Cultural Geography, 12*(8), 947–963.

McMurtry, R., & Curling, A. (2008). *The review of the roots of youth violence: Volume 1*. Government of Ontario.

Ontario Ministry of Education. (1988). *A synopsis of public responses to the report of the provincial advisory committee on race relations: "The development of a policy on race and ethnocultural equity."*

Ontario Ministry of Education. (2009). *Who's responsible for your child's education?* http://www.edu.gov.on.ca/eng/document/brochure/whosresp.html

Ontario Human Rights Commission. (n.d.). *Human rights settlement reached with the ministry of education on safe schools*. http://www.ohrc.on.ca/en/human-rights-settlement-reached-ministry-education-safe-schools

Puxley, C. (2007, April 10). Ontario to scrap zero-tolerance at schools. *The Star*. http://www.thestar.com/news/2007/04/10/ontario_to_scrap_zerotolerance_at_schools.html

Toronto Board of Education. (1988). *Education of Black students in Toronto schools*.

Toronto District School Board (1988). *Education of Black students in Toronto schools*. Toronto: Toronto Board of Education.

Toronto District School Board. (2013a). *TDSB Facts. Programs of study: An overview*. http://www.tdsb.on.ca/Portals/research/docs/reports/ProgramsOfStudyAnOverview%20FS-%20FINAL.pdf

Toronto District School Board. (2013b). *Who are our students with special needs in the TDSB? A descriptive overview 2013–14*. http://www.tdsb.on.ca/Portals/research/docs/reports/SpecialEducation2013-14Factsheet.pdf

Toronto District School Board. (2014). *About us*. https://www.tdsb.on.ca/About-Us

Toronto District School Board. (2016, October 24). *Black student achievement advisory committee*. http://www.tdsb.on.ca/Community/HowtoGetInvolved/CommunityAdvisoryCommittees/BlackStudentAchievementAdvisoryCommittee.aspx

United Nations Human Rights Office of the High Commissioner. (2016). *Statement to the media by the united nations' working group of experts on people of African descent, on the conclusion of its official visit to Canada, 17–21 October 2016*. https://www.ohchr.org/EN/NewsEvents/Pages/DisplayNews.aspx?NewsID=20732&LangID=E

Walcott, R. (2003). *Black like who? Writing Black Canada* (2nd rev. ed.). Insomniac Press.

Walcott, R. (2018). Against social justice and the limits of diversity: Or Black people and freedom. In E. Tuck, & K. W. Yang (Eds.), *Toward what justice? Describing diverse dreams of justice in education* (pp. 85–100). Routledge.

Contributors

RICHARDSON ADDAI-MUNUNKUM teaches in the Department of Psychology and Education at the University of Education, Winneba, Ghana. He has expertise in teaching and research in the field of curriculum and pedagogy. He has published in a number of reputable international journals and plays an active role in the ongoing curriculum reforms in Ghana's education sector. Richardson welcomes collaborations in the areas of curriculum and pedagogy.

PAUL BANAHENE ADJEI is an associate professor and the chair of the PhD program at the School of Social Work, Memorial University of Newfoundland, Canada. Paul's research and scholarship draws on anti-Black racism theory, critical race theories, critical Whiteness studies, and anticolonial theory to ask new questions as well as to identify potential answers to what W. E. B. Du Bois described as "colour-line problem" in Euro-American, Canadian, African, and Caribbean society. He also draws on African Indigeneity as rich cultural sources of knowledge to (re)imagine a new future for social work education.

ANTHONY AFFUL-BRONI is currently a professor and vice chancellor of the University of Education, Winneba, Ghana. He was a consultant to the Academic Quality Assurance Unit of the University of Ghana. Professor Afful-Broni is the editor in chief of the *International Journal of Educational Leadership*, Ghana. He is a specialist in time management and still facilitates workshops on time management, staff development, and leadership in universities locally and internationally. Professor Afful-Broni led a team that ran training for the West African College of Physicians and Surgeons.

JOPHUS ANAMUAH-MENSAH is a science education expert and a tertiary education consultant with more than 45 years in academia as university researcher, teacher, administrator, policy analyst, and national and international consultant. Professor

Anamuah-Mensah's university leadership positions have included six years as the head of the Department of Science Education, three years as the dean of the Faculty of Education, two years as the pro-vice chancellor of the University of Cape Coast, and nine years as a principal and foundation vice chancellor of the University of Education, Winneba. His contributions to national development include chairing and producing the blueprint for the 2002 President's Committee on Review of Educational System in Ghana. Professor Anamuah-Mensah research has centered on crafting the concept of community knowledge system to improve STEM (science, technology, engineering, and mathematics) education that has now been introduced into the school science curricula to gradually create awareness of the value of our endogenous activities.

LOUIS ATSIATORME is a professional teacher and an environmental and science education specialist. His expertise is in the area of curriculum development and pedagogy in science and environmental education. Dr. Atsiatorme is a lecturer in the Department of Development and Environmental Studies, School of Research and Graduate Studies, Wisconsin International University College, Ghana.

JANELLE BAPTISTE-BRADY is an educator, researcher, and early activist scholar. She teaches at various postsecondary institutions as a sessional lecturer in Toronto in the fields of sociology, women and gender studies, and social justice education. She enjoys community work, organizing activities, and learning from elders.

ISAAC NORTEY DARKO is an assistant professor of education at Burman University, Alberta, Canada. Dr. Darko work is in innovative classroom teaching with his integrative approach to teaching and learning, examining the intersectionalities of the teaching profession as it relates to engaging multiple epistemologies, technology, social justice, morality, and adult education. He currently focuses on understanding the significant role of Indigenous knowledge in the holistic development of the learner within the frameworks of inclusivity, anticolonialism, antiracism, equity, respect, recognition, and historical context through which knowledge is engaged primarily in the academy. His recent publications include *African Proverbs as Epistemologies of Decolonization* (2018); "Concealed Markets and the Commercialization of Education: Implication on Inclusivity," in *Inclusive Education in African Contexts: A Critical Reader* (edited by N. Phasha, D., Mahlo, and G. S. Dei., 2017); "The Effect of Colonialism on Policing in Ghana," in the *International Journal of Police Science & Management* (with F.D. Boateng, 2016); and *Critical Pedagogy and Youth Education: The Relevance of Indigenous African Cultural Stories* (2015).

Ghanaian-born **GEORGE J. SEFA DEI** is a professor of social justice education and the director of the Centre for Integrative Anti-Racism Studies at the Ontario Institute for Studies in Education of the University of Toronto. He is a fellow of the Royal Society of Canada. In June 2007, Professor Dei was installed as a traditional chief in Ghana, specifically as the Gyaasehene of the town of Asokore, Koforidua, in the New Juaben Traditional Area of Ghana. His stool name is Nana Adusei Sefa Tweneboah.

NYUIEMEDI AGORDZO EDOH-TORGAH is part of the faculty in the Department of Psychology and Education at the University of Education, Winneba, Ghana. Her teaching and research are rich in experience in counseling psychology and teacher education, which have influenced her areas of interest and publications on trauma and abuse, childhood experiences, counseling needs of the vulnerable, and curriculum evaluation. She is also a licensed counseling psychologist with the Ghana Psychology Council and a member of the Ghana Psychological Association.

SULEMANA FUSEINI is a PhD candidate at the School of Social Work, Memorial University of Newfoundland. He has more than eight years' experience as a child welfare services worker with Children, Seniors, and Social Development in Newfoundland, Canada. His PhD research focuses on how social workers in the Child Welfare systems in Canada name, define, and manage the seemingly competing demands imposed by (1) Child Welfare agencies' rules and regulations and instruments of assessments, (2) the diverse sociocultural values of recipients of Child Welfare services, and (3) the social work professional expectations (which are formed and shaped by the Professional Code of Ethics, years of training, and personal values).

ROWENA LINTON is a PhD student in social justice education at the Ontario Institute for Studies in Education of the University of Toronto. Her research interests include anti-Black racism in education, decolonizing education teaching and practices, Black students schooling experiences, and resistance.

ABIGAIL ADUBEA MILLS is a lecturer at the Department of Social Work, University of Ghana. Her current research focuses on caregivers' experiences with children with disabilities as well as the role of social workers in inclusive education.

RUKIYA MOHAMED is a Somali Muslim educator, researcher, and community member. She is currently an MEd student in the Department of Social Justice Education with a collaborative specialization in educational policy at the Ontario Institute for Studies in Education of the University of Toronto. Her research interests focus on rethinking the sociocultural purpose of education, race, and resistance, African-centered schooling, and the decolonial solidarities within anti-Blackness and anti-Muslim racism.

NAKANYIKE MUSISI is an associate professor at the University of Toronto, Canada. She is a former director of Makerere Institute of Social Research at Makerere University, Kampala, Uganda. Her research interests are in gender, colonialism, missionary work in Uganda, social change, and education. Her publications include "Uganda," in *African*

Higher Education: An International Reference Handbook (edited by D. Teferra and P. G. Altbach, 2003); *Makerere University in Transition 1993–2000* (coauthored with Nansozi Muwanga, Oxford, James Currey, 2003); "Rethinking the Public-Private Mix in Higher Education: Global Trends and National Policy Challenges" (coauthored with S. Kim, Z. Gilani, P. Londani, and P. Teixiera) in *Higher Education in the New Century: Global Challenges and Innovative Ideas* (edited by P. G. Altbach and P. Peterson, 2007); *Growing Up by Accident: Challenges in Handling Adolescents in Uganda Schools* (coauthored with Deborah Kasente, 2007); and "Financing Higher Education in Uganda" in *Higher Education Financing in East and Southern Africa,* (edited by P. Pilly, 2010). Her articles have also appeared in *Signs: Journal of Culture and Society,* the *Journal of African History, History in Africa, Gender and History,* and in various edited collections.

PATRICK RADEBE teaches at Lakehead University. His research interests revolve around Afrocentric schools, Black students' education, and African Canadian studies. As an educator, watching his students succeed and their confidence grow is one of his many rewards.

KOLAWOLE RAHEEM is the head of the Centre for School and Community Science and Technology Studies at the Institute for Educational Research and Innovation Studies, University of Education, Winneba, Ghana. He worked for many years as a special researcher at the Institute for Educational Research and the Department of Biological and Environmental Science, University of Jyvaskyla, Finland. Professor Raheem is a member of the advisory board for the Lagos State University, Africa Centre of Excellence, for Innovative and Transformative STEM Education.

CHLOE WEIR is an assistant professor at Burman University, where she teaches in the School of Education. Her passion for teaching can be traced to her second-grade teacher who had a profound influence on her life. She is devoted to teaching and enjoys learning new ways of engaging her students in meaningful classroom activities. Her research interests intersect Indigenous ways of knowing and doing, teacher identity, and professional development. She is a strong proponent of the view that there is a space for understanding how Indigenous ways of knowing and doing can contribute to human development.

SAMIERA ZAFAR is a South African living in Canada. She currently works as a policy and advocacy advisor at Save the Children Canada. She is a PhD student in the social justice education program with a collaborative specialization in comparative international and development education at Ontario Institute for Studies in Education, University of Toronto. She plans to anchor her research in anti-racism education and to reconnect with her nascent research efforts in this field and initiated during her employment at the Centre for Education Policy Development in South Africa.

Index

D

E